EMBASSIES
UNDER SIEGE

EMBASSIES UNDER SIEGE

Personal Accounts by Diplomats on the Front Line

An Institute for the Study of Diplomacy Book

Edited by Joseph G. Sullivan

BRASSEY'S
Washington • London

Library of Congress Cataloging-in-Publication Data

Embassies under siege: Personal accounts by diplomats on the front line/edited by Joseph G. Sullivan.
    p.   cm.
"An Institute for the Study of Diplomacy book."
Includes index.
ISBN 1-57488-022-5
1. Diplomatic and consular service, American—Buildings—Security measures. 2. Embassy buildings—Security measures—United States. 3. Embassy takeovers. I. Sullivan, Joseph G.
JX1683.P7E42   1995
363.11'93272'0973—dc20   95-6820

10 9 8 7 6 5 4 3 2 1

Printed in the United States of America

The exertions which a nation is prepared to make to protect its individual representatives or citizens from outrage is one of the truest measures of its greatness as an organised State.

—SIR WINSTON CHURCHILL

Contents

FOREWORD

Anthony C. E. Quainton,
Assistant Secretary of State for Diplomatic Security

What is it that brings an embassy under siege? The events described in this remarkable compendium of personal reflections on crisis events are set in the period of the Cold War; yet, interestingly enough, few had anything to do with the profound ideological conflict that provided the basic underpinning of our post–World War II foreign policy. To be sure, the Salvadoran civil war had a heavily Marxist dimension, and Ambassador Adolph Dubs was killed in an assault carried out with Russian advice in a Soviet satrapy. But the other events have an uncannily post–Cold War feel about them, reflecting the breakdown of certain societies in Africa and the profound hostility of extremist Islamists to American values, culture, and Middle East policy. The challenge for policymakers and historians in analyzing these disparate events is to separate truly ephemeral, idiosyncratic events from longer-term trends. Are we to see more embassies at risk in the years ahead, or fewer? And if so, why?

Recent months have provided much evidence that the phenomenon of besieged embassies is not about to go away. Almost from the day it reopened in 1993, our mission in Mogadishu has been under attack from hostile Somali clans. Our diplomats there, as in Sarajevo and Sanaa, live and work in a war zone. Repeated evacuations in the Congo, Burundi, and Sudan and the suspension of embassy operations in Rwanda in the midst of genocidal killing testify to the extraordinary breakdown of institutions and the vulnerability of our embassies to violence, terrorism, and urban disorder. Embassy Bogotá and Embassy Lima are still armed fortresses confronting relentless hostility from narcoterrorists in Colombia and the Shining Path in Peru. Beirut continues to be under constant threat, with our diplomats living in what is surely the most intensely guarded diplomatic mission in the world. In many other posts around the globe, criminal violence is so common that diplomats feel themselves under siege in their own homes.

While much of such violence in the years ahead will be sporadic and unanticipated, far more is predictable. We can expect three sources of violence: (a) the breakdown of institutions resulting from the devastating pressure of people on resources in what were once called the Second and Third Worlds; (b) the more aggressive assertion of ethnic or tribal identity; and (c) alienation of significant segments of Muslim societies from their own societies and leaders and from Western values, which extremists will exploit in violent and destructive ways.

The breakdown of social and political institutions is dramatically seen in Africa, where several countries have no or few governmental structures; Somalia, Liberia, and Angola lead the list, but they are not alone. Throughout the world, the level of criminal violence is rising in the face of urban scarcities, created both by internal migrations and by relentless natural increases in population. The State Department's own semiannual threat list rates a total of seventy-seven posts as high or critical for crime. Twenty-five posts have been added to these levels in the last two years alone. Scarcity of employment, even in the informal sector, is the rule rather than the exception for young urban Third World males. For many, their only activity is robbery, often against Westerners—on the street, in their homes, even in the very environs of our embassies. With skillful manipulation, these youths can also be provoked to participate in large demonstrations and mob violence, which can find as their focus the symbols of Western power and affluence: our embassies.

Linguistic and cultural fragmentation is nothing new, but it has surely accelerated in the last decade. We have not seen the end of it and can expect Americans both official and nonofficial who reside in multiethnic societies to be dramatically affected. The recent massacres in Rwanda are graphic reminders of this phenomenon; but Bosnia, Somalia, Liberia, Angola, Georgia, and Azerbaijan have also provided further evidence of the breakdown of multiethnic, multitribal states.

Violence by extremist Islamists has many roots—alienation from political leaders, lack of social or economic justice, and the Arab-Israeli conflict. There is hardly a Muslim country where religious leaders are not denouncing the corruptness of the West and the inappropriateness of its materialistic acquisitive values to Muslim society. In some countries, significant political parties or movements share that view. Algeria is an extreme example, where armed Islamist groups have been attacking foreigners as part of their efforts to overthrow the current regime. States such as Iran or the Sudan, where fundamentalists are in power, denounce Western culture and lifestyle in general and seek to export that view throughout the Muslim world. Often the United States is a target of their animosity, although the genuine source of dissatisfaction is usually closer to home. The events in Pakistan and Beirut described in this book are precursors of what we may see in the future. At least a part of the motivation of those events was a sense of Muslim alienation and grievance against American policies and values.

Reading these illuminating essays, one might well say, "We have seen the future and it is now." American embassies have come under siege since the days of the Boxer Rebellion. But the number of facilities besieged has grown over the years. We can expect more of the same. Coping with increasing levels of violence will require a new generation of diplomats, accustomed to living in conditions of instability and violence rather than in the orderly nineteenth-century world of balance-of-power diplomacy.

We will have to adapt security policies to protect diplomats not only in the fortresses where they work but in their homes and on the street. In the resource-constrained environment in which we live, that will be no easy task. A first step is understanding that we face a new world disorder. This book is a useful and instructive primer for the Foreign Service of the future.

PREFACE

To further its mission of contributing to education in diplomacy, the Georgetown University Institute for the Study of Diplomacy (ISD) has produced a series of useful studies on the varied experiences of diplomats serving in embassies abroad, the roles they play, and the objectives they pursue. These works, drawn principally from U.S. experience, deal with ambassadorial, consular, commercial, public affairs, and political roles, and relations between diplomats and the media. Beginning in 1990, these works, including this book, constitute the Martin F. Herz Series on United States Diplomacy.

In 1993, during a hiatus in my career as a Foreign Service officer, I spent a semester as an ISD diplomatic research associate at Georgetown. The institute's director at that time, Hans Binnendijk, persuaded me to organize a book with other career diplomats recounting and analyzing some of the searing incidents of recent decades in which embassies of the United States have come under direct threat of physical harm or worse. The purpose, as with all ISD books, was to draw from these experiences constructive lessons, in this instance lessons to help guide diplomats and others unfortunate enough to confront such situations in future.

The questions I asked each of my fellow authors to address were pointed. On the policy environment at the time of the specific crisis covered I asked: Did U.S. policy precipitate the crisis? Did the embassy have input to that policy? Were there acceptable policy changes that could have averted the crisis? What were the arguments against such changes? Similar questions covered the political situation in the country or region, its implications for the crisis the embassy faced, and the impact on the embassy of U.S. relations with the host government.

Central to the book's focus were questions on the embassy's handling of the crisis, especially what worked and what didn't. How did the embassy organize itself to deal with the crisis? How did it communicate with Washington, and how did Washington respond to embassy requests? Where relevant, was the embassy's size at the onset of the immediate crisis appropriate? How were the drawdown of personnel and evacuation managed? What special problems arose? And how did the embassy deal with the local American community? Finally, what lessons would each draw in retrospect, especially what would each have the embassy or the U.S. government do differently in preparing for and managing such a crisis in future?

As the project progressed and before I departed that July to head the U.S. Interests Section in Havana, the authors who were available came together at the institute to share their insights with me and one another. After my departure, Margery Boichel Thompson, the institute's longtime editor and director of publications, took on the principal work of editing, communicating with authors, and arranging publication of the resulting book. She has my thanks and appreciation, as does William Bradley Burks, who assisted her.

To all of my Foreign Service colleagues who contributed their efforts and their often extremely limited time to the research and writing of their chapters, the institute and I owe a great debt. For some, the work evoked painful memories. Thanks go as well to Assistant Secretary of State Anthony Quainton for contributing the book's foreword and to the *Foreign Service Journal*, which published an earlier version of Jim Bishop's chapter on Somalia. In every case, the views expressed are those of the authors and do not necessarily reflect the views of the Government of the United States or the Institute for the Study of Diplomacy.

My thanks go also to the institute and its Martin F. Herz Memorial Fund for making possible what we all hope will be a useful contribution to the literature on diplomacy, including the increasingly cogent aspect of diplomacy's cooperation with its military counterparts. The latter have not only shared the crises of embassies under siege; they were often pivotal players. In recounting these experiences this book is thus a tribute to the many fine officers, diplomatic and military, who faced real danger and handled tough situations with courage, skill, and determination.

EMBASSIES
UNDER SIEGE

In the State Department's Operations Center in the summer of 1990, a crisis management task force coordinates the U.S. response to the conflict in Liberia. At the far end of the table (second and third from left) are Donald Hester, Liberia desk officer, and Stephen Kelly, task force coordinator. *State Department*

1 | Embassies at Risk: Learning from Experience

Joseph G. Sullivan

The June 1985 report of the Secretary of State's Advisory Panel on Overseas Security headed by Admiral Bobby R. Inman reviewed the long tradition and principles of international law governing diplomatic immunity, occasional violations thereof, and the swift punishment that generally followed such violations. At the time the United States achieved its independence, it had accepted these concepts of international law; when its own envoys suffered insult or injury, it expected and usually received appropriate apologies and redress. Occasionally, when local authorities abroad were unable or unwilling to provide protection or apprehend offenders, the U.S. government used military force to back up its legitimate demands. On a number of occasions, it sent Marines to capture offenders, to be tried by local courts or to carry out what was known as "condign punishment."[1]

From the beginning of the republic, in fact, United States diplomats and embassies overseas have had to cope with crises. Early American diplomats had to deal with rulers on the Barbary Coast who lived by tributes, piracy, and kidnapping. In 1796, after five American hostages held by the local ruler had died, U.S. Consul to Algiers Joel Barlow negotiated and secured the release of 145 surviving hostages.[2] In the late nineteenth and early twentieth centuries, several incidents resulted in the endangerment or death of U.S. officials overseas. In 1896, Siamese government troops assaulted the U.S. vice consul in Chiang Mai.[3] In 1900, during the Boxer Rebellion, the American legation in Peking was besieged, along with those of other Western powers and Japan, for eighty-one days. The diplomats, their families, missionaries, and other civilians, as well as the Marine guard detachment, were rescued by an international expeditionary force, and the Chinese government was forced to pay reparations.

In 1924, on the streets of Tehran, a mob attacked and killed the U.S. vice consul. In 1927, the invasion of Nanking by Nationalist Chinese troops endangered U.S. consulate officials and other U.S. citizens, along with nationals of other countries. Some had been captured, but all avoided death as their countries' naval vessels interposed a curtain of fire to facilitate their escape.[4] In a 1932 incident in Mukden, three Japanese soldiers attacked and severely bruised U.S. Consul Culver B. Chamberlain en route to his post in Harbin, China. What followed ironically demonstrated the traditional respect for diplomats: upon protest by the U.S. consul general, the Japanese consul general in Mukden visited his U.S. counterpart to express regret over the incident and to assure him that the responsible soldiers would be disciplined.[5]

CONTEMPORARY THREATS TO DIPLOMATIC MISSIONS

The 1985 Inman panel concluded that although past U.S. officials overseas had suffered occasional violence of one sort or another, only recently had there been any real pattern of politically inspired violence. After World War II, a new phenomenon emerged in Eastern Europe of large demonstrations against U.S. establishments and state-directed harassment against U.S. diplomats. The number of attacks on U.S. Foreign Service personnel overseas increased dramatically in the 1960s and early 1970s, attacks mostly by hostile forces in Southeast Asian war zones but also by the anti-American revolutionary terrorist groups increasingly prevalent in the 1970s and 1980s.

The Inman report noted the emergence in the fifteen years prior to 1986 of newer, more violent tactics and weapons than previously and more frequent kidnappings and murder attempts. "In sum, what we have seen in recent years is an expansion of the threat from physical violence against diplomats—often private, incidental, even furtive—to the beginnings of calculated terror campaigns, psychological conflict waged by nation or sub-group against nation, with an ever-broadening range of targets, weapons and tactics."[6]

Some comparisons illustrate the heightened degree of danger to U.S. embassies and Foreign Service personnel overseas. Of the 186 personnel commemorated on Department of State plaques for their deaths overseas in service to their country, 110 died between 1965 and 1993, far exceeding the total killed in the previous 185 years of United States diplomacy. Moreover, violent circumstances surrounded only two of the deaths before 1900 and five of those between 1900 and 1964. By contrast, the great majority of the post-1965 deaths occurred in violent circumstances, even after the end of the wars in Southeast Asia that had cost so many Foreign Service lives.[7]

A New Policy Emerges

U.S. policy toward terrorism was not always one of absolute refusal to make deals with hostage-takers. When U.S. Ambassador to Brazil Charles Burke Elbrick was kidnapped in September 1969, the Nixon administration pressed the reluctant Brazilian government to meet the kidnappers' demands for the release of political prisoners. When Elbrick had been freed in exchange for the release into exile of fifteen political prisoners, the U.S. government thanked the Brazilian government for placing its concern for Ambassador Elbrick's life above all other concerns. In all, 129 political prisoners were released in exchange for kidnapped diplomats in Brazil in the years 1969 and 1970. Following the 1970 kidnapping of U.S. police adviser Dan Mitrione in Uruguay, however, both U.S. and Uruguayan governments declined to deal with the kidnappers, and Mitrione was killed.[8]

The kidnapping and murder of Israeli athletes by Palestinian Black September terrorists at the 1972 Munich Olympics shocked the world. Thereafter, the U.S. government began organizing its terrorism policy in a more systematic fashion. David Korn, in his book *Assassination in Khartoum*, writes that the Munich Olympics terrorist attack sparked the crystallization of a new U.S. policy on terrorism based on "no negotiations with hostage-takers, no deals with them, and no concessions to them."[9]

According to Korn, however, the new U.S. policy was not widely publicized until the 1973 Black September attack on U.S. diplomats in Khartoum, capital of the Sudan. That March 1973 kidnapping and murder of U.S. Ambassador Cleo A. Noel, Jr., his deputy George Curtis Moore, and Belgian Chargé Guy Eid at the Saudi embassy in Khartoum marked a new and dangerous turn toward the internationalization of terror against diplomats, often with the support, sponsorship, or tolerance of governments.

In response to the growing number and intensity of terrorist attacks against U.S. diplomatic missions in the late 1960s and early 1970s, the Nixon administration conceived a counterterrorism program and justified it to Congress in 1973. This period saw increased emphasis on defensive driving, varying one's route to work, and other security precautions. But the new and growing element that made terrorism and security far more difficult problems was the internationalization of terror. This new and dangerous period parallels the crises discussed in this book.

A problem as difficult for diplomats as international terrorism was the reluctance or inability of host governments, sometimes out of political weakness, to confront dangerous threats to foreign embassies and their personnel. A government's reluctance to deal harshly with domestic or international antiforeign or anti-American actions was one manifestation of such weakness. In other cases, the proliferation of weaponry had made local mobs and political groups increasingly formidable for host governments to confront. In addition, some of the weaker states—particularly in Africa, including Liberia and Somalia—began to unravel in the 1990s in ways that put our embassies at grave risk.

The revolutionary, anti-Western movements that grew and spread in the 1970s and 1980s had little or no regard for the traditional notions of respect for the status of diplomats. Rogue or revolutionary regimes, such as those in Iran and Libya and in China during the Cultural Revolution, "can also be extremely bad news for diplomats and consuls."[10] Violent mob assaults on U.S. embassies in Tehran,

Islamabad, and Tripoli in late 1979 and the demonstrated inability or unwilling-ness of the governments in those and other foreign capitals to provide effective protection to U.S. missions abroad resulted in the initiation of major programs at a number of posts to increase security against this threat.

After a series of suicide-vehicle bombings against U.S. installations in the Middle East, the State Department began a large program to strengthen security programs and construct new embassies to replace those that could not be ade-quately strengthened.[11] The Inman panel concluded in 1985 that facilities in 126 of the State Department's 262 overseas posts did not meet the department's cur-rent minimum physical security standards and thus required replacement.[12] The enormous building program undertaken in the ensuing years will take many years to complete.

The increase in attacks on U.S. personnel and facilities overseas coincided with a marked increase in international terrorist incidents, from 124 in 1968 to highs of 672 in 1987 and 648 in 1988. Finally, the number of international terrorist inci-dents began to decline substantially, to 406 in 1989 and 456 in 1990.[13] After increasing to 557 in 1991, when half of the incidents occurred during Operation Desert Storm, the declining trend resumed for the remainder of 1991, reaching 362 in 1992, the lowest number of international terrorist incidents since 1975.[14]

"The United States is a prime target," says the State Department, "because its policies, values and culture are directly opposed by many terrorist groups and because the U.S. has an extensive official and commercial presence overseas."[15] For similar reasons, the United States has been a prime target of violence-prone mobs. From 1980 to 1991, about 2,500, or 40 percent, of the 6,500 recorded inter-national terrorist incidents were against American targets. American casualties since 1980 have totaled 587 dead and 627 wounded.[16]

The tremendous increase in terrorist incidents in the 1970s and 1980s stimulat-ed the development of a clear and strongly articulated U.S. policy of counterter-rorism. This policy is similar to, but more carefully articulated than, the policy originally proclaimed in 1973. The United States makes no concessions to terror-ists holding official or private U.S. citizens hostage. At the same time, it will make every effort, including contact, to obtain the release of the hostages without mak-ing concessions. The United States also works with other countries to isolate states that support terrorism and cooperates with friendly countries in developing practical measures to counter terrorism.[17]

The department clearly states U.S. policy toward terrorist incidents. The United States holds that the country in which the offense occurs, and where the victim is located, retains the primary responsibility for the safe release of the vic-tim and punishment of the perpetrators. The United States will seek to extradite those who take U.S. citizens hostage. It will not pay ransom, release prisoners, change policies, or make substantive concessions, including publishing manifestos or arranging safe-conduct for terrorists out of the country. The United States encourages other nations to adopt the same stance.

State Department Coordinator for Counter-Terrorism Thomas McNamara testified in early 1993 that the growth of international cooperation, particularly pressure on state sponsors of terrorism such as Iraq and Libya, had been the main reason for the steady decline in international terrorism. Citing the positive impact of the massive changes in the former Soviet Union and Eastern Europe, McNamara also addressed the need to monitor closely the dangers that could result from the intensification of ethnic conflicts in this area.[18]

Emergency Action Preparedness

U.S. embassies overseas have generally given mixed reviews to the State Department *Emergency Action Manual*, designed to prepare embassy personnel for emergency situations. Though almost no crisis develops exactly as written in the manual, the State Department has devoted a great deal of effort in recent years to updating its manuals and conducting crisis management exercises. The *Emergency Action Manual*'s table of contents provides a useful indicator of crisis preparations required in today's world: "hostage taking"; "aircraft hijacking"; "bomb plan"; "civil disorder"; "disaster"; "major accident"; "internal defense"; "destruction"; "major casualty"; "fire"; "drawdown" (of personnel); "evacuation"; and "safehaven" (in government usage defined as "a secure location of last resort").

The manual's key guidelines provide that all posts must establish emergency action committees, designate personnel for specific crisis-related functions, and prepare special office space. Clear discipline is to be established under the ambassador. Posts are instructed to draft emergency action plans, send them to Washington, update their lists of U.S. contacts, and test their plans through drills. As readers will see, managing the crises recounted in the following chapters involved assigning responsibility for virtually all the elements the manual prescribes: evacuation, transportation, embarkation, consular services, internal defense, disaster relief, destruction of documents and classified material, administration, public affairs, rumor control, medical matters, and liaison (with the host government).

Emergency Consular Services to U.S. Citizens[19]

In the early days of the U.S. Consular Service, as Charles S. Kennedy comments in his book on the subject, "untrained men were acting on their own with minimal guidance, responding to local events, each according to common sense and instinct."[20] In the ensuing years, consular history was marked by numerous dramatic and improvised efforts to assist U.S. citizens—in France during the Franco-Prussian War, in Spain at the outbreak of the Spanish Civil War, and elsewhere.

With the need for emergency assistance to U.S. citizens growing as their presence overseas continues to increase, the delivery of such assistance has become more organized and effective in recent years. Easier communications with

Washington and the greater feasibility of sending in a team of consular or other experts have markedly enhanced the magnitude and speed of resources that can be concentrated on a crisis. Forever changed by the downing of Pan Am Flight 103 over Lockerbie, Scotland, in 1988, the Consular Affairs Bureau now provides consular officers substantial training in responding to emergencies.

The *Disaster Assistance Handbook on Consular Assistance to U.S. Citizens Involved in Disasters Abroad*, produced by the bureau's Citizens' Emergency Center, provides guidelines for consular officers. It instructs them to cable and call reports of any disaster immediately to the Department of State; to send one or more consular officers to the scene of the disaster; to establish a task force at the embassy and a control center at the site, if necessary; and to identify U.S. citizens involved, maintain a log of all activities, and report daily on the situation, among other duties. Even in crises that primarily affect the U.S. embassy community, embassies are increasingly concerned for and attentive to the unofficial U.S. community, as this book's cases demonstrate.

This concern reflects, in part, the shrinking world, in all parts of which U.S. citizens are likely to be residents or visitors. It also responds to congressional mandates calling for the Department of State to prepare and respond more effectively to emergencies overseas. The U.S. government is charged to effectively advise U.S. citizens and those with U.S. permanent resident status of the dangers they face overseas and to assist those who wish to depart from a dangerous situation. When normal commercial transportation modes become unavailable, access to evacuations offered to U.S. government officials is now also offered to private U.S. citizens.

While not directly responsible for providing a secure environment in which private U.S. citizens can work, the U.S. government "has a moral obligation to provide assistance, advice, guidance and information that can enable citizens, business, or other organizations to enhance their own protection."[21] In 1985, the State Department established a formal organization, the American Private Sector Overseas Security Advisory Council, to promote coordination between U.S. overseas business and private sector interests and State Department overseas security programs.

LOOKING AT CASES

U.S. embassies have always faced crises in periods of internal or cross-border wars, natural disasters, or other calamities. Beginning in the early 1970s, however, they faced new and growing dangers as terrorism went increasingly international, traditional respect for diplomats and diplomatic installations was increasingly violated, and weak governments failed to fulfill their responsibilities for protection. At the same time, the means of violence available to terrorists and mobs had greatly increased, along with their inclination and ability to use violence against embassies and embassy personnel.

This volatile combination of circumstances has made for a highly dangerous period for U.S. embassies and their personnel. In the changed environment since the early 1970s, many more embassies have faced serious crises than could be accommodated in a single volume—even after excluding the Southeast Asian crises, about which many others have already written. For this volume the cases selected present crises of varying types faced by U.S. embassies around the world and show how individual embassies coped with their particular crises.

The March 1973 kidnapping and murder of Cleo Noel and Curt Moore by Black September terrorists in Khartoum marked a new and dangerous phase in international terrorism and a change in U.S. policy toward terrorism. The calculated killing of Noel and Moore is the subject of David Korn's book. The first case study in this volume, the decision later in 1973 to close the U.S. embassy in Kampala, Uganda, flowed from the Khartoum assassinations. Embassy Kampala recommended its own closing because Ugandan ruler Idi Amin failed to condemn the killings in Khartoum and the embassy's analysis concluded that he would not oppose similar international terror operations in Uganda. Although the State Department did not accept the embassy's recommendation until seven months later, the embassy showed itself prescient in predicting the sort of terrorist activities Amin would tolerate, as demonstrated several years later in the crisis that led to the raid on Entebbe.

The closing of Embassy Kampala was an effective case of crisis avoidance, although Robert Keeley, who was then chargé, notes that the decision to close the embassy was made easier by the absence of any vital U.S. interests in Uganda. The management of the closure provides some rare lessons in how to close embassy operations in an efficient and orderly manner, something that was easier in 1973 Kampala than in several violence-ridden capitals described in later chapters. Keeley's chapter also reveals the substantial scope given embassy officials to evaluate and manage local factors in the closure, duties made easier by the embassy's correct judgments of the local environment and reactions.

The next three cases examined are examples of weak host governments unable or unwilling to protect U.S. embassies and diplomats against security threats: the continuing crisis affecting the U.S. embassy in Tehran between its February 1979 temporary takeover by Islamic militants and the prolonged embassy takeover that began in November 1979; the February 1979 kidnapping and murder of U.S. Ambassador Adolph Dubs in Kabul, Afghanistan; and the razing of the U.S. embassy in Islamabad, Pakistan, in November 1979. (In Tehran, the Iranian government went further and actually identified itself with the militants holding the U.S. embassy and its personnel hostage.)

These three incidents were the work of domestic groups attacking a U.S. embassy to advance their own political agendas. As was not the case in Uganda, the United States had significant policy interests in maintaining influence and a diplomatic presence in Iran, Afghanistan, and Pakistan. The three cases presented difficult dilemmas for U.S. policy and security interests.

Victor Tomseth, author of the chapter on Tehran, concludes that critical foreign policy decisions are based on U.S. domestic considerations as well as on foreign policy concerns. An embassy, he says, has the responsibility to evaluate the likely consequences of such decisions and to recommend appropriate steps to diminish the dangers to the embassy.

The 1983 bombing of the U.S. embassy in Beirut, Lebanon, illustrated the host government's inability to provide adequate protection to the embassy in that war-torn country. In this case, the U.S. policies of strengthening the Lebanese government and helping to broker an agreement between it and Israel were anathema to some groups within Lebanon, especially Hizballah, as well as to neighboring Syria. This bombing, and the subsequent bombings of U.S. Marine quarters in Beirut, the new Beirut embassy building, and the U.S. embassy in Kuwait, led in summer 1984 to creation of the Inman panel, whose report in June 1985 spurred major efforts to build or rebuild secure embassy facilities around the world.[22]

The Beirut bombing displayed in powerful and tragic fashion both the dangerous commitment of terrorists to using violence to advance their ends and the sophistication of their weaponry. Richard Gannon discusses the special needs for coping with large-scale tragedy presented by the great loss of life in this episode.

The November 1989 military moves by the Salvadoran guerrillas and their call for popular insurrection posed special dangers for the U.S. embassy in El Salvador. For the first time, the guerrillas launched major attacks on the capital, San Salvador, including neighborhoods where embassy families lived and hotels that housed temporarily assigned U.S. personnel. William Walker discusses the U.S. embassy's efforts to cope with the crisis occasioned by these guerrilla assaults, in a country where the United States had a large physical presence and a major policy commitment to the economic and military support of the elected Salvadoran government.

The El Salvador case in some ways reflected the traditional crisis situation in which a revolutionary movement tries to topple a U.S.-supported government. The chapter discusses the importance of the U.S. community's security concerns and U.S. reluctance to give the appearance of abandonment, in addition to the U.S. government's real need for personnel on the ground to manage its policy interests.

The crisis in Embassy Kuwait described by Barbara Bodine flowed directly from the decision of the United States and most other governments to refuse to recognize the legitimacy of Iraq's invasion in August 1990 or its claims of sovereignty over Kuwait. During the months after the Iraqi invasion, the situation of U.S. embassy personnel and private U.S. citizens and third-country nationals inside and outside the embassy compound was precarious. Bodine's account reveals that situation's emotional impact. And although the Iraqi government could be held responsible for the fate of the embassy and its personnel, that government had already shown itself disrespectful of such fundamental international norms as Kuwaiti sovereignty and the lives of Kuwaiti and third-country civilians.

Similar dangers for U.S. embassies and for U.S. and third-country personnel resulted from strictly internal battles over power in Liberia and Somalia. Dennis Jett describes the efforts in the spring and summer of 1990 to secure and finally evacuate Embassy Monrovia, and James Bishop tells how Embassy Mogadishu handled the 1990 crisis and early 1991 evacuation there. The success of such evacuations depended critically on U.S. military support and close coordination between our embassies and those support elements.

The El Salvador, Kuwait, and Liberia chapters also illustrate the great importance, and the great difficulty, of extending protection to the very large number of private U.S. citizens living and traveling overseas today, even in countries where the prospects of military action are building. These difficulties are compounded in places like El Salvador, where many U.S. citizens deliberately maintained their distance from any contact with the U.S. government. Modern communications also pose their own problems. As one author put it, the one dissatisfied U.S. citizen will inevitably appear on CNN.

The U.S. and other governments and embassies have made many adjustments in their security precautions and procedures since the early 1970s, increasing the number of security officers overseas and the resources devoted to the security of embassies and their personnel. Resources for security have again begun to decline, however.[23] James Taylor's account of the 1979 kidnapping and assassination of Ambassador Dubs notes the absence of a specific threat to Dubs's life. The large security budgets available some years later most likely would have provided a bodyguard detail for an ambassador in an environment as violent as that of 1979 Kabul, even without a specific threat. There are no guarantees, of course, that the presence of such a bodyguard would have prevented the kidnapping.[24]

DRAWING LESSONS

It is not possible to protect against every danger. We often prepare well for the last war or the last crisis. Although Embassy Mogadishu was newly constructed to Inman standards and provided a measure of protection, eventually it had to be abandoned when all semblance of order broke down in Somalia. Terrorists, and even mobs, can be flexible; they often adapt their methods to shift to new, less well guarded targets, as they did in the 1980s in attacking vulnerable consulates and other facilities, for example when Arab gunmen wounded U.S. Consul Robert Homme in Strasbourg and murdered Leamon Hunt, head of the Sinai Multinational Force Observer Mission based in Rome.

This book's authors recommend stepped-up efforts to systematically debrief participants in embassy crises. Lessons learned should be disseminated to embassies worldwide and to newly arriving staff in posts that have suffered previous assaults.

In their testimony before Congress in 1993, senior State Department officials responsible for terrorism policy primarily credited enhanced international cooperation against terrorism for the reduction in international terrorist attacks, including those against U.S. citizens. International consensus in repudiating and punishing terrorist acts has grown.

Nonetheless, the breakdowns of the regimes in Liberia and Somalia and other ethnic clashes of the 1990s could be as dangerous as the terrorism of the 1970s and 1980s. The horrors are too recent, the dangerous weapons in the hands of those who would use violence to advance their ends too many, and the renegade regimes too disrespectful of international norms for us to do other than maintain vigilance and anticipate and prepare, as best we can, for the next crisis.

These nine cases of embassies in crisis do not all suggest the same lessons. In some instances the lessons conflict, depending on the particular type of crisis. But there is a substantial amount of commonality in the lessons learned, including these frequently mentioned ones:

• Good and well-drilled emergency action plans were found useful in several cases, although not relevant in another.

• The difficulty of getting sufficient focus in Washington when a crisis happens in the middle of the night or simultaneously with other crises was mentioned by several authors, although there have been some improvements in this regard.

• The tendency of ever-optimistic embassies to suspend belief, to engage in wishful thinking, or not to notice subtle policy shifts is a danger. (It is too simple to recommend hoping for the best while planning for the worst.)

• Planners must recognize that foreign policy decisions will be made for a combination of domestic and foreign policy reasons. Concomitantly, both Washington and its diplomats abroad must carefully assess and plan for the likely effects of foreign policy decisions made in Washington on our embassies and personnel abroad.

• It is difficult to manage a crisis when policy decision processes are drawn out, particularly when several agencies have strong interests. Needed are improved efficiency in that decision process and uniform application and discipline once the policy decision is made.

• In instances of personnel drawdowns, close attention must be paid to functional needs, to the strengths of remaining personnel, to clear roles and responsibilities, and to the evolution of a cohesive embassy crisis team.

• Embassies should manage short-term crises largely on their own, because Washington support takes time to organize.

• Washington support is more important in longer-term crises, but embassy input into what support is needed and what provided should be heavy. (Washington agencies, for example, gave Embassy San Salvador a menu of evacuation options and worked the logistics on each, so that when Ambassador Walker chose an "authorized departure" the necessary charter aircraft could be sent.)

• State Department support is vital. It is almost always good in the immediate aftermath of tragedy, but less good in prolonged and contentious situations.

• It is important that there be a single channel of communication.

• Communications are critical, and backup systems are needed in case of failures.

- The management of evacuations and evacuees is important and generally improved, but the exceptions can be devastating.

In some instances, the lessons from earlier crises have already been put into practice, as for example in improving crisis planning and security preparations—and the budgets necessary to support them. U.S. military capability to respond to crises in far-flung locations has similarly improved, as has coordination among the various U.S. government elements required for responding effectively to crises. Although problems remain and new crises arise, as in Rwanda in 1994, these lessons from the past can contribute to that effectiveness.

The president of Uganda, Idi Amin Dada, poses with the Kampala diplomatic corps. West German Ambassador Wilhelm Kopf is standing directly behind Amin, and U.S. Chargé d'Affaires Robert Keeley is behind Kopf. *Uganda Ministry of Information*.

2 Crisis Avoidance: Shutting Down Embassy Kampala, 1973

Robert V. Keeley

In October 1973 the United States government decided to close its embassy in Kampala, Uganda, to avert a crisis considered highly probable in the ominous atmosphere generated by General Idi Amin Dada's misrule. I was the chargé d'affaires at the time, the ambassador having been recalled eight months earlier. No acute crisis for the embassy or its personnel resulted from the closing, but its careful management provides a lesson in crisis avoidance.

In March 1973, deteriorating Ugandan domestic security conditions increased the vulnerability of official American personnel, freshly heightened by the recent kidnapping and assassination of U.S. Ambassador Cleo Noel and Deputy Chief of Mission Curt Moore by Palestinian Black September terrorists in Khartoum, capital of neighboring Sudan. After prolonged consideration by the embassy's country team and in view of limited U.S. government interests in Uganda, Embassy Kampala recommended, in cable number 900 of March 9, 1973, that the State Department seriously consider withdrawing its diplomatic presence from Uganda by mid-1973. Kampala 900 stressed the absence of motivation shown by the security organs of the Government of Uganda (GOU) to protect U.S. officials. "What stands out in Uganda today," it concluded in part, "is that (a) GOU security organs are themselves the greatest danger to public order; (b) General Amin publicly condones actions of Palestinian extremists such as Black September (BSO) terrorist operations and is prepared to plead for leniency for [the] murderers of two American diplomats; [and] (c) terrorist groups such as [the] BSO are aware of Amin's favorable attitude toward them, which could well incline them to use Ugandan territory with good hope of impunity. . . ."

13

The Department of State decided in March not to accept the embassy's recommendation that it begin preparations to close the mission by June 30. New developments in late October 1973, however, moved the department to order the embassy to be closed as quickly as possible.

AMIN'S OCTOBER SURPRISE

In the afternoon of October 29, 1973, I was summoned to meet with the new Ugandan foreign minister, Colonel Michael Ondoga, recently ordered back to Kampala from his post as ambassador to Moscow. As he greeted me in his office, Colonel Ondoga could not hide his nervousness, and I soon understood his apprehension. Amin had instructed him to inform me of the expulsion of our Marine security guards from Uganda, allegedly for having engaged in "subversive activities," though more likely the expulsion was Amin's riposte to alleged U.S. intervention on the side of Israel in the recent "October War." The order gave the Marines forty-eight hours to leave the country. It is doubtful that Amin had thought about the probable consequences of his action in terms of how the United States would respond, but perhaps he did not care.

Radio Uganda announced the expulsion that evening, though it did not spell out the allegations against the Marines. The explanation given was consistent with the line Colonel Ondoga had taken with me and confirmed that the Marines had until 6:00 P.M. on Wednesday, two days later, to leave Uganda.

I reported the expulsion order to the State Department by "Immediate NIACT" (night action cable), stating the obvious—that we had no choice but to comply. The department concurred and instructed us to effect the departure of the entire Marine detachment as a group as soon as it could be arranged. The department also instructed me to close the embassy, with all personnel departing as soon as possible. They suggested that forty-eight hours would not be too soon. Amin's expulsion order had been the last straw.

Next Steps—October 30

The first cable I sent out on October 30 went to Embassy Nairobi, asking it to brief my wife, Louise, on the expulsion of the Marines and the order from Washington to close the post. All of our dependents had already been relocated to Nairobi in the previous weeks. She would be able to brief the other wives staying there and caution them to be as discreet as possible in talking by telephone to their spouses in Kampala.[1]

The next cable replied to the department's instructions. We had no quarrel with the decision to close the post, but the order for an extremely rapid (to my mind, precipitate) exodus greatly bothered me. My preference was to leave in as orderly, comfortable, and dignified a manner as could be arranged. As no one felt in particular danger at this time, I pressed for a longer period to close the embassy, allowing us time to pack up and to dispose of our automobiles, and in two cases dogs, as best we could.

14

The Marines were booked to leave on the next day's morning flight to Nairobi. Two communicators had already left as part of our earlier drawdown, and another officer would depart with the Marines. That left nine of us, each of whom would depart as soon as he had completed what he had to do with his effects and car. I would of course depart last, after arranging the turnover of our affairs to the chosen protecting power.[2]

I thought it best not to inform the Ugandan government officially of our action until just before my own departure, though it would probably have surmised what was up long before that. I preferred not to discuss anything with the embassy of the prospective protecting power unless and until that government had agreed to assume the role. I also wished to delay informing the private American community until closer to the end.

As for our official vehicles, it made no sense to drive them to Nairobi as the department had proposed. They were in such a deplorable state that I doubted they could make it to the border; moreover, they could still be sold locally for a good deal more than they were worth. Our best vehicle, a Toyota Land Cruiser, was already in Nairobi being serviced, while our USIS post had just received two brand-new vehicles that could profitably be sold in Kampala.

The department had asked that nonessential personnel be ordered to depart immediately. I deemed all remaining nine persons essential, among other reasons because they were needed to share the standing of guard duty in the chancery in the evening and night hours, as substitutes for the Marine guards. I also informed the department that we would begin confining our reporting to matters affecting our own situation plus one general wrap-up on each day's antics of General Amin.

The Ugandan government seemed to have decided on a program of harassing us right to the end. At 10:30 A.M. the previous day, it had shut off electric power to the USIS Center and to the entire Embassy House building, whose sixth and seventh floors were our chancery. Repeated calls to the power company had been unavailing. In addition, some army personnel cut the telephone line at the house occupied by the head Marine. Before leaving they told his steward that the embassy-owned house now belonged to the Ugandan government.

To reinforce my argument that we should not hasten our departure unduly, I stressed the risk of serious losses from theft and diversion unless we packed our personal effects before leaving. There was only one moving company still in business in Kampala, and its personnel could handle only one packing job at a time.

Problems Pile Up—October 31

The Marines got off for Nairobi as scheduled on the morning of the 31st. One of their last concerns was that they would be unable to host the traditional Marine Birthday Ball on November 10, a date observed in this way by U.S. embassy Marine detachments worldwide on the anniversary of the founding of the Marine Corps. It was agreed, after some sticky negotiations, that our Marines would cohost the ball in Nairobi and invite all of our Embassy Kampala personnel, as we expected to be there by November 10.

The department urged us to speed up the departure of our personnel. I concurred that James Haase, our political officer, could go, since we were cutting our reporting to the bare minimum. I needed Philip Ringdahl, our consul, as we still had the major chore of informing the private American community of our plans. We certainly needed a communicator to send and receive telegrams till the end; the one who stayed was Edward Nosko, who worked from my typed drafts, as no secretary remained.

One problem remained in the communications area, a common one in the Foreign Service. Despite the department's having imposed a "minimize" order—supposed to restrict communications traffic for Embassy Kampala to essential messages only—we continued to receive long cables we could very well have done without, such as a status report on the Law of the Sea negotiations and the full text of Secretary Kissinger's speech on agricultural policy.

Our classified file holdings had already been nearly eliminated, and we now shipped out by diplomatic courier all that remained of the embassy's permanent archives. We planned to burn the traffic of the final days after we closed down communications on the last day.

Most of our closing-down problems were administrative, so I needed some additional experienced "admin" talent to augment our staff in the closing days. We were in particularly dire need of someone with budget and fiscal know-how. Even better would be someone who had had experience closing a post. The department obliged and sent me two excellent people, James Mark from Dar es Salaam, one of the Africa Bureau's very best admin people, and Patrick Kennedy, one of the ablest people I have known in the Foreign Service. What we lacked in numbers we made up for in skill, dedication, and hard work.

With word of our imminent closing spreading through the private American community, we were beginning to receive requests for assistance in communicating with various missionary headquarters in the United States. As we passed messages, it became clear that the missionaries would follow our advice to leave Uganda only if ordered to do so by their home offices. They did not want to leave, but would do so if ordered out.

Electric power at our chancery remained cut off for more than forty-eight hours, but this did not disrupt our communications because we had an emergency generator. (I declined the department's discretionary advice to establish a formal record of GOU harassment by sending low-key notes to the Foreign Ministry about these "intolerable conditions.") When power was restored, we received a written apology from our Embassy House landlord about the prolonged outage. It was hard to tell whether it had been a case of harassment or merely another of the now frequently occurring breakdowns in public services. The cutting of the phone line, however, appeared to have been the personal inspiration of the soldiers in a barracks near the head Marine's house.

Much more serious for our personnel—and for everyone else in Uganda who owned anything movable—was the continuing threat from attacks by gangs of armed criminal robbers, known locally as "kondos." These were often serving military personnel, freelancing with their weapons. One encounter with such a gang nearly ended in grief for one of us. Four armed thugs, including at least two in army uniforms, attacked Jim Haase as he was returning with his household employees in his Rover sedan after a farewell dinner. He managed to escape after a zigzag high-speed chase through downtown Kampala, with the kondos shooting out one of his taillights in the process. Haase flew off to Nairobi the following day feeling lucky to have escaped this last adventure unharmed.

THE PROTECTING POWER PROBLEM

By this time the State Department had decided to ask the Federal Republic of Germany to act as protecting power for the United States in Uganda. The West German Foreign Office agreed in principle and so instructed Ambassador Wilhelm Kopf in Kampala.

Ambassador Kopf raised a number of questions, which the German Foreign Office then took up with our embassy in Bonn. He wanted us to leave behind one or two men "with technical qualifications" to work in the West German embassy in Kampala on matters affecting U.S. interests. He had in mind an administrator to deal with property questions and a communicator to operate our radio and telegraphic equipment. The Germans did not hide their designs. They relied entirely on the Ugandan telex system and wanted us to turn over our much more advanced, independent, and reliable communications equipment for them to operate if we could not leave our own operator behind; but we told them we could not leave our communications equipment behind.

The German ambassador was also concerned that assuming the role of the United States' protecting power had potentially negative consequences for his own personnel and for German relations with Uganda, given Amin's unpredictable and emotional nature. Kopf proposed to "smooth" the transfer process by carrying out the notification to the Ugandans in two stages—first a note from us announcing our closure and the withdrawal of our personnel, then one from his embassy, a short time later, announcing its assumption of responsibility for U.S. interests. Our embassy in Bonn pointed out that despite some political-psychological advantages, this procedure would leave a short time gap during which the Ugandans might "legitimately" assume no one was responsible for U.S. property.

In subsequent days there ensued a seemingly interminable exchange of messages between Kampala, Washington, and Bonn over this issue of how we and the West German embassy would inform the Ugandan government about our embassy's closure and the Germans' assumption of protecting power status. But Washington now set November 10 as the day by which all U.S. embassy personnel must be out of Uganda, and this issue and all others had to be settled by then, regardless. The deadline may have helped push these discussions and disagreements to a resolution, but in the event it was a close call.

17

Ambassador Kopf hoped that we would evacuate all the American missionaries from Uganda before we departed, fearing that Amin might move against them after we had gone. He also urged that we discourage American tourists from visiting Uganda, something we had already been doing.

We could not be sure what Amin might do about the private American community. He might decide to expel all Americans from Uganda, perhaps as a reaction to our closing the embassy. Retaliation was a basic instinct with him, an outlet for his own frustrations and paranoia. Based on his behavior when he expelled the Israelis and the Asian Ugandans, as well as our Marines, we anticipated that Amin would allow a reasonable time for their safe departure. But after observing the general for two years and four months, I still found him totally unpredictable.

The State Department declined to leave any American officials behind to work in the West German embassy, citing the security dangers to our personnel that were causing us to close our embassy. Kopf's proposed two-stage notification procedure did not appeal to us because we wanted the Ugandan government to understand clearly, *before* we closed up shop, that the West Germans were being entrusted to protect our interests in Uganda. Since we were not breaking relations, only closing our embassy, and were not asking the Ugandans to reciprocate by closing their embassy in Washington, we would continue to deal with them through that embassy (provided Amin kept it open) as well as through the West Germans in Kampala.

The department asked Embassy Bonn to express its "very deep gratitude" to the German Foreign Office for its cooperation and assistance in agreeing to represent our interests in Uganda. We would do our utmost to keep the work performed on our behalf to a minimum and hoped the Germans would find it possible to handle our workload with their own staff and facilities. Anticipating the additional workload, the German Foreign Office accelerated the filling of two vacant positions in its Kampala embassy.

MORE DIPLOMATIC NICETIES, NOVEMBER 3

On November 3 the department sent me the text of the note I was to deliver to an "appropriate GOU official" prior to my departure but only after we had final German government agreement to assume representation of our interests. After delivering it I was to notify the department as fast as possible, perhaps via telephone to Embassy Nairobi, which could then send an "immediate" cable to Washington. As soon as I had done the deed, the department wished to inform the Ugandan chargé d'affaires in Washington. The note began:

Upon instructions from the Government of the United States, the Embassy wishes to inform the Government of Uganda that all diplomatic and consular representatives of the United States are being withdrawn from Uganda. This decision by the United States Government results from actions of the Government of Uganda contrary to its international obligations which have created intolerable conditions for the conduct of diplomatic relations in Uganda. These have included, inter alia, official threats against the safety and dignity of diplomatic representatives of the United States Government in Uganda, unfounded accusations by high Ugandan officials, and the precipitous and unjustified expulsion from Uganda of American personnel responsible for the protection of the Embassy. . . . The United States Government intends to entrust the Government of the Federal Republic of Germany with the protection of its interests and property in Uganda. . . .

Also on November 3, Ambassador Kopf renewed his effort to have the notification take place in two stages. He got his Foreign Office to propose that our note be changed to state that we had merely "requested" the Federal Republic of Germany to assume responsibility for our interests. The West German embassy would then follow with a note saying it had agreed to do so. Kopf argued that otherwise the Ugandans would think we and the Germans were engaging in some sort of "collusion."

The department accepted this argument and told Bonn it would supply new language for that portion of the note. I disagreed but failed to use the strongest argument with the department, which was that the host government has to approve the selection of the protecting power; if the GOU did have an objection, we should know about it and act accordingly before we closed our embassy.

I thought Kopf and his Foreign Office with their two-step scenario were trying to be too subtle with General Amin. Amin was not a sophisticated man; in my experience the best way to deal with him was to be absolutely candid, to "lay it on the line," as he said he preferred. There was no point pretending that our request to the West Germans to act as protecting power was something like an afterthought, to be arranged after we pulled out. I thought it especially important that the Ugandans understand we had arranged for a protecting power prior to our departure.

In the interest of tidiness I thought our note should include the date by which all embassy personnel would have left Uganda and the effective date on which the West German embassy would assume the protection of U.S. interests. If that date was not in the note, I suggested that I state it orally when delivering the note. I proposed to request an appointment with Foreign Minister Ondoga on November 9, to present the note to him or whomever else I could see that day, and then to leave on the evening flight for Nairobi on Saturday, November 10, at which point West German protection would begin.

There was some method in this proposed schedule of final events, though I did not explain it to the department. I anticipated that Ondoga would be so upset by the news I brought him, and so fearful of Amin's reaction (punishing the messenger for bringing bad news was his usual custom), that he would put off informing Amin as long as possible, hoping the general would learn of our action from some other source first. I counted on at least a twenty-four-hour delay, and perhaps as much as forty-eight hours, during which time we would have left the country and escaped his possible wrath.

The department acceded to the West Germans' suggestion that we change the text of the note to read we had "requested" them to take over and to substitute "protecting power" for the explicit reference to the FRG embassy. The department remained concerned about a potential time gap during which U.S. citizens in Uganda would be technically "unprotected," so I was instructed to make the point orally, when delivering the note, that we would be withdrawing within twenty-four hours after delivery of the note. During that twenty-four-hour period, the West German embassy was to deliver its note announcing its assumption of responsibility.

Meanwhile, I had picked up some useful information from a Ugandan policeman assigned guard duty at our chancery. (It is always good policy to be kind to the guards provided by the host government.) This guard's inspector had told him that Amin would soon be calling in the U.S. chargé to discuss embassy security following the Marine guards' expulsion. During Amin's recent visits to Rwanda and Burundi, the inspector had also told him, Amin had urged their presidents to expel any U.S. military personnel and Peace Corps volunteers.

GETTING READY FOR SHUTDOWN

I began giving the department and other interested posts daily status reports on our progress in closing the embassy. We were now down to seven persons, including Pat Kennedy on temporary duty. On Monday, November 5, Phil Ringdahl began notifying U.S. private citizens that we were closing down. It would take him three days to complete the process, via phone calls to our wardens and the heads of various groups, as well as telegrams to remotely located individuals asking them to telephone or come in to see the consul. Some of the missionary groups had already been hearing from their U.S. headquarters, and some, such as the Medical Mission sisters, had asked to confer with me about their plans.

On Monday I also called on Archbishop Bellotti, papal pro-nuncio and acting dean of the diplomatic corps, to inform him of the closure. Bellotti thought some Catholic missionaries would leave, further complicating the church's staffing problems, already grave because of the GOU's refusal to renew the residence and work permits of a number of priests and nuns. The only other diplomat I briefed at this stage was the acting British high commissioner, who kindly offered to send any classified cable traffic for us if we experienced communications problems during the final days.

That same day I informed the embassy's Ugandan employees of our plans. With all the packing, shipping, selling, and leaving they certainly knew the score already, and further delay in informing them officially would be senseless and wrong. I explained why we had decided to pull out, gave them a detailed outline of their termination benefits, and offered some the hope that they would be reemployed by the protecting power's embassy. They expressed appreciation for the good treatment we had accorded them in the past and understanding for our decision. A number voiced concern over delays they anticipated in receiving their final checks and their retirement contribution refunds.

Phil Ringdahl's phone calls would spread the word of our impending departure fast and wide throughout Uganda, but I wanted to hold off informing the Ugandan Foreign Ministry officially until the end of the week, on the presumption that so long as it had not officially received the news it might not feel a need to react. I had as yet made no personal contact with Ambassador Kopf, pending receipt of authorization from the department to begin discussions with him.

His DCM, Hartmut Hillgenberg, asked to see me and informed me that his government had in principle agreed to represent our interests in Uganda. He wanted to know what that would entail. I briefed him and gave him a photostat of our ten pages of regulations on the subject. He hoped that not many U.S. citizens would remain behind and that few if any American tourists would be coming in. He also said that Ambassador Kopf was surprised that I had not yet called on him to discuss the turnover to the protecting power.

I hastened to explain that our regulations specifically forbade any discussions at field posts until authorized by the department. This saved embarrassment in the field if, for example, the ambassador of the country receiving the request advised against assenting. As soon as I was authorized, I would call on Ambassador Kopf. The authorization arrived within three hours, telling me to discuss all aspects with Kopf and to resolve as many problems as we and the Germans could foresee prior to my departure.

In the midst of the uncertainty at this stage, David Newsom, the assistant secretary for Africa, sent me a morale-boosting message. He commended our handling of the withdrawal and closure, gave us positive feedback on the value of our reporting, analysis, and recommendations, and expressed welcome empathy for our difficult circumstances.

Suddenly and without notice my night guard, or *askari*, was changed on November 5, not the first time this had happened. This time, however, I had to assume the new man was actually an employee of the Special Branch. There was no point complaining to Securicor, the private company that supplied our guards, as it could only comply with police orders. A policeman in uniform also appeared that night, removing any doubt that I had been placed under close surveillance.

The policeman and the *askari* stationed themselves just outside my bedroom window on chairs borrowed from the terrace, probably in order to be able to listen in on any phone calls I made or received during the night, by now a fairly common occurrence. I walked out to where they sat and lectured them sternly, telling them their duty station was at the front gate, to protect me and my house, not at my window to spy on me. They moved fast.

As expected, word was spreading rapidly that we were pulling out of Uganda. It was quite possible that General Amin would hear about it and call me in to ask what we were up to. If he did call me in, my best tactic would be perfect candor, telling him what we were doing and why and informing him that I intended to notify the Foreign Ministry officially on Friday, at which time I would also name the country that would be assuming responsibility for our interests in Uganda. If he reacted by saying he was kicking us out rather than letting us quietly withdraw, I planned to ask for seventy-two hours to pack up and leave, which was all we really needed at that point.

Protective Pussyfooting

On November 6 the first order of business was to confer with Ambassador Kopf. He accepted my apology for being unable to discuss the matter with him earlier because of the strictures imposed by our regulations. I spent more than two hours with him, with DCM Hillgenberg joining us for the last part of the meeting.

At Kopf's request I gave him a detailed account of the ups and downs, mostly downs, of our relations with General Amin. Kopf was keenly interested in the rationale for our choice of his country as the protecting power. Though he said he was willing to do the job, he was not especially happy about it.

Kopf read to me the instructions he had received from Bonn to the effect that in the interests of both the Federal Republic and the United States the Foreign Office hoped the Germans' role as protecting power would do no harm to the good relations existing between the West German government and the Ugandan government. Kopf alluded to West Germany's "special relationship" with Israel as one complicating factor, given Amin's anti-Israel fanaticism. Everything I had told him about the responsibilities of a protecting power was news to him, he said, as Bonn had sent him little information on it. I gave him the text of the note I planned to deliver, indicating that his government had not yet signed off on the department's modifications.

We had a long discussion about the scenario for the delivery of our respective notes at the end of the week. I told Kopf my timing was pretty well fixed in concrete, as my instructions were to have everybody, including myself, out of Uganda by Saturday night, November 10. Kopf suggested I deliver my note as late as possible on Friday afternoon, just before close of business at the Foreign Ministry, in the hope that our action could be kept off the news broadcasts that evening. He accepted my reasoning that I could not deliver my note Saturday morning, since the ministry would be closed and there would be no one there to receive it.

Kopf's tentative decision was to deliver his note Saturday morning, in the hope that it would not be noticed until Monday. He proposed that we sign the necessary transfer documents on Saturday morning after he had delivered his note. He and Hillgenberg would work out how to deliver their note to a closed Foreign Ministry.

Kopf was particularly concerned that the Ugandans would learn prematurely that he was taking over as protecting power. We were doing our best to keep it secret, by telling those who were aware of our impending closure that we were still negotiating for a protecting power. Kopf suggested that it would be better to have

Amin bear the onus of kicking us out; but, as the "kickee" who would catch the "onus" or whatever else he delivered, I demurred.

Word of our closure was spreading through the Kampala diplomatic corps less rapidly than I had expected. I continued to receive requests for appointments and social invitations for the following week from usually well-informed diplomats who should have known better. I answered each by saying I planned to be in Nairobi that week.

We suggested to Washington that we keep three or four of our best Ugandan employees on our payroll to look after our affairs, rather than terminate them and ask the West Germans to rehire them. We would terminate on Friday those not being retained.

Complications

On Wednesday, November 7, at my second meeting with Kopf and Hillgenberg, Kopf translated for me the instructions he had just received from Bonn. Overriding my counterarguments, he insisted that I obtain the Ugandan government's assent before he would take over from me. He was also fearful about publicity identifying his embassy as the protecting power, and I was unable to convince him that the publicity would center on our pullout.

We were in a dilemma. Under the scenario we had worked out the previous day, with me delivering my note late Friday afternoon, we could not obtain the Ugandans' assent prior to my departure Saturday evening. I told Kopf that I and all remaining staff had to be out of Uganda by Saturday night, and there was no leeway in that plan. To get the Ugandans' assent before I turned over to Kopf I would have to inform the GOU earlier than desired or risk not obtaining the assent prior to my departure. If I did inform the GOU earlier, we ran the risk of being stuck too long in Kampala following delivery of the official notification.

After much discussion, Kopf and I worked out a new scenario. I would now plan to deliver my note early Friday morning. Instead of identifying the FRG, we would substitute a sentence saying the embassy would advise the ministry, without delay, of its intentions regarding a protecting power. On Friday afternoon I would deliver a second note stating that the U.S. government would like to ask the Federal Republic of Germany to protect its interests and property in Uganda and asking the Ugandan government's concurrence to the FRG's so serving. I would ask whoever received this note to please let me have at least an oral answer by Saturday noon, to be followed by written confirmation from the ministry. In a telephone conversation with Wendell Coote at the State Department, he and I settled on a revised text for our initial note that avoided any mention of the FRG or its embassy in Kampala.

Also on Wednesday, Phil Ringdahl reported on his efforts to notify all resident U.S. citizens of our impending closure and advise that they also leave Uganda. He had succeeded in reaching nearly all of them except for the four registered in far-distant West Nile District, Amin's home territory, to whom he had sent telegrams. Most of our citizens, particularly the missionaries, had to consult their home offices for instructions. The most common response was that they would wait to see how Amin reacted to our closure.

By this time the American community was nearly down to what could be termed the "hard core": about 150 missionaries and teachers whose life work was in Uganda, Americans married to Ugandans, and the children of those marriages. These would not leave except under the most extreme provocation and harassment or an expulsion order.

At the Soviet embassy's national day reception that evening I found that a number of the diplomats present had figured out that we were closing our embassy. A few even had the date. Amin attended the reception, exchanged toasts with the Soviet ambassador, and in his rambling, extemporaneous remarks praised the Soviets for helping the Arabs with arms in their fight against Israel. The Middle East dominated all post-speech conversation among the diplomats.

Toward the end of the reception, Mr. Oseku, the chief of protocol, sidled up to tell me that the foreign minister wished to see me at 10:30 the following morning, Thursday. I said I would be there. I phoned Hillgenberg and informed him that I would most likely be delivering the revised note to Foreign Minister Ondoga in the morning. I said I would try to see Kopf before the meeting with Ondoga to get his concurrence to this revised timing.

DOUBLE SURPRISE AT THE FOREIGN MINISTRY

On arriving at the chancery office on Thursday morning, November 8, I hurriedly retyped the note to reflect the changes agreed with Kopf and Coote. I then typed a second brief note, expressing my government's intention to ask the FRG "to assume the protection of its interests and property in Uganda" and asking for written confirmation that the GOU had no objection. My plan, assuming Ondoga did not expel me from Uganda forthwith and ship me over the border, was to call on John Ntimba, the senior career officer at the ministry, in the afternoon and deliver this second note, asking him to try to give us an answer by close of business on Friday.

I walked from Embassy House over to the Foreign Ministry, unsure of exactly what was going to happen in the meeting with Ondoga and whether the situation would be such that I ought to deliver the note to him. Since he had initiated the meeting, he had something on his mind and would not be aware that I had a note to deliver to him. I knew my message would be a surprise.

As I was on the way to the Foreign Ministry a big black Mercedes limousine flying the East German flag pulled up alongside me. Out jumped the East German ambassador, Hans Fischer, who grasped my right hand in both of his and shook it vigorously. "I am very, very sorry to learn that you are leaving. Very sorry to see you go. Saturday night, is it? I will not be able to say goodbye at Entebbe. So . . . you have my very best wishes. And kindest regards to Madame Keeley."

He jumped back into the car, which sped away, leaving me speechless. So much for our well-kept secret. The East Germans, in cahoots with the Ugandan Special Branch, most likely had been tapping our phones or Kopf's or both and knew every detail of our meticulous planning for the embassy closure. It therefore seemed ridiculous to delay notifying the Ugandans any longer, so I decided to proceed with Ondoga forthwith.

When I arrived at the foreign minister's office at 10:30, the waiting room already contained a full panoply of media people, a television crew, a movie crew, still cameramen, and a press reporter. This was normal for my sessions with General Amin but was a first for a meeting with Foreign Minister Ondoga. I concluded he was going to announce our expulsion, for the benefit of the media.

After a ten-minute wait, Colonel Ondoga arrived, accompanied by Oseku and a note-taker. As the camera crews went to work, the minister gravely recounted a series of serious incidents, threats, and burglaries affecting the security of the Ugandan mission to the United Nations. The Government of Uganda insisted that the Government of the United States do something to improve security for Ambassador Grace Ibingira and his mission.

Ondoga assured me the incidents were recent and limited to New York, then handed me a note to read. The language was quite strong but otherwise unimpeachable. Among other things the note referred to the articles of the Vienna Convention stipulating the duty of the host country to protect the person and property of foreign diplomats. As I read the note, I found the situation most surreal and thought, "The pot is calling the kettle black"; but I decided not to voice the thought, as this was not an occasion for levity.

Improvising, I said to Ondoga: "The United States government takes very seriously its obligation to provide protection, both to foreign embassies in Washington, consulates elsewhere, and all the missions accredited to the United Nations. I will immediately inform my government and will ask that steps be taken to help Ambassador Ibingira's situation."

As the cameras continued to hum softly, I changed the subject, handing my note to Ondoga with the simple statement that I was delivering it "on instructions from my government." The minister read the note in silence, while Oseku and I chatted about the Soviet reception of the previous evening. I observed sweat breaking out on Ondoga's forehead and suddenly felt sorry for him. Less than two weeks on the job and nothing but bad news to take to the general. Ondoga finished the note and then read it over again from the beginning.

I waited until he had finished his second reading and then said, "I would like to add one thing orally. When something like this happens, we need to arrange to have a protecting power take charge of protecting our interests and property in Uganda." (On hearing the words "protecting power," Oseku nearly fell off his chair. He knew what *that* meant.) "This can be a time-consuming process," I continued, saying I hoped it would not be. I said I hoped very shortly to be in touch with Mr. Ntimba to give him a request for the minister's "concurrence in the selection of a protecting power," so that we could "make a transfer to the ambassador of the protecting power before I leave on Saturday evening."

"I will tell Mr. Ntimba to expect you. Are all of your people going to be gone by Saturday?"

"Yes, Mr. Minister, all the official Americans, all the staff of our embassy are leaving, and the last group, which includes me, will be flying out of Entebbe on the Saturday-evening flight."

I rose and we shook hands, and Oseku escorted me out without comment. I walked back to the chancery, sent a two-line telegram to the department ("Note delivered to Foreign Minister Ondoga at 1045 November 8. Details by separate telegram"), and then phoned Ambassador Kopf to tell him the deed had been done. We agreed to meet again in the afternoon, by which time we hoped to have received instructions on step two from Washington and Bonn.

By now we had scheduled the serial departure of our remaining staff. Phil Ringdahl would leave on the Friday-morning flight to Nairobi, two other officers on the Friday-evening flight, Jim Mark on Saturday morning back to Dar es Salaam, and Pat Kennedy, Ed Nosko, and I on the flight to Nairobi leaving Entebbe at 8:45 P.M. on Saturday.

At an hour-long meeting with Kopf and Hillgenberg that afternoon, I first briefed them on the meeting with Ondoga before watching the evening news with them to see how the story was played. Kopf proposed a new notification schedule. I would deliver my note about the protecting power to Ntimba on Friday morning, asking for an answer by close of business Friday. If no answer had been received by five o'clock Friday afternoon, Kopf would telephone his Foreign Office to ask if he could take over from us "provisionally." He would then sign the key turnover document, the "Protocol de Remise," around noon on Saturday.

The media treatment of my meeting with Ondoga was as surreal as the meeting itself. There was no mention anywhere of the impending closure of our embassy. Who would want to be within eyeshot or earshot of General Amin when he got the news? Fortunately Amin was out of town. Kopf thought he would fly back to Kampala the minute he got the news, but I doubted that very much.

All reports of the meeting covered only the portion dealing with the Ugandan complaint about the security problems being experienced by Uganda's mission in New York. The evening television news showed me handing my note to Ondoga and him reading it, with no explanation as to what this scene was all about. The *Voice of Uganda* published on its front page a picture of me handing my note to Ondoga, with a caption indicating the note concerned security for Ugandans in the United States. Much bigger play was given to a telegram from Amin to President Nixon supporting his refusal to resign his office.

COUNTDOWN

Friday, November 9

Overnight the department overruled me on the question of the text for my second note to the Ugandan Foreign Ministry, saying we would be asking for trouble if we requested the Ugandans' explicit approval of the West Germans as the protecting power. The Ugandans might not give an answer or, if pressed, might refuse to approve our choice. The department thus favored simply informing the ministry of an agreed-upon arrangement we had made with the Germans, with the clear implication that Ugandan silence would constitute tacit approval.

The department also accepted new language, agreed upon by Bonn and Washington after considerable negotiation. So I redid my second note to say that the United States had asked the FRG to assume the protecting power role and that the FRG was "prepared to assume this responsibility, and it is assumed that this arrangement is satisfactory." Instructions along these lines had been sent to Kopf, who would follow them by delivering his note to the Foreign Ministry confirming that the FRG had agreed to serve as our protecting power in Uganda.

Meanwhile, two Catholic missionaries serving in Fort Portal had been robbed in the Kampala area the evening of November 8 by two armed kondos, who absconded with the missionaries' vehicle and all their personal belongings. These included the victims' own passports and those of three other American missionaries that they were bringing to the embassy for renewal. Because missionaries who traveled in Uganda without passports risked arrest by the military authorities if caught without identification, Phil Ringdahl issued them new though defective passports. We reported all this to Embassy Nairobi, which would have to straighten matters out by mail once the fathers had safely reached home in Fort Portal. Personal appearances we suggested be waived for the other passportless missionaries, as they could not safely travel to Nairobi without passports.

Ambassador Kopf asked me to stop by for yet another chat before I delivered the second note to John Ntimba. During the hour I spent with him and Hillgenberg, I showed him the text of the note. He became very upset, finding the language "provocative" and likely to stimulate a negative reply from General Amin. I assured Kopf that I would indeed meet with the general if he called me in prior to my departure, but I doubted that would happen.

I then showed him the text of a circular note I had prepared informing the other diplomatic missions accredited to Uganda of the closure of our embassy and asked if he would deliver these notes on Monday. Kopf agreed to do so, but only after insisting I change the text to say we were only "asking" the FRG to take over from us. Given the time constraints and my own weariness, I agreed with no further discussion.

Kopf volunteered nothing about how or when he would deliver his own note to the Foreign Ministry. His instructions were to deliver it before my departure, and I guessed he would wait till Saturday when the ministry would be closed and slip it under the door, hoping it would not be found before Monday at the earliest. We agreed to sign the Protocol de Remise in his office at around noon on Saturday.

I strolled over to the Foreign Ministry to deliver the note to Ntimba, who said he had been expecting my call. He read the note without comment and said he would pass the information to Ondoga right away. I told Ntimba that I intended to turn our affairs over to Ambassador Kopf at noon on Saturday.

Ntimba asked what withdrawal of our personnel meant. I explained that it did not mean a break in diplomatic relations and that we hoped Uganda would keep its embassy in Washington open. There would be no U.S. "interests section" in the German embassy, I said, and no U.S. diplomatic or consular officials would remain in the country. The USIS Center would be left in the custody of the German embassy, which would also provide consular services for U.S. citizens remaining in Uganda and look after our government-owned properties.

In response to Ntimba's question as to what had motivated our decision, I referred to our note and stressed the expulsion of the Marine guards. Our twenty-five-minute meeting ended on a personally friendly note, with mutual expressions of appreciation and thanks.

Chief of Protocol Oseku later phoned me to ask for a list of all the American missionaries in Uganda and their locations. We complied immediately, although we had no idea what function this list was going to serve for the ministry, or for General Amin. We would learn the reason before the day was over.

Ed Nosko started the process of closing down the embassy's communications systems. He submitted a detailed report of how and where he was disposing of all the key items—sending out classified equipment in courier pouches, shipping other things to Nairobi, burning his cryptographic tapes and other classified flammables, turning our leased telex equipment over to the Germans, and terminating the contract for our leased circuit. Pat Kennedy assisted Nosko with the chore of incinerating all our remaining classified documents.

Nosko planned to shut down finally at 1:00 P.M. on Saturday. Four key elements of our code machines and the pouch seal would be put in a courier pouch, which he or I would hand-carry on the flight to Nairobi. Nothing classified could be left behind.

Friday Night and Saturday Morning

I informed Eugene Schreiber, our desk officer in Washington, in case he needed to reach me by phone outside office hours, that in the evening I would be moving from my house to the vacant ambassador's residence, where our remaining staff would camp out until time to go to Entebbe to catch our flight for Nairobi. Before leaving my house for good, I had to dispose of the remaining supplies in our storeroom, mainly food and liquor. The liquor I sold to Nico Calo, the Greek manager of the local Coca-Cola franchise, along with some European delicacies. The remaining food supplies I divided equally among six boxes, which I presented to the household servants and gardeners when I called them together to inform them of my impending departure. I invited them to take any remaining supplies before they could be looted. It was an emotional farewell for us all.

Phil Ringdahl and two other officers took the Friday-evening flight to Nairobi, leaving four of us in Kampala: Ed Nosko, Pat Kennedy, Jim Mark, and me. We moved into the ambassador's residence for the last night to be together, out of harm's way, and to be able to move together if a hasty strategic retreat or flight was called for. We had our before-dinner drinks while watching the evening news in the living room.

It was an unforgettable program, the longest Ugandan television news broadcast in memory, containing two lengthy diatribes against the United States more venomous in content and tone than anything we had previously experienced. Both were stimulated by the news of our closure having finally reached General Amin. One was a speech by the general himself to his senior security types at military police headquarters at Makindye; the other, similar in tone, was a statement attributed to a "government spokesman," who was of course the general himself.

In his speech at Makindye, Amin accused all Americans, including missionaries, of being spies against his country. He called upon all Ugandans to "report any dirty activities by the two hundred Americans who have been posted in missions by the American government to confuse people" and said he had directed the Foreign Ministry "to make a detailed list of these two hundred Americans available to all battalions throughout the country." He also warned the West German embassy it too would be under close surveillance "because it is widely known that whoever the Americans put in charge of their interests is a notorious saboteur."

Well now! We had finally succeeded in getting Idi Amin's goat, but it had taken the closure of our embassy to accomplish the task. Putting aside the general's charge that our sole mission in Uganda was to spy, this was his most threatening public outburst in a long time, especially the accusations directed against the remaining American missionaries. We were leaving, so this was the general's last opportunity to threaten us; but the missionaries were another matter. They would be very wise to get out as soon as possible, but I doubted many would do so. Those most in danger were the missionaries associated with churches other than the Roman Catholic and Anglican, because in his bigotry Amin recognized those two as the only "legitimate" Christian sects and had taken steps to outlaw all the other, less "establishment" church groups.

Of even greater immediate concern to me was how Ambassador Kopf would react to being branded a "notorious saboteur" and placed under close surveillance for having agreed to take charge of our interests in Uganda. We reconstructed the content of these attacks from notes made during the broadcast, and Ed Nosko and I hustled down to the chancery to inform the department, Nairobi, and Bonn of these latest developments. I feared Kopf would now want to back out of the deal and sought reassurance from the department that the West German ambassador would sign the Protocol de Remise on November 10 prior to my departure. The Foreign Office in Bonn provided the assurances sought. I was instructed to take the protocol with me to Nairobi if any complications developed, and it would be signed in Washington or Bonn.

From New York, Ambassador Ibingira must have been counseling Amin by cable to "cool it," for a separate announcement indicated Ibingira had been summarily "recalled" to Kampala. Wisely, he did not return.

On Saturday morning we all went down to the chancery together, the "final four" as we had taken to calling ourselves. Nosko and I discussed when he could begin his final communications shutdown. I asked him to send as unclassified cables the full texts of Amin's declarations of the previous day, as reported on the front page of Saturday's *Voice of Uganda*, and then to send one final classified cable for me, following which he could dismantle the coding machines. After that we would need to send only two unclassified messages, one saying I had signed the protocol with Kopf and a second saying we were closing down our official communications.

My final classified message to the full "Kampala circuit" on the closure of the embassy reported on the timing of the remaining tasks and departure of remaining staff, commended the outstanding performance of embassy staff and the "immense assistance" of Pat Kennedy and Jim Mark, and thanked the department for its efforts with the West German government. In a parting thought, I expressed the hope that it would be possible "to reestablish this post in the not too distant future, not because we need it particularly—the United States can get along without Uganda—but because it would most probably mean that General Amin had departed from the local scene. The real tragedy in this whole business has not been that General Amin has been unable or unwilling to get along with us; the tragedy is what one man, who is unfit for the office he holds but whom nobody apparently has the guts to remove, has done, is doing and will continue to do to ruin this country of Uganda and its ten million people."

OUT AT LAST

At noon I walked down the Embassy House stairs to the West German chancery and was escorted into Ambassador Kopf's office. He glanced through the thick sheaf of documents with the brief Protocol de Remise on top. Attached were an inventory of our diplomatic and consular property, an inventory of property of other U.S. federal agencies and departments, and a list of U.S. nationals considered entitled to protection. Kopf gave all of these only a cursory review, saying simply, "I take it all of these are in order?" I assured him we had done a careful job, but he might want to have someone check it out. "That won't be necessary," he said.

So at ten minutes past noon we signed the protocol and a custody receipt for the embassy's real property, consisting of five houses in Kampala. There were four copies of everything. Kopf kept one set, one was for me, and the other two would be delivered to Embassy Nairobi and the department in Washington. After all my worrying, the final ceremony went off without a hitch. Hillgenberg opened a bottle of champagne and we all toasted German-American friendship.

Ed Nosko himself composed Embassy Kampala's final message, telegram number 3357 of 1973, "Closure of Embassy Kampala." Announcing "This is final message from AmEmbassy Kampala. Circuit terminated at 1000 hours Zulu Nov. 10," he closed with "Last one to leave will turn off the lights," signed "Keeley."

The story of our departure from Entebbe for Nairobi has circulated within and without the Foreign Service for some years, the highlight being that I displayed my disdain for Idi Amin by wearing a tuxedo for the departure. While it is true that I left wearing black tie, there was a practical motivation. Our Kampala Marines were joining their Nairobi colleagues in hosting the Marine Birthday Ball at the Nairobi Intercontinental Hotel, and dress for the ball was full-dress uniform for the military and black tie for the civilians.

The ball began at 6:00 P.M., included dinner and dancing, and would last till after midnight. Since our flight from Entebbe would not touch down in Nairobi until about 9:45 P.M., Nosko, Kennedy, and I would miss a good deal of the ball. I thought I ought to turn up in black tie to honor our Marines in style, but there was no time for changing clothes. So I asked Louise to meet me at the airport dressed for the ball and I would arrive wearing my tuxedo. That way we could go straight from the airport to the Intercontinental.

No one from the Government of Uganda showed up at Entebbe Airport to see us off, as I had expected none would, though it was customary for someone from Oseku's protocol staff to do the honors for departing chiefs of mission of whatever rank. I was a bit surprised, however, to find that only one lonely diplomatic colleague showed up, Henri Dupuy, counselor of the French embassy. The others apparently considered me a pariah. Who would want to be seen in public with a person who had aroused the supreme ire of Idi Amin? My friends Niko and Aliki Calo had offered to see me off and to drive me to Entebbe, but I said goodbye to them in Kampala at their house.

Louise met the three of us at the Nairobi airport and we went straight to the Intercontinental. We entered the ballroom to a literally thunderous ovation from our Marines and our colleagues who had reached Nairobi ahead of us, as well as some applause of greeting from the Nairobi crowd. I gave a short speech thanking, congratulating, and lauding the Marines and then cut their birthday cake with a sword, both actions that the chief of a diplomatic mission is called upon to perform at a Marine ball. It seemed a fitting way to end our tour in Uganda. The expulsion of our Marines, after all, had been the cause of the closure of Embassy Kampala, and of the termination of that phase of our lives.

LESSONS LEARNED

On the evidence given here, this story does not belong in a compendium of American embassies in crisis, because there was actually no crisis, no disaster, no tragedy. The closure of Embassy Kampala went quite smoothly, especially when one considers the increasingly chaotic condition of the country at that time, the awful state of relations between Uganda and the United States, and the character of the host government and its brutal leader—mercurial, bloodstained, and absurd. About the only criticism of the closure operation that one heard afterward was to ask why it had not taken place sooner—for example, back in June, as the embassy itself had recommended.

There were several factors that contributed to the relatively trouble-free out-come. One was that the U.S. side held the initiative during the entire process. The decision to close up shop was taken unilaterally, in reaction to the Ugandans' expulsion of our Marine detachment, and was not something forced on us by events or actions over which we had no control. The *timing* was therefore strictly in our hands.

Secondly, the action was not precipitate and thus allowed sufficient time for a smooth transition. Although the Department of State initially wanted everyone out of the country within forty-eight hours, Washington accepted the embassy's contention that that was unnecessary. It gave the embassy sufficient time—nearly two weeks—to effect an orderly shutdown, with all absolutely necessary adminis-trative tasks accomplished prior to the handover to the West Germans.

We tried very hard to keep what we were doing secret for as long as we could, so as not to arouse the Ugandan leadership to take some action against us that would interfere with our plans. In essence this meant keeping one person in the dark—General Amin—and for that we counted heavily on his habit of blaming the messenger who brought bad news, which meant that anyone figuring out what we were up to would do his utmost to keep from having to inform Amin.

We also counted on our correct analysis of Amin's behavioral syndromes. He loved to throw out threats in all directions but was fundamentally afraid to go too far with someone much more powerful than he for fear of swift, brutal, and per-haps total retribution against his own person. Thus he enjoyed bullying the weak and fearful, including all of his own subjects; but when it came to the United States government, he would think more than twice about harming a hair on a U.S. diplomat's head, because that could lead to his undoing.

The Department of State's general policy is: "We open embassies. We don't close them." It was on the basis of this general principle that the department did not take Embassy Kampala's advice in March 1973 that the mission be shut down by June 30. It was easy to reach a contrary conclusion in late October 1973 because the domestic Ugandan situation, including security conditions, had dete-riorated further, and our displeasure with the regime of Idi Amin Dada had grown.

The most essential factor, however, had remained unchanged: we had no vital interests in Uganda to protect and very few interests of any kind beyond protect-ing the resident American citizens, who were mainly devout, fearless missionaries. By November anyone would have been very hard put to come up with a reason why we should keep our embassy in Kampala open.

By the time we decided we had been harassed enough, we had already reduced our official presence in Kampala to the absolute minimum, making our shutdown that much easier. The Peace Corps program had been shut down two years previ-ously, the AID program had been terminated earlier in the summer, the post had been without an ambassador since the recall of Thomas Melady in February, and the embassy was already operating with a skeleton staff, with officers departing at the end of their tours not being replaced unless their positions were deemed essential. The lesson from this might be that all embassies should be smaller, easier to manage, and better able to weather a crisis should one arrive unexpectedly.

As for me personally, it was a wonderful learning experience that I hoped not to have to repeat. About a year and a half later, however, on April 12, 1975, under much different circumstances, I helped manage the evacuation by Marine helicopters of the entire American mission in Phnom Penh, Cambodia, where I was serving as deputy chief of mission. After months of careful planning, followed by about five and a half hours of execution, that operation enjoyed total success in terms of no lives lost. There was no Protocol de Remise to sign and no one to whom to turn over protection of our interests. We simply said goodbye with broken hearts and abandoned that tragically oppressed country to the Khmer Rouge.

A Sad Footnote

The chief victim of this episode in Ugandan-American relations was probably Colonel Michael Ondoga, whom General Amin dismissed as foreign minister in February 1974. In March it was reported in the press that Ondoga's body had been found floating in Lake Victoria near the Jinja source of the Nile River. There was well-informed speculation that he had paid the full price for the closure of the U.S. embassy in Kampala, probably blamed by Amin for having "mismanaged" Uganda's relations with the United States. Other cabinet ministers had received equivalent death sentences on other occasions, and Ondoga's cousin Kay, one of Amin's four official wives, had herself been brutally murdered and dismembered, according to quite believable reports.

If the motive for the killing of Ondoga was scapegoating for the closure of our embassy, then he had become the innocent victim of Amin's own decision to expel our embassy's Marines.

The U.S. Embassy in Tehran the day after its November 1979 seizure startled the world.
AP/Wide World Photos.

3 | Crisis After Crisis: Embassy Tehran, 1979

Victor L. Tomseth

In the months between February 14 and November 4, 1979, the United States government was attempting to adjust to the new reality in Iran created by the fall of the shah and to develop a relationship with his successors that would allow continued pursuit of basic U.S. interests in the Persian Gulf region. Good relations with prerevolutionary Iran had been a linchpin of U.S. policy in the area. This chapter deals with U.S.-Iranian relations between a February 14 attack on the U.S. embassy in Tehran and a second attack on November 4, which began the infamous hostage crisis that lasted till January 20, 1981. (Not dealt with here to any extent are the periods before February 14 and after November 4, which constitute crises in their own right.) I was the embassy's political counselor, having served previously as principal officer in Shiraz.

U.S.–IRANIAN TIES

Iran had occupied an important place in U.S. foreign policy in the gulf region since the 1940s, initially as a link in the effort to contain Soviet expansionism and later as a bulwark against the forces of instability in the volatile Middle East. For nearly four decades, the shah of Iran, Mohammed Reza Pahlavi, who ascended the Peacock Throne in 1941, represented continuity to the United States as it pursued its policy objectives.

Not surprisingly, the personal relationships the shah developed with a series of U.S. leaders, from Franklin Roosevelt to Jimmy Carter, came to be closely associated with U.S.-Iranian bilateral relations, in the eyes of both Washington and the shah's countrymen. Reinforcing this personalization of the bilateral relationship was the nature of the Iranian regime itself—one of the world's last absolute monarchies. The longer the shah remained on the throne, the more blurred the distinction became between his personality and the policies of the Iranian state.

In the 1960s and especially the 1970s, the shah undertook a series of policy measures embodied in the so-called White Revolution, thanks in part to the vastly increased oil revenues that gave him the wherewithal to pursue his ambitions. The new measures included land reform, a push to transform the country's agriculturally based economy into an industrial one, expansion of education, emancipation of women, secularization of the law, and creation of a variety of new governmental and social welfare institutions. Iranian and foreign liberals initially applauded the shah's intent, and the United States supported many of his initiatives with development programs of its own. At their core, however, these policy measures represented the shah's highly personalized vision for his country, formulated and implemented with little reference to the views of the Iranian people. Key elements of Iranian society, significantly including the Islamic clergy and large segments of the tradition-bound population, rejected both the shah's objectives and the manner in which he sought to achieve them.

The United States viewed the shah's program in relation to its own policy objectives in the Persian Gulf. Reasoning that a modern and prosperous Iran could contribute more effectively to those objectives, Washington sought to reinforce the shah's efforts to develop his country. In the process it came to be closely associated with both the programs of the White Revolution and the shah himself.

By 1978 the United States and the shah had emerged as the tangible targets of deep popular frustration in Iran. For many Iranians, the highly visible U.S. presence (there were upwards of fifty thousand U.S. citizens living and working in Iran by the late 1970s) symbolized their dissatisfaction with the Pahlavi regime. In Iranian minds, the United States shared responsibility with the shah in his refusal to yield to popular aspirations for greater participation in the political process, the free rein he gave to the oppressive state security apparatus, the dislocations occasioned by the overrapid expansion of the economy during the 1970s, and the mimicry among members of the ruling elite of foreign manners at the expense of traditional values.

Throughout 1978, the United States government adjusted only slowly to Iran's increasingly rapid slide into revolution. Constrained by historical inertia and past success, U.S. policy did not for the most part respond in a timely fashion to developing events. There was deep reluctance to abandon a longtime ally and to embrace the unknown. The shah had survived other crises, and U.S. policymakers were reluctant to conclude that he would not survive this one.

In the decade prior to 1978, moreover, the United States had allowed its contacts with Iranian political dissidents to attenuate. In the midst of the unfolding revolution, U.S. diplomats made efforts to reestablish contacts with relatively moderate elements among those opposed to the shah. But by then it was probably too late for these elements to have much influence on the revolution's course. Disorganized and weakened by years of political oppression, Iranian political moderates were ill prepared to lead a transition to more representative government. In the waning months of 1978, radicals were clearly gaining the upper hand.

SLOUCHING TOWARD REVOLUTION

As the crisis in Iran deepened in 1978, the U.S. embassy in Tehran faced a continuing dilemma. On one hand, members of the official and nonofficial U.S. communities alike grew increasingly apprehensive about the deteriorating security situation. On the other, there was concern on the part of Ambassador William H. Sullivan and his senior staff that panicked flight by U.S. residents would exacerbate the rapid collapse of the Pahlavi regime and provide momentum to the revolutionary forces arrayed against it. The tendency was to temporize.

By September 1978, however, U.S. firms began to make staffing decisions independent of embassy advice. They drew down personnel and sent dependents home, a process that accelerated as the year drew to a close. In early December, Washington authorized the voluntary evacuation of all U.S. mission dependents who wished to depart. Most chose to leave.

At the eleventh hour, Washington established an indirect dialogue with Ayatollah Ruhollah Khomeini, still resident in France, through Ibrahim Yazdi, a member of his entourage (and later foreign minister).[1] This initiative, however, did not dispel the deep antipathy toward the West in general and the United States in particular that Khomeini harbored. At the very time contact with Khomeini's Paris entourage was undertaken, the United States was reiterating its support on a daily basis for the shah's last government, headed by Shapour Bakhtiar.

A few weeks later—and ten days after Khomeini's return to Iran on February 1, 1979—Bakhtiar was swept aside in a brief armed uprising. The Provisional Revolutionary Government (PRG) that succeeded it contained elements willing to work with the United States, but they were constrained by the widespread suspicion of U.S. motives that characterized the Iranian revolution.

A Violent Valentine's Day

After Bakhtiar had fallen, a collection of radical militants stormed the United States embassy on February 14 (the same day as the kidnapping and murder of U.S. Ambassador Adolph Dubs in neighboring Afghanistan). The attack left six dead, including one Iranian Foreign Service National and embassy contract employees, none U.S. citizens.

The attackers' motivations were rooted in long-standing popular views about the role of the United States in the 1953 overthrow of the contentiously nationalist government of Mohammed Mossadeq and the restoration of the shah to his throne. Both Britain and the United States had supported the Iranian coup leaders who overthrew Mossadeq and invited the shah to return from his European exile, and many Iranians attributed the coup entirely to British and American machinations. The militants thought that the United States might be plotting to repeat history and stormed the embassy to disrupt any such plans.

The Provisional Revolutionary Government intervened to restore the embassy to U.S. control, with PRG Foreign Minister Yazdi rushing to the embassy to take charge of the situation. He returned control of the embassy to Ambassador Sullivan and placed an armed security force on the compound to guard against further attack. But the attack marked a watershed in Washington's approach to Iran.

RESHUFFLING THE EMBASSY

Events in the early weeks of 1979 had further accelerated the departure of the resident U.S. community, both official and nonofficial. In early January the embassy advised U.S. firms that any remaining nonessential employees should leave, and later that month all remaining official dependents were ordered home.

After the fall of the Bakhtiar government and the February 14 attack on the embassy, a massive airlift was organized to evacuate most of the several thousand remaining U.S. citizens who wished to leave or were no longer needed in Iran. By the end of February, the number of U.S. citizens in the country had fallen from nearly fifty thousand in 1978 to perhaps less than a thousand, most of whom were dual nationals. The consulates in Isfahan, Shiraz, and Tabriz had been closed and the U.S. mission staff reduced to a few dozen American personnel.

In Washington, where each agency approached the situation from its own perspective, it was collectively agreed that a fresh start was needed in Iran. As part of this approach, virtually the entire U.S. mission staff was replaced in the weeks and months following February 14. The process was almost completed by autumn. Only five officers present in Iran prior to the February 14 attack remained at the time of the November 4 attack: political officer (and former principal officer in Tabriz) Michael Metrinko; defense attaché Thomas Schaefer; Army attaché Leland Holland; press attaché Barry Rosen; and myself. All were Farsi speakers (Metrinko and Rosen had been Peace Corps volunteers in Iran).

Initially, the embassy was staffed by a small number of officers who had stayed on and a constantly shifting mix of temporary employees assigned to help fill gaps until permanent replacements could arrive. Ambassador Sullivan remained until early April, after which his deputy, Charles Naas, became chargé d'affaires *ad interim* until his own departure in June. The chief of the Joint United States Military Advisory Group (JUSMAG)[2] and the senior military attachés stayed, but with substantially reduced staffs. The heads of most other units had departed.

I assumed leadership of the political section, joined by Metrinko, my counterpart from Tabriz, and one temporary holdover. Former deputy section chiefs took charge of the economic and consular sections for the next few months, operating with a small number of holdovers and temporary duty personnel until replacements began to arrive in the summer. The much-reduced administrative section focused initially on restoring communications and making the tear gas–filled chancery building habitable once again.

Restaffing the mission proved a complex problem. In some cases, replacements for personnel scheduled for transfer in mid-1979 were already identified and in training. Most of them were given the option of going ahead with the assignment to Tehran or being reassigned elsewhere, and most chose the former. In the majority of cases, however, recruits had to be found on short notice for unanticipated vacancies. By late summer, most positions had been filled. But among those on hand at the embassy on November 4 were several staff members still on temporary assignment.

NEW EMBASSY PRIORITIES

Deputy Chief of Mission (soon to be Chargé) Naas returned to Tehran on April 1 from Washington consultations at which the embassy's new tasks for the coming months had been decided. These included (1) demonstrating resolve to remain engaged in Iran; (2) taking steps to establish a new kind of relationship with the PRG and the new political order; (3) analyzing that order to determine where real power lay; (4) improving the embassy's physical security; (5) collecting and disposing of the belongings of former mission staff and cleaning up the debris and repairing the damage from the February 14 attack; (6) resolving outstanding contractual issues, both commercial and military; and (7) readying a new facility to provide a full range of consular services as soon as possible.

This agenda largely determined mission organization and responsibilities in the succeeding months. The charge, assisted by a totally reconstituted political section staffed by the best available language officers, was to concentrate on establishing solid working relations with the PRG as well as making contacts among the new political elites, most importantly the Islamic clergy. The political section would also provide Washington with analyses of the still-evolving political process. Meanwhile, the economic section and JUSMAG would concentrate on the large volume of contractual cases, working both with representatives of the U.S. firms involved and the relevant Iranian government agencies.

As new staff arrived, the U.S. Information Service would resume operations at its binational center, including the enormously popular English-language teaching program, and undertake new outreach programs targeting the postrevolutionary elites. The administrative section, assisted by military personnel attached to JUSMAG, would collect the household effects, personal vehicles, and even pets left behind by departing staff. These would be disposed of through sales or packed and shipped as appropriate.

With the help of a constantly rotating stream of engineers, security specialists, electronic technicians, and Seabees, administrative personnel would also oversee and coordinate the effort to restore embassy communications, purge the main chancery building of the tear gas used to slow down the attackers on February 14, improve the building's physical security measures, and convert a building in the main embassy compound, formerly used for a recreation facility and administrative offices, into a secure, full-service consular section. Until the new consular section could be completed, the small consular staff would provide services to the relatively small number of U.S. citizens remaining in Iran or visiting, as well as issue visas in "emergency" cases.

Pending restoration of the embassy compound to full U.S. control, security officers and a substantial contingent of Marine security guards would work with the paramilitary units assigned by the PRG following the February attack to provide security inside the compound.

Picking Up the Pieces

Carrying out this mandate proved a daunting task. At its peak the official community had numbered over five thousand employees and dependents. The personal belongings they had left behind were scattered in houses and apartments throughout the city, usually in areas controlled by self-appointed, largely autonomous revolutionary committees, or *komitehs*. Gaining access to each of these homes and taking possession of their contents typically required protracted negotiations with *komiteh* members, who were invariably suspicious of anything involving the United States government. Once the personal effects had been secured and sorted, it was often necessary to conduct more negotiations with other *komitehs* that claimed authority to approve sales or exports.

Resolving the hundreds of contracts worth billions of dollars between U.S. firms and assorted Iranian entities proved equally challenging. The economic section and JUSMAG frequently found their Iranian interlocutors had little substantive background for understanding the issues involved. Coupled with their deep suspicion of *any* agreement reached with the United States during the shah's time, this meant that negotiations on even seemingly innocuous points were typically lengthy and frequently acrimonious.

Even the small consular operation, with seemingly well-defined and limited interim responsibilities, was sorely tested. In the years immediately prior to the revolution, the consular section in Tehran and the consulates in Shiraz, Isfahan, and Tabriz had been issuing more than 100,000 nonimmigrant visas a year. The events of 1978 and early 1979, and the fundamental change they wrought in official U.S.–Iranian relations, did not diminish the demand for visas, however.

In the fluid situation following the shah's downfall, more Iranians than ever viewed possession of a visa to enter the United States as the ultimate insurance policy against the instability gripping their country. Consular officers were subjected to constant pressures, ranging from the intervention of senior PRG officials and religious figures on behalf of visa applicants who invariably seemed to face some "emergency" to offers of bribes and threats of bodily harm.

Political Minefields

Achieving the mission's political objectives also proved elusive. As part of the general changing of the guard in the aftermath of the February 14 attack, Washington quickly nominated Walter Cutler as a replacement for Ambassador Sullivan. Cutler's fate was emblematic of the difficulties the United States experienced in trying to deal with an Iran whose revolutionary tide had not yet run its full course.

In May, following Cutler's confirmation, while he was being briefed to assume his new responsibilities, the United States Senate passed a "sense of the Senate" resolution sponsored by Jacob Javits of New York. The resolution sharply criticized Iran's revolutionary courts, which had recently condemned to death a leading Jewish businessman as a spy for Israel.

These courts were usually constituted ad hoc and operated under no standardized rules of procedure save the Islamic *sharia*, as interpreted by the Muslim clerics who presided over them. Internationally accepted norms of due process were nowhere in evidence; the accused had no right of appeal, and sentences were frequently carried out immediately. From February onward, executions at the hands of these courts were widespread. Gruesome pictures showing the condemned being shot or their bullet-riddled corpses were flaunted in the Iranian press and subsequently carried in the international media.

The Javits Resolution, a reaction against what was going on in Iran, passed overwhelmingly; but it is doubtful that its supporters expected it to have much impact on the courts' activities. Its primary purpose was to demonstrate to their domestic constituents that the senators shared U.S. popular concern about human rights abuses in Iran.

Passage of the resolution did, however, produce an Iranian reaction. Almost immediately, massive demonstrations erupted outside the United States embassy in Tehran and continued for several days. Deputy Prime Minister Amir Entezam summoned Chargé Charles Naas and advised him that Ambassador Cutler should delay his arrival until the public tension caused by the resolution had subsided.

A week later, Entezam called in Naas once again, this time to inform him that the PRG had reconsidered its earlier decision to grant *agrément* for Cutler's appointment. It had reexamined his curriculum vitae, Entezam told Naas, and had concluded that Cutler's earlier service in Iran during the shah's reign and in U.S. client states such as Vietnam and Zaire would prove a sore point with many Iranians, who identified with peoples of countries oppressed by Western imperialism. It would be better to propose a new nominee.

POLITICAL DISARRAY

Whether or not the PRG had genuine second thoughts about Cutler's prior service is not particularly important. The real lesson of the Javits Resolution experience lay in how it demonstrated the government's relative weakness vis-à-vis the many groups in society then engaged in a struggle for influence in shaping the Iranian polity after the shah. These groupings were legion, ranging from the neighborhood *komitehs* to the Revolutionary Guards, a parallel army created to check the power of the regular armed forces, which were suspected of harboring Pahlavi loyalists. They were frequently able to prevail over government authority, at least in situations where crowds in the street or firepower were the deciding factors.

There was in fact a parallel government, represented not only by the *komitehs* and organizations like the Revolutionary Guards, but also by the powerful Revolutionary Council. Members of this shadowy body were never named but were assumed to include some of the people who had been with Khomeini in France and powerful Muslim clerics. Most preferred to remain at Khomeini's "court" in Qom, a religious center one hundred miles from the ostensible political capital in Tehran.

The PRG interacted with foreign governments, including the U.S. government, but the U.S. embassy in Tehran could never be sure that the PRG had full authority to speak for Iran in its foreign relations, or in any other area. Prime Minister Mehdi Bazargan himself summed up the situation on one occasion when he described the PRG as "a knife without a blade."

The surprising speed of the shah's fall was a major contributing factor to the ensuing fluidity. Substantial casualties were sustained in an escalating series of anti-shah demonstrations throughout 1978 and in the bloody February 1979 confrontation with regime loyalists that ended the Pahlavi monarchy. But the shah, with over 500,000 men in his security forces, had put up surprisingly little resistance to the rising revolutionary tide. Victory had come so quickly that the shah's opponents had had insufficient time to develop a coherent consensus on the shape of Iran's political future.

Khomeini had provided those opponents both a convenient focus and the rhetoric to articulate the popular cultural angst that fueled the revolutionary movement; but beyond their common dislike of the shah and his regime, there was little that united the revolutionaries' disparate political points of view. The so-called Islamic fundamentalists wanted to purge Iranian society of all "foreign" (meaning non-Islamic) influences. At the other extreme were the secular Marxists, whose political agendas were as divergent as those of the mainline communist Tudeh Party adherents and the radical terrorists of the Fadayan-e-Khalq. In between was a hodgepodge of less extreme but still anti-shah nationalists who viewed their partners and even Khomeini quite cynically: they sought to leverage their own influence through manipulation of Khomeini's popular appeal and ultimately to dominate the political process.

The speed with which the revolution had unfolded also meant that the shah's opponents had little time to organize themselves for running the country following victory.[3] After the collapse of the Bakhtiar government in February 1979, local mosques active in 1978's anti-shah demonstrations reemerged as focal points for organizing the many neighborhood *komitehs*. Moreover, the disintegration of much of the shah's military and security forces had put large numbers of weapons in the hands of militant radicals, ordinary students, and criminal gangs, among others.[4] Some of these now well-armed groups either organized their own *komitehs* or attached themselves to *komitehs* centered on mosques or government offices.

These councils presumed to substitute locally for the holdover national administrative apparatus, now in disarray and frequently suspected of insufficient revolutionary zeal. Many *komitehs* provided needed community services and a degree of law and order in the neighborhoods where they operated, but they also quickly emerged as rivals to the PRG for power and authority. They often ignored government decisions and enforced their own edicts on matters ranging from women's dress to contract disputes. Some seemingly existed primarily for their members' profit, raising funds by intimidation and extortion.

EMBASSY OPTIONS IN A VOLATILE ATMOSPHERE

In the aftermath of the February 14 attack, the U.S. embassy in Tehran became the reluctant host to three armed groups, installed there by the Provisional Revolutionary Government ostensibly to protect the embassy from further attack. One group was composed of fifty to sixty air force *homafars*.[5] Another was headed by political radicals who may actually have participated in the February 14 assault. The third was a personal faction led by former butcher Mashallah Kashani, whose pious pretensions hardly masked his essential venality.

Reflecting the atmosphere beyond the embassy compound's walls, where a myriad of armed groups were vying with one another for a share of power, these groups, too, were rivals deeply suspicious of one another. Their inability to cooperate in carrying out the mandate given them by the PRG created a potentially dangerous situation, balanced somewhat, however, by a certain sense of security their presence provided ("Better to have them inside shooting out than outside shooting in," as one veteran of February 14 put it).

Within a few weeks the *homafars* were withdrawn for duties elsewhere, with the radicals also removed soon after by the PRG.[6] That left only Mashallah's faction, which increasingly neglected its security responsibilities to intrude on embassy operations. By late spring, the embassy concluded it would be better off without Mashallah's "protection." Mashallah, however, had come to regard the embassy as his group's personal cash cow and stoutly resisted suggestions that the embassy could now provide for its own security inside the sprawling compound.

Unfortunately, by that point the PRG was largely powerless to remove Mashallah and his thugs. Repeated embassy requests were met only with repeated PRG promises that the group would leave but with no action. Not until mid-August did the PRG evict Mashallah and his merry band, and then only at gunpoint. To do so the PRG had been obliged to turn to one of the unofficial paramilitary forces that had emerged after the shah's downfall. By now, the PRG itself had neither the authority to order Mashallah out nor command of its own armed personnel to enforce such an order.

In the midst of the crisis following the Javits Resolution in May, Chargé Naas convened several "skull sessions" among embassy staff to consider the situation and possible options. The Iran Desk at the State Department, which in 1978 had been ahead of the embassy in recognizing the severity of the opposition to the shah and concluding that his regime would not survive, in 1979 was inclined to focus on positive developments. The PRG was in place and behaving like a government, even if it was sometimes challenged by the *komitehs* and other nongovernmental centers of power. Khomeini continued to give rhetorical support, albeit often tepid or ambivalent, to Prime Minister Bazargan. Efforts to draft a constitution, a preliminary step toward national elections and the formation of a permanent government, were proceeding. While progress was painfully slow, negotiations to resolve the huge volume of commercial and military supply contracts left from the Pahlavi era had at least begun.

Embassy veterans of 1978 still in Tehran in the first half of 1979 tended to see the situation differently. In their view, the fall of the shah had not marked the culmination of the revolution, but merely the beginning of a new phase in which former anti-shah allies were now locked in a struggle with one another to determine Iran's political future. The political landscape was highly fragmented, riven in several directions by religious, regional, and ethnic differences, as well as by ideological diversity among the contending factions. The authority of the PRG was constrained by the power of parallel organizations, such as the *komitehs* and Revolutionary Council, often enforced at gunpoint or by organized mobs. While the PRG was working with the embassy in an effort to resolve contractual issues, there was no guarantee that negotiations would succeed in the face of Iranian hostility and suspicion.

This more pessimistic viewpoint was thoroughly aired in Naas's skull sessions with his staff. There was deep apprehension that the effort to build a new kind of relationship with postrevolutionary Iran would ultimately fail. Although the protest marches outside the embassy provoked by the Javits Resolution were essentially nonviolent, they demonstrated the embassy's vulnerability to another attack.

Security in fact depended upon the host government, in this case a weak government frequently challenged by the contending political forces that continued to sweep Iran. At one point a participant in Naas's meetings suggested that it might be prudent to reduce the embassy staff drastically—perhaps to no more than a half-dozen U.S. personnel led by a chargé d'affaires, not an ambassador—and wait for the revolution to run its full course.

In the end, however, the embassy agreed with Washington that too much was at stake to abandon the effort to build a relationship with postrevolutionary Iran or even to "hunker down." It simply was not possible to write off the billions of dollars involved in commercial contracts and military supply agreements concluded during the shah's reign. Iran remained a potentially important market for the

United States. Moreover, while oil production had plummeted in the latter part of 1978 and was only beginning to recover, Iran had been and could be again the world's second-leading producer. It also commanded the world's second-largest natural gas reserves and sat astride the entry to the Persian Gulf, through which much of the petroleum bound for international markets had to pass.

Iran's size and location gave it considerable strategic importance also in U.S. containment policy. While Iran would no longer be prepared to join the United States as an active partner in containing Soviet power, perhaps traditional Iranian concern about Russian expansionism could still be used to serve U.S. interests. In any event, the embassy concluded, the effort had to be made.

THE SHAH DILEMMA

From the earliest days of the Khomeini era, which began in February 1979, the status of the former shah hung like a sword of Damocles over the relationship between Iran and the United States. When the shah decided to leave Iran in January 1979 for a "vacation," he asked Ambassador Sullivan about going to the United States. Washington agreed that he could, and a prominent Republican offered him the use of his private residence in California. The shah's plane would refuel in New England and fly on directly to the West Coast, with no meeting between the shah and senior administration officials.

When he departed Iran, the shah instead went first to Egypt to visit his longtime friend and supporter Anwar Sadat. There, most likely with Sadat's encouragement, he tarried. Perhaps he recalled 1953, when he had fled the political turmoil at home only to be called back from Rome following the coup that overthrew Mossadeq. The shah may have hoped that the military would prevail once again,[7] or even that the United States would intervene.

Following the February 14 attack on the embassy, Washington's enthusiasm for admitting the shah diminished substantially. Allowing him to come would have severely complicated the Carter administration's efforts to catch up with swiftly moving events in Iran and build a new relationship with postrevolutionary Iranian authorities. The shah eventually moved on to Morocco, where he was bluntly told that, for the time being, Washington could not agree to his settling in the United States. From Morocco, the shah traveled to Barbados and then to Mexico.

Even before he arrived in Mexico, a number of the shah's American friends—notably former secretary of state Henry Kissinger and David Rockefeller—had criticized the Carter administration's handling of the Iranian crisis and its treatment of the shah, a longtime ally. New salience was given to their criticism when medical tests in Mexico revealed that the shah had cancer.[8] This was news to his American backers, who now argued that the shah deserved to come to the United States not only because he was an old friend but also because he needed access to the best treatment for his disease. Pressure rapidly increased on the Carter administration to admit the shah.

In July, Washington asked recently arrived Chargé d'Affaires Bruce Laingen to assess the likely impact on the embassy's security should the shah be admitted to the United States for medical treatment. (The new chargé had been thrown into the breach created by the PRG's second thoughts about Walter Cutler.) Laingen replied that, prior to the establishment of a permanent Iranian government with a firmer basis of authority than the PRG's and a clear signal, such as appointment of an ambassador, that the U.S. government accepted the results of the Iranian revolution, admission of the shah for *any* reason would risk provoking another attack on the embassy.

Two months later, Washington again asked Laingen the same question, and he gave the same reply. In the meantime, Washington had informed him, first, that it wished to put his name forward as the next U.S. ambassador to Iran and, later, that his name was no longer under consideration, as the nomination "would not be the right signal" at that juncture.

Shortly thereafter, on October 22, Laingen received a message from Washington informing him that the shah was being admitted to the United States for urgent medical treatment and instructing him to seek the PRG's understanding and its assurance of security for the embassy. Laingen called on Prime Minister Bazargan, who promised him only that his government would do its best, a clear indication—if one were needed—that the PRG was hardly in full control of the situation.

Inevitably, the decision to admit the shah, like the Javits Resolution before it, provoked a hostile reaction.[9] Khomeini railed from Qom, and angry crowds filled the streets in Tehran in a steadily escalating round of anti-American demonstrations. On November 1, however, it appeared that a critical point in the crisis had come and gone without producing the direst consequences anticipated. The largest demonstration yet had been scheduled for the streets around the embassy compound that day, but was moved some distance away at the last minute at the direction of leading clerics. Although a number of angry demonstrators arrived at the compound's walls, a police contingent was on hand to keep them under control, and larger crowds congregated at the designated alternate site in vocal but otherwise peaceful protest.

The embassy interpreted this development as indicating that even the religious leadership did not wish to provoke a complete break in relations, notwithstanding deep unhappiness with the decision to admit the shah into the United States and suspicion that it might represent some sinister purpose other than the "urgent humanitarian treatment" Washington claimed had been its only motivation.

SEIZURE

Three days later a previously obscure group of university students seized the embassy and initiated a new crisis that was to last for more than fourteen months. Ironically, November 4 began at the embassy with the usual senior staff meeting in which discussion focused on the danger posed by a demonstration scheduled that day at Tehran University to commemorate the deaths of several students a year earlier during an anti-shah protest on the campus. The university was about a mile from the embassy, but some of the participants would pass along the streets outside the embassy compound en route to the demonstration.

There were suggestions that the embassy be closed for the day and the staff released to avoid possible risks. In the end, though, a counterargument prevailed: Were the embassy to close its doors every time a demonstration was scheduled somewhere in Tehran, it might as well close them permanently. The embassy was thus open for business and fully staffed when the student militants arrived and stormed the compound two hours later.

Following the seizure of the embassy and the capture of more than sixty U.S. hostages, the students demanded, *inter alia*, the shah's return to Iran for trial. The evidence suggests, however, that the shah's admission to the United States was little more than a pretext for their action.

The actual trigger was more likely another event—a meeting in distant Algiers of Iranian Prime Minister Bazargan and Foreign Minister Yazdi with President Carter's national security adviser, Zbigniew Brzezinski, during the twenty-fifth anniversary celebration of the Algerian revolution. The embassy had urged that such a meeting be arranged, not only to provide assurances at a high level about U.S. intentions regarding the shah but also to signify the progress made toward constructing a new and mutually beneficial bilateral relationship between Iran and the United States.

The meeting took place on Thursday, November 1, the same day the crisis provoked by the shah's admission to the United States for medical treatment had appeared to peak. Wire service reports of the meeting and an accompanying photograph of Bazargan shaking hands with Brzezinski reached Iran late that evening. But newspapers there did not publish on Friday, a weekend day. Thus the story and photo did not appear until Saturday morning, when the embassy was closed. Splitting the difference between the Iranian and the U.S. weekends, it reopened on Sunday, November 4.

The Daneshjuyan-e-khat-e-Imam—"University Students in the Line of the Imam"—were among literally hundreds of tiny groups seeking to have some impact on the unfolding Iranian political process in 1979. The core cadre numbered hardly more than a hundred young men and women. Like many other groups of similar composition, they looked for guidance, both spiritual and political, to a Muslim cleric, in this case a minor member of the *ulema* whose views did not necessarily reflect those of the senior clerical leadership.

Like the vast majority of such groups, these students were virtually unknown as an organized group outside the narrow confines of their individual campuses. The embassy had never heard of them before November 4, 1979; nor is there any reason to believe that the PRG or senior members of the *ulema* had either. Khomeini appeared to be genuinely surprised when he learned of the students' action, although in his usual politically astute fashion he quickly positioned himself to use it for any perceived advantage.

It is clear from statements the students themselves made to their U.S. captives that their original intention was neither to force the United States to return the shah nor to engage in a protracted standoff. Rather, they hoped that by seizing the embassy and holding the staff hostage for a few days they could seriously embarrass the PRG and perhaps bring it down. Their objective was to break relations irrevocably between Iran and the United States. They feared that the relationship that was developing would eventually undermine the revolution's achievements, including the independence gained from the perceived U.S. manipulation of Iran practiced during the Pahlavi era. They saw in the photo from Algiers proof that the United States was once again subverting Iranian aspirations, and it galvanized them into action.

The students succeeded spectacularly, probably well beyond their expectations. Not only did the PRG collapse within forty-eight hours of the embassy's seizure, the hostage crisis ultimately led to a complete rupture of official relations between Iran and the United States, a situation that has endured for fifteen years at this writing. What the students did not anticipate but soon recognized was that possession of the U.S. embassy and control of its staff as hostages gave them power to affect the national political process far out of proportion to their numbers and position as otherwise inconsequential university students.

LESSONS LEARNED

The lessons of the interval between the two attacks on the United States embassy in Tehran in 1979 are of several varieties. Some decisions made during the period were not based on past experience so much as they were on the perceived needs of the moment. Nonetheless, with the perspective of hindsight, certain lessons, both positive and negative, might be drawn from the experience and applied to future situations.

Staffing

Whatever the views of individual embassy officers on the shah and the revolutionary forces arrayed against him, the experience of the revolution and the February 14, 1979, attack on the embassy deeply affected almost all American personnel. With rare exceptions, the experience of these traumatic events had impaired the ability of those involved to view the Iranian scene dispassionately.

In the circumstances, when Washington decided that it needed to forge a new relationship with postrevolutionary Iran, it was logical to look to new personnel to achieve this policy objective. Whatever expertise from past service in Iran might be lost would be compensated for by gains in assessments of current developments uncluttered by distortions born of witnessing the preceding violent events.[10]

Disposing of Documents

In at least one case the experience of the February attack led the embassy to take the wrong decision in November. The destruction of files and communications software during the February 14 attack, together with the residue of tear gas used to slow the attackers, severely handicapped the ensuing efforts to resume normal embassy operations. The memory of the hardship of trying to work without files, of being dependent on less than state-of-the-art telecommunications, and of having to operate out of makeshift offices created a hesitancy to repeat the experience.

Over the course of the summer and autumn of 1979, as the embassy gradually resumed normal operations, it accumulated a growing body of records. When the shah was admitted to the United States in October, embassy offices were ordered to review their file holdings and reduce them to the extent possible. By November 4, however, the embassy's classified files were still far greater than could be disposed of in the time the embassy's physical defenses could be expected to hold against a concerted attack.

Chargé Bruce Laingen learned of the attack while leaving the Iranian Foreign Ministry following a meeting. Advised of the situation by the embassy security officer over the radio in his limousine, Laingen went back into the ministry to seek help. His hope was to get the PRG to intervene as it had in February, when the embassy had been quickly restored to U.S. control and there had been no significant compromise of classified documents. Unfortunately, his efforts to convince senior ministry authorities that their government was obliged to intervene to protect American personnel at the embassy produced nothing more than vague assurances.

In the meantime, precious time was lost before the order to begin destruction of classified holdings was given to the besieged staff at the embassy. Moreover, the equipment available for destruction of file holdings was inadequate for the task. Embassy shredders were generally of a "nonterminal" type—that is, they cut paper fed into them into thin strips instead of reducing the paper to a fine confetti-like substance. The students who seized the embassy later laboriously pasted the shredded document strips together, re-creating a substantial body of documents.[11]

The embassy had "learned" the wrong lesson from the first attack. It should not have viewed the destruction program as an encumbrance to resumption of operations but as a mandatory procedure in any situation where an attack could occur, whether or not local authorities had the capacity to intervene quickly and restore control. In the Iranian case, the experience of the months prior to the second attack on the embassy had repeatedly demonstrated the weakness of the PRG and a steady erosion of its authority. It was probably unreasonable to expect in November that the PRG could intervene as decisively as it had done in February.

A related lesson concerns the issue of the embassy's chain of command. From early April until November 4, the embassy was headed by a chargé d'affaires with no formal deputy chief of mission. In practice, as the embassy's political counselor, I served as Laingen's informal deputy, but on the day of the attack I had accompanied the chargé to the Foreign Ministry.[12] Thus, when the attack began, there was no one clearly in charge at the embassy compound. Laingen attempted to give instructions via radio and telephone to various embassy officers while simultaneously pressing Foreign Ministry officials. In these circumstances, command and control at the embassy was confused.

It was extremely imprudent on the embassy's part to maintain a volume of records beyond what could be destroyed in a matter of minutes. Moreover, as hindsight again reveals, there should always have been someone present at the embassy formally designated to take command in the absence of the chargé d'affaires, with the authority to direct a defense against attack, including authority to initiate destruction of classified holdings.

Physical Security

Decisions on physical security based on the February 14 experience proved largely irrelevant. Following that first attack, the embassy undertook an ambitious program to consolidate operations in the embassy compound and to harden the physical facilities. The chancery was fitted with massive steel doors; the windows were barred and equipped with sand boxes to stop incoming gunfire. A building on the compound was converted into a consular section with elaborate security controls, replacing the leased commercial space several blocks away that the consular section had formerly occupied. Consular staff would work behind a "hardline" separating it from the Iranian public who entered the waiting area directly from the street.

The concept of buying enough time for Iranian authorities to intervene in the event of future attack may have been sound enough. On November 4 the student militants were not immediately able to penetrate the main chancery building (though they managed to get in more quickly than had the February 14 attackers). Defenses at the new consular section held for more than an hour. But in the absence of will and capacity on the part of the PRG to live up to its obligation to protect foreign diplomatic missions, the post–February 14 physical security measures proved meaningless.

Personnel Numbers and Deployment

It is worth noting that both the layout of the embassy compound and the large number of U.S. staff working and living there made the embassy particularly vulnerable to the kind of action carried out on November 4 by the student militants. Their most effective weapon was to threaten violence against embassy personnel who fell into their hands. As soon as the first hostage was taken, the lack of timely intervention by the Iranian authorities virtually assured capture of the entire compound and its staff.

In addition to the main chancery building and the recreation center–cum–consular section, the compound contained a variety of administrative offices, the motor pool, a commissary, and a number of residences, including those of the ambassador, the DCM, and communications staff. Only the wall surrounding the compound and the small contingent of Iranian police stationed outside protected the personnel working or living in these buildings. In addition, off-duty Marine security guards and personnel in transit used a leased apartment building across a narrow alley directly behind the rear compound wall for living quarters.

Although U.S. mission staff in Iran was drastically reduced following the February 14 attack, on November 4 it still numbered more than seventy U.S. personnel, making the embassy one of the largest diplomatic establishments in Tehran. In addition to those manning the consular, economic, and political sections, these personnel included a Marine security guard contingent numbering more than a dozen, a substantial administrative support staff, a defense attaché office, and a residual JUSMAG operation working on military supply contracts.

At any given moment of the day (or night), a significant portion of these personnel would be on duty in areas *outside* the hardened chancery building and consular section or resting in one of the compound's several residences and the nearby apartment building. In sum, it was hardly necessary for the embassy's attackers to penetrate the main chancery building and consular section to find a sufficient number of U.S. captives to serve their purposes.

At the time of the Javits Resolution crisis in May, as noted above, the embassy had debated the wisdom of maintaining a relatively large U.S. staff in Iran, given the volatility that continued to grip the country and the questionable power of the PRG to provide adequate security. Despite deep concern about the embassy's potential vulnerability to another attack, the consensus then had been that U.S. interests in Iran were so compelling that an official presence was needed to protect and advance them.

In retrospect, it is doubtful that this collective judgment was correct. Subsequent developments not only in Iran but elsewhere suggest that there are times when an official presence simply is not tenable. However, again with the advantage of hindsight, even when it is deemed essential to maintain some kind of presence in uncertain circumstances, the Iranian experience demonstrates the need to keep the numbers to an absolute minimum. Was it really necessary in Tehran to preserve the full range of consular and visa services and the relatively large economic and military staffs? How many security officers and Marine guards were really needed? And how many political officers?

There is no guarantee that the outcome on November 4 would have been different had the embassy's U.S. staff been smaller than it was. The critical element in the situation was the willingness and ability of the government of the day to carry out its duty to protect accredited foreign diplomatic missions. As documented above, by November 4 the PRG's capacity for intervention to provide the embassy security had eroded considerably.

The lesson for future situations, however, is that smaller numbers in tightly consolidated facilities with good physical security are likely to be able to hold out longer than was the case in Tehran. There were simply too many personnel scattered throughout the sprawling compound and beyond for hardened areas to serve their intended purpose.

51

Domestic vs. Foreign Policy Considerations:
Weighing Advice from the Scene

A seemingly obvious lesson lay in the Carter administration's decision to admit the shah for medical treatment, a decision contrary to the explicit advice from the United States government's highest-ranking representative and most seasoned diplomatic observer on the scene in Iran. Given that the seizure of the embassy on November 4 resulted in a protracted hostage crisis that ultimately contributed significantly to President Carter's defeat in the 1980 elections, it would appear that elected officials would in future want to give greater weight to the views of trained professionals on important questions of foreign policy. To conclude so, however, largely ignores both U.S. political reality and the inexactitude of the "science" of diplomatic analysis.

In October 1979, as he viewed the coming election campaign, President Carter had to be focused more on the jockeying for political advantage then already underway in both the Republican Party and among potential Democratic Party challengers than on the possible reaction in Tehran to *any* decision he might make on matters of concern to Iran's new authorities. Kissinger, Rockefeller, and others were increasingly vocal in arguing for the shah's admission, and they had a strong case: the shah *had* been a valuable ally and he *was* sick.

Their arguments, moreover, were reinforced by the U.S. public's impression of what was then going on in Iran. By comparison with Iran's new leadership and the conditions it presided over, the shah and the police state he had operated appeared relatively benign. President Carter's decision to protect his flank from Republican attack on the issue of the shah was not only logical, it was a political imperative.

The embassy's view of the likely consequences of a decision to admit the shah ultimately proved prescient, but, as noted, the shah's admission served essentially as a pretext for the November 4 attack. The more probable catalyst was the November 1 meeting in Algiers between the PRG's premier and foreign minister and President Carter's national security adviser, a meeting the embassy itself had advocated. Furthermore, after debate in the daily senior staff meeting on the morning of November 4, the embassy opted to remain open for business rather than close and send staff home (as Embassy Kampala had done six years earlier). A contrary decision would not have precluded the attack two hours later, but there would have been fewer U.S. citizens on hand to become hostages of the student militants. One can only speculate what course the ensuing crisis might have taken had only a few U.S. personnel been captured while the bulk of the staff remained free.

The more relevant point is that even well-trained and astute professionals are far from infallible. Their analyses and policy recommendations can at best be no more than well-informed estimates. Moreover, decisions of whatever sort frequently produce unforeseen consequences. U.S. political leaders responsible for foreign policy and national security do need to take seriously the views and recommendations of foreign affairs professionals, but it would be unreasonable to expect that they would be the only factors weighed in decisions.

In an open, democratic, and participatory political system such as that of the United States, domestic considerations more often than not will take precedence in the foreign policy decision-making process. That is the key lesson from the Iranian experience, and the posture of U.S. representation abroad must be adjusted accordingly.

The embassy in Tehran knew throughout the period from February to November 1979 that it was operating in volatile, potentially dangerous circumstances. It understood that actions taken in the United States for essentially domestic political purposes could have serious repercussions in Iran. It foresaw that a decision to admit the former shah would risk a new attack on the embassy. It even sensed that reducing the size of the staff still further could diminish the embassy's vulnerability to some extent (although it did not go so far as to recommend such a reduction). Neither Washington nor Embassy Tehran, however, amalgamated these insights with the relevant domestic political considerations weighing on the Carter administration to forge a diplomatic posture consistent with political realities in *both* Iran *and* the United States.

U.S. Ambassador Adolph "Spike" Dubs, murdered in Kabul on February 14, 1979.
State Department

4

The Murder of Ambassador Dubs, Kabul, 1979

James E. Taylor

Shortly before 9:00 A.M. on February 14, 1979, in front of the American Center, four men seized U.S. Ambassador Adolph "Spike" Dubs in downtown Kabul as he was being driven to his embassy office and took him to the nearby Kabul Hotel, where he remained for nearly four hours in Room 117 on the second floor. They did not hold Dubs's chauffeur but sent him instead to inform the embassy of the ambassador's "arrest."

Moments later the embassy's deputy chief of mission, Bruce Amstutz, notified Afghan authorities and requested their assistance. He then dispatched an embassy team to the hotel, where Afghan forces had just appeared on the scene, led by Kabul police chief Lal Mohammad. The embassy group succeeded in temporarily dissuading these forces from launching an immediate assault on Room 117.

Over the next few hours, the embassy entreated the Afghan authorities to take no action that would endanger the ambassador's life or welfare. Embassy officers established contact with the Foreign Ministry, and personal messages from Secretary of State Cyrus Vance reinforced their appeals. The embassy had sporadic access to tactical officials at the hotel but effectively none with the two key Afghan security and political figures making the crucial decisions, Foreign Minister Hafizullah Amin, who was also deputy prime minister, and Interior Minister Daoud Taroon. Amin was virtually never accessible to U.S. officials, while Taroon made one specious pledge but otherwise simply refused to meet waiting embassy political officer James Taylor (myself). Despite U.S. appeals, at about 12:30 P.M. the U.S. team at the hotel saw that Afghan forces, with critical tactical assistance from Soviet embassy security officers, were preparing to assault the hotel room. Urgent embassy efforts to forestall this move proved fruitless.

At 12:50 the Afghans unleashed a devastating fusillade of automatic fire at the room from a building across the road and from the hallway outside the room. After the firing, Afghan security officials prevented the waiting U.S. team from entering the room until they had determined the results of their assault. As the embassy team waited in the hallway outside Room 117, they heard the sound of several single shots within, fired from a small-caliber gun.

Upon being allowed to enter the shattered room, members of the team found Ambassador Dubs slumped in a chair, dead from multiple gunshot wounds. They also saw the crumpled bodies of two of the kidnappers. A third kidnapper, apparently captured earlier in the lobby, was removed from the hotel by Afghan security forces along with the bodies of his mates. The whereabouts of a fourth man wearing a police uniform was never firmly established, but the regime produced four corpses that evening for identification by embassy officers, who agreed that three of the dead were definitely those seen at the hotel.

The kidnapping and murder of Ambassador Dubs was a unique crisis compared to others faced by Embassy Kabul between the communist coup of April 1978 and the Soviet invasion of December 1979. A brief crisis, this one posed no overt threat to other members of the American community, in contrast to the full-scale military battles that had been and would be endured by the entire population of Kabul during those turbulent months. While U.S.–Afghan relations had previously continued more or less normally despite the drastic changes following the 1978 coup, the murder of Ambassador Dubs had an immediate and devastating impact on bilateral ties.

The Soviet role in those hours in Kabul precipitated an angry exchange between Washington and Moscow over what the United States viewed as totally inappropriate behavior by Soviet embassy officials. This chill in superpower relations previewed the U.S. reaction to the Soviet invasion ten months later.

BACKGROUND TO THE CRISIS

U.S. Policy Before the Crisis

The April 1978 "Saur Revolution" that destroyed Afghanistan's *ancien régime* was carried out by a small group of Afghan leftists of the People's Democratic Party of Afghanistan (PDPA), led by military officers trained and indoctrinated in the Soviet Union. Though significant reform was necessary to lift Afghanistan's society and economy out of the "bottom ten" of the world's least developed, the new leaders soon revealed their brutality, their heavy-handed approach to domestic reforms, and their devotion to and dependence upon Moscow.

U.S. policy since the 1978 coup had been to work as much as possible with the new PDPA government in areas of mutual concern. The United States recognized the negative character of the regime, but sought to provide an alternative to a tightening Soviet embrace. The Peace Corps maintained an active contingent, AID continued its programs in an increasingly dangerous countryside, and the U.S. Information Service (USIS) offered what views and information it could to offset the regime's anti-American propaganda to the degree possible.

It was rough going for all, and support for this policy was not unanimous in Washington. Some observers argued that in Afghanistan the United States confronted another Third World repressive leftist regime and should not squander U.S. resources by supporting a hostile government fundamentally unreceptive to U.S. generosity.

Spike Dubs did not share this negative view. He had arrived in Kabul in the summer of 1978 following senior-level appointments in the State Department and our embassy in Moscow. It was his belief that if U.S. efforts were ever going to help the majority of the Afghan people, we as a mission had no choice but to work with the host government as best we could, no matter how deplorable that government might be. As it happened, if U.S. policy had been to strike a hands-off stance toward the new Afghan regime by, for example, withdrawing the ambassador, downsizing all agencies' operations, and terminating many programs (more or less what followed the Dubs killing), the crisis at issue would not have happened as it did. Ironically, that approach was one that Dubs himself rejected.

An incident about two months after the April 1978 coup illustrates that period's official U.S. policy of working with, not against, the new regime. A representative of a nascent resistance group composed mainly of medical doctors (thereafter known in Kabul as the "Doctors' Plot") clandestinely contacted the embassy seeking assistance in some move against the regime. Washington decided that we should inform the doctors' representative that the U.S. government could offer no support for his group's efforts. The regime discovered this particular group several months later and executed many of its members.

A Regime in Trouble

By the beginning of 1979, the infant PDPA regime faced increasingly serious problems on a number of fronts. Its ham-handed treatment of needed reforms had produced little progress, its brutal repression of all perceived opposition had terrified the urban population, and its unrelenting support of Moscow and communism alienated many strongly Muslim Afghans. In less than a year, armed mujahaddin resistance forces in the countryside, organized in mid-1978, had become capable of mounting increasingly ambitious hit-and-run attacks against the government's military and security forces. While the mujahaddin's strength was at that time concentrated in the more remote areas of the country, operations were moving ever closer to major population centers. In addition, a number of tiny Marxist splinter factions were struggling against the regime.

The PDPA regime was composed of several distinct circles of power, notably the Khalq and Parcham factions, and stresses within the regime had also produced many schisms among those competing for control. Those involved in the political jockeying, particularly Hafizullah Amin—officially number two in the regime, but the de facto dominant power—and Interior Minister Daoud Taroon, fiercely loyal to Amin, were not averse to using violence to achieve their objectives. (Amin had already maneuvered President Nur Mohammad Taraki into a powerless position and later had him killed.) A standard quip at the time asserted that attending the regime's cabinet meetings was a particularly risky undertaking, what with participants having to check their guns at the door before entering. The violent character of Afghan political leaders and their underlying anti-American convictions were to make a tragically deadly combination as the Dubs crisis unfolded.

EMBASSY RESPONSE

Surprise

In contrast to crises involving coups d'état, revolutions, and invasions, which are generally foreshadowed by some sort of intelligence or signs, the Dubs crisis was totally unexpected. There had been no indication of any threat aimed at U.S. officials, and despite the outbreaks of violence over the preceding ten months, there was no reason to anticipate that Afghan authorities would respond to this crisis with total disregard for high-level U.S. appeals for patience. Nor could we have foreseen that with Soviet tactical assistance they would launch an assault virtually certain to leave no survivors—or that the host government itself would emerge as the party most likely, in my view, to have been responsible for the murder of our ambassador.

Initially, there was some understandable confusion at the U.S. mission upon hearing of the ambassador's abduction, because we had no idea what we were facing. The lack of accurate information was to plague both us and Washington throughout the crisis.

My boss, political counselor Bruce Flatin, arrived at the office shortly before 9:00 A.M. declaring, "The ambassador has been arrested." Even given the highly anti-American attitudes of the regime, this report of an arrest sounded farfetched, though it could not be completely dismissed. The source of the report was the ambassador's driver, who had gone at once to the embassy after leaving Dubs and his captors at the Kabul Hotel.

On the way to the embassy a few minutes before, the driver recounted, the ambassador's car had been stopped by a man in a traffic police uniform. With the ambassador's permission, the driver lowered his bulletproof window to determine what the officer wanted. At that point, the man thrust his revolver at the driver and three other armed men scrambled into the now unlocked limousine, directing the driver to take them to the Kabul Hotel. The embassy soon concluded that this was not some crazy action by the regime, but a full-scale terrorist operation of unknown origin and unclear goals or demands.

In a report issued several months later, the State Department Office of Security underlined the element of surprise, saying it had had "no indication of a possible threat or kidnapping plot directed against Ambassador Dubs prior to the incident." As the report noted, "The Ambassador did not normally have personal bodyguard protection while traveling in his vehicle, . . . which was partially armored and afforded a degree of protection from weapon fire. The Ambassador's chauffeur had been instructed on defensive driving techniques, and as instructed, routinely varied his driving routes when transporting the Ambassador." Noting further that "Dubs enjoyed complete diplomatic immunity, and detention and searches of his person or vehicle were not permissible," the Security Office investigators inferred that the ambassador's decision "to open the vehicle's door to the inspecting policeman permitted the kidnappers to proceed with their plans unrestricted" and that "had he declined to unlock the door, the abduction might have been avoided."[1]

Deploying Embassy Resources

DCM Amstutz at once called the Foreign Ministry chief of protocol, who subsequently reported that he had informed Hafizullah Amin. Amstutz then convened the senior members of the embassy's country team to consider what steps we should take. Among those participating were Bruce Flatin and me as the political officers, economic counselor Jay Freres, and the consular and defense attachés. Our goal was to try to head off precipitate action that would endanger the life of the ambassador.

Amstutz immediately dispatched an embassy team to the Kabul Hotel. The team included, among others, Bruce Flatin, security officer Charles Boles, and Jay Freres (the last took minute-by-minute notes on everything that happened at the hotel, a crucial function because his notes were a key element of the embassy's complete reporting a few hours after Dubs's death). Also part of the team were the embassy's doctor, Lloyd Rotz, and several of our more burly staff members to serve as possible stretcher bearers.

A number of these officers spoke Dari (the Afghan dialect of Persian), and together they were competent in Russian, German, and Arabic, so language was no barrier to communication with the Afghan forces and their Soviet advisers on the scene. The communication problem was broader and more vexing: the Afghans and Soviets, at the hotel and throughout Kabul, refused to provide U.S. officials with critical information regarding the regime's intentions.

The embassy sent FLASH (highest precedence) telegrams to late-night Washington and notified the American community through the warden system. Meanwhile Amstutz sought unsuccessfully to contact Amin and Deputy Foreign Minister Shah Mohammad Dost. Amstutz then sent our administrative counselor, Bernie Woerz, to Amin's office, but Amin refused to see him—Amin, according to his aides, was tied up with the Iraqi foreign minister's visit. Afghan leaders were singularly uncooperative, and all our efforts to reach key officials proved frustrating and fruitless.

At about 9:30 A.M. I took a radio call from Chuck Boles at the hotel, who said the authorities wanted to mount an immediate attack to "rescue" the ambassador. (At this point, the number holding Dubs in the hotel room had been reduced to two because the other one there had wandered alone down to the hotel lobby and been quickly overpowered by security officials.) I told Boles that, in keeping with known U.S. policy, the embassy team should urge the authorities at the hotel in the strongest terms not to take any precipitate action that would endanger the ambassador's welfare. They should urgently insist that the forces at the hotel do nothing until the United States government had made contact with the Afghan government at the highest levels to reinforce this message and determine whom the kidnappers represented and what they wanted.

Bruce Flatin conveyed this message at 9:50 A.M. to the Soviet adviser and Afghan police at the hotel. The Afghans and Soviets acknowledged the U.S. request and professed to agree with the wisdom of a patient course. At 10:15 A.M. the Soviet embassy security officer, KGB colonel Sergei Bakhturin, arrived and added further assurances of a strong Soviet interest in the ambassador's safety.

Pursuing our efforts through normal channels, the DCM sent me to the Foreign Ministry to make a similar appeal for restraint. I met with Deputy Foreign Minister Dost, who served chiefly as the highest-ranking contact for most embassies in Kabul. (The Soviet ambassador, however, dealt almost exclusively with regime strongman Hafizullah Amin, who was almost always "unavailable" to meet with U.S. officials.) Dost seemed receptive to the U.S. position and said he would pass it on to his superiors. I recall a feeling of complete futility, since Dost's lack of political power was well known and his expressions of understanding of the U.S. message were virtually meaningless. All embassy efforts to reach Amin directly proved unavailing.

Deciding to try to reach the Afghan officials who really mattered, the DCM next sent me to deliver the U.S. message to Interior Minister Daoud Taroon, who was also police commandant and in security matters second in power only to Amin. A rough customer, often described simply as a thug, Taroon ran the extensive Afghan security forces that had brutalized the population, in particular all those perceived as opposition, since the April 1978 coup.

Upon reaching Taroon's waiting room at 11:15 A.M., I was told quite firmly by two heavily armed and formidable-looking male "receptionists" that Taroon was busy with the "situation" and that I should wait. Taroon was known to have even more heavily armed bodyguards with him at all times, and I had no choice but to give a hastily written version of the U.S. position to one of these receptionists to take to Taroon. He entered Taroon's office and returned without the paper, but I have no idea what took place inside. I could hear constant radio chatter from Taroon's office and several voices responding as Taroon directed the actions of his security forces at the hotel.

At 11:35 A.M., just over an hour before the assault would be launched, Taroon informed the embassy by phone that the regime had no intention of making any move that would threaten the ambassador and that the DCM would be consulted before any major action was taken.

During the remaining time before the eventual assault, the embassy remained deployed in much the same manner: DCM Amstutz and most of the staff at the embassy were evaluating and disseminating the skimpy information provided by the regime, maintaining contact with Washington as best they could, and directing action by the team at the hotel and staff elsewhere in Kabul. The team at the hotel were trying fruitlessly to garner whatever they could from the stonewalling Afghan authorities and their Soviet collaborators regarding those forces' intentions, and continually pressing for patience and forbearance on the part of the regime. A looming responsibility of this team was to try to rescue the ambassador following any violent assault on the room.

I remained at the Interior Ministry, cooling my heels in Taroon's waiting room. Pressing as far as possible in a highly charged atmosphere, I convinced Taroon's gatekeepers three times to take U.S. messages in to Taroon, including a personal appeal from Secretary Vance for additional time to consider all aspects of the crisis.

Communications with Washington

Keeping Washington informed on developments up to the minute was a serious problem for Amstutz and his staff throughout the crisis. Even though we sent all our reporting cables by FLASH precedence, we were working in the precomputer Foreign Service. All these messages had to be typewritten on the old green telegram forms and taken to the communicators, who then had to retype them on appropriate tape for sending. This was a clumsy process in a fast-moving situation; there always seemed to be "one more event" to be added before each message was released.

Although the embassy support staff did yeoman work, our cable reporting system guaranteed that Washington would never be aware, in real time, of what was currently happening in Kabul. Our first reporting message, for example, sent via FLASH at 9:30 A.M. (exactly midnight Washington time), was received, according to Operations Center records, about fifteen minutes later (9:45 Kabul time). Thus, the four-hour crisis was already one hour old by the time our initial alerting message hit the State Department.

To exacerbate everyone's frustrations, the Afghan telephone system was abysmal. Even in the best of times, a call to Peshawar, just over the border in Pakistan, was always difficult and many times impossible. Once completed, the connections were usually bad, and shouting was the normal mode when calling anyone outside Kabul, not an ideal means to send or receive precisely tuned instructions.

At the outset of the crisis, the embassy immediately tried to establish telephone contact with Washington. It was several hours into the crisis, however, before this could be done, and then the quality of the connection was bad. At one point I passed the ambassador's office and observed an officer yelling strenuously, trying to make himself heard in Washington. What if anything he could hear in response I have no idea.

Notwithstanding the difficult communications, a department task force established under the direction of Anthony Quainton, then director of the Office for Combatting Terrorism, did succeed in establishing phone contact with the embassy. One message counseling restraint was sent from Secretary Vance for the Afghan leadership, and a second was dispatched following renewed preparations for assault. But Embassy Kabul continued to have great difficulties finding any Afghan with genuine authority who would receive the message, much less heed it.

THE END COMES

Whatever the reasons for the delay following the apparent earlier intention to assault the hotel—whether because of U.S. pleas or for the Afghans' own reasons—the team at the hotel observed new preparations for assault at 11:20 A.M., when Afghan authorities began sealing off the streets and putting ladders up to the buildings. At 11:40 A.M., Bruce Flatin conversed briefly with Dubs in German through the door of Room 117, but declined the Afghans' request to warn him of an imminent assault, again arguing instead for patience.

Soon, however, at about 12:30 P.M., the team saw alarming signs that the Afghan forces, with the open help of Soviet security officials, were preparing to assault the room. Heavily armed commandos were moved to the first floor of the building across the street from the hotel, where they received tactical advice regarding the best means of deployment via hand signals from Soviet officials. Photographs of Dubs were circulated among the assault forces, presumably with the hope they would not mistake him for a terrorist, and firemen with picks and axes joined the commandos.

Ignoring further frantic pleas from the embassy team not to launch an attack, at 12:50 Afghan troops unleashed a barrage of heavy automatic fire into the room from across the street and from the hallway.[2] This fusillade, started and stopped on Soviet instructions, lasted almost a minute, devastated the room, shattered water pipes, and left a heavy pall of smoke and dust in the air. It killed the two kidnappers in the room (the one captured earlier and a fourth individual not recognized by embassy officers also turned up dead that evening). But the fusillade did not kill the ambassador.

Once the firing stopped, the embassy team members ran to enter the room with the first Afghan forces, but were ordered to remain in the hallway. Several Afghan officers entered the room; then shots from a small-caliber gun rang out from inside. (Given the tension of the moment and the barrage they had just heard, team members understandably differed on the number of shots each remembered hearing.) When the embassy officers were finally admitted to the room, they found visibility extremely hampered. They saw the crumpled bodies of the two Afghan abductors and found the ambassador with multiple gunshot wounds and powder burns. Dr. Rotz confirmed that he was dead.

From the Interior Ministry I could just barely hear the outbreak of heavy firing. As soon as it stopped, a man in civilian clothing—a Soviet, as I believed then and so reported—emerged from Taroon's office. He turned at the door and spoke, in Russian, back into the office. He had been with Taroon for at least an hour and forty minutes.

Within seconds, Taroon emerged with several bodyguards toting AK-47s and moved past me without a word. When I caught up with him and asked what had happened, he replied, "It is over," and moved on. I pressed him for details but got the same reply—no word of explanation or expression of regret about the outcome.

IMPACT ON THE AMERICAN COMMUNITY

The death of Ambassador Dubs had a traumatic impact on the U.S. community, which had held Dubs in very high professional and personal regard. Perhaps it was the suddenness—many members of the community were unaware of the events until well after the four-hour crisis had ended. Clearly, it was the finality, but it was also the completely unexplainable: Why? There were simply no plausible reasons available in the first days following the crisis to account for the ambassador's death. Emotionally, many people were fearful and sought answers that did not exist.

Into this psychological and emotional context several days later came the official Washington delegation accompanying the ambassador's widow, Mary Ann Dubs. The delegation was led by the director general of the Foreign Service, Harry Barnes, and included the senior leadership of the Near East Bureau. Also in the group was the State Department's in-house psychiatrist, presumably to address some of these widely felt fears and concerns. The delegation held a meeting the night of its arrival with all interested members of the community to answer questions and provide whatever support it could.

Because Mary Ann Dubs invited me to represent the embassy at the funeral, I left the next day on the plane with the delegation. I thus had no opportunity at the time to discuss the impact of this visit with colleagues. Upon my return two weeks later, however, I heard from many in the community that the department psychiatrist had greatly upset the group with some inappropriate remarks and left many mission members feeling even worse than before the delegation's visit. It was only through some extraordinary efforts by the embassy leadership, the embassy's own resident psychiatrist, Dr. Elmore Rigamer, and the community itself that morale was eventually repaired. As one example, the little theater group, after some deliberation, pressed on with a full production of *Oklahoma*, in which Dubs was to have had a part. It was important to keep people occupied and help them move beyond the tragedy.

Although these harsh judgments by our community may seem unfair, they were openly voiced at the time by many colleagues and family members. Perhaps no one could have responded successfully in the aftermath of this particular crisis. One might conclude, nonetheless, that officials asked to respond to the needs of a traumatized American community should be most carefully selected. If the widely held feelings in Kabul in the weeks following the Dubs murder serve as any guide, occupying a senior position does not necessarily guarantee effective interpersonal skills.

THE INVESTIGATION

According to the official State Department investigation into the incident, the U.S. embassy shortly after the ambassador's death submitted a diplomatic note to the Democratic Republic of Afghanistan (DRA) "requesting an official report on the kidnapping and death of Ambassador Dubs." The note specifically requested "an explanation of the circumstances leading to the decision to assault the room in which the Ambassador was held."[3]

The report's conclusions castigated the DRA's response and enumerated unanswered questions. Reading it evokes the maddening frustration that has lingered on many years later:

> The Afghan government to date [late 1979] has refused to cooperate with U.S. government efforts to clarify the circumstances of Ambassador Dubs' death. The account of the Ambassador's death as provided by the DRA is incomplete, misleading, and inaccurate. Some of the actions taken by DRA authorities during the events preceding the Ambassador's death may be attributed to Afghan inexperience in handling kidnapping incidents. However, sufficient evidence has been obtained to establish serious misrepresentation or

suppression of the truth by the government. Consequently, the following significant questions surrounding the circumstances of Ambassador Dubs' death remain unanswered:

1. Why was the Ambassador the target of the kidnapping?
2. Who were his abductors? Who do they represent? What were their demands?
3. Why did the DRA assault the room where the Ambassador was held?
4. Who fired the weapons which resulted in the Ambassador's death, especially the unidentified .22-caliber weapon? Why has the DRA refused to allow U.S. government officials to examine the weapons?
5. Why was at least one of the terrorists killed by DRA authorities while in captivity? What information if any did he provide before his death?
6. What were the circumstances regarding the death of the fourth terrorist? Was this individual actually one of the Ambassador's abductors?
7. What was the involvement of the Soviets in the decision making process in the operation directed against the terrorists?
8. Why was the DRA not more cooperative with U.S. Embassy officials during the hours immediately preceding the Ambassador's death and with the subsequent investigation?
9. Why has the DRA provided incomplete, misleading and inaccurate information to the U.S. government?[4]

Who Were the Kidnappers and What Were They After?

In the absence of Afghan government cooperation, no definitive information on the identity or motivation of the kidnappers has ever emerged. Several theories exist, including the argument that the operation was an elaborate scheme by the PDPA regime to remove Dubs because he was effectively bridging the differences between the leftist Afghan government and the United States. In addition, his Soviet expertise posed a nuisance in the context of the regime's growing ties with Moscow. (In this scenario, the four abductors were regime dupes not expecting to end up dead.)

Some observers contend that Moscow was responsible for the planning as well as the execution of the entire kidnapping and murder. I have never seen any evidence that would point to a Soviet role in the conceptual stages of this affair, but there is irrefutable proof that Soviet officials performed key functions during the preparations for the assault on the hotel room. These activities were clearly contrary to official U.S. pleas and contributed to the subsequent chill in U.S.–Soviet relations.[5]

In my view, the most plausible explanation, based on subsequent intelligence, is that the group behind the operation was a radical leftist rival of the regime and that the four abductors were terrorists demanding release of several colleagues held in prison. This report fits with information, acquired shortly after the event, that the kidnappers were trying to barter the ambassador for some imprisoned dissidents named "Wahez, Majid, and Faizani." This information later paralleled, in part, several of the versions provided by the regime. Such a group might have mounted a flawed operation, with Keystone Kops overtones, in the belief that taking the U.S. ambassador hostage would somehow give them leverage over the anti-American regime in Kabul. (In this analysis, Soviet behavior on the scene, in keeping with Moscow's close and broad ties with Kabul, would reflect the Soviets' efforts to crush all opposition to their Afghan allies from whatever quarter.)

Most observers believed, in fact, that Amin's determination to destroy all opposition should have led rational men to conclude that a violent and immediate response was inevitable. Tragically, not all violent extremists can be counted on to be rational. Moreover, Amin's documented anti-Americanism, coupled with a determination to prevent the ambassador from reporting whatever he may have learned about the existence or activities of this rival group, could have made it easy for him to decide that no one was to survive.

Who Killed the Ambassador?

Subsequent forensic and ballistics reports remain inconclusive. What is certain is that Dubs suffered no potentially fatal wounds from the high-powered military weapons used during the barrage on the room. Autopsy and forensic examinations show that Dubs died as a result of at least ten wounds inflicted by small-caliber weapons, at least five of them by a .22-caliber weapon. None of the weapons the Afghan government reported finding in the possession of the terrorists were .22-caliber weapons, nor could any have caused the .22-caliber wounds.

To explain the fatal shots, some observers contend that one of the terrorists had been positioned next to the ambassador, that once the firing started he had held his position and shot the ambassador repeatedly with a pistol that somehow disappeared, and that he himself was then shot at some point.

In my personal view, the individual shots the embassy team heard as they were detained in the hallway provide compelling evidence that the regime's forces had been instructed to eliminate any possible opponents of Amin and all witnesses to what had happened in that room, including Dubs. Those in charge of the operation may have feared that Dubs knew enough Dari to understand the terrorists' demands and might thus reveal information potentially embarrassing to the regime had he survived.

Amin and Taroon had no regard for the norms of international relations and were thus unconcerned with the possible impact of their actions on U.S.-Afghan relations or what that might mean for the Afghan people. Amin's power in this crisis was, in effect, unfettered, and he may have had a number of reasons in his mind as to how he might benefit from the actual outcome. We are unlikely ever to know precisely who gave what orders and for what reason—the key Afghan participants all met violent ends later the same year. Taroon was killed during one of the famous "OK Corral" cabinet meetings; Lal Mohammad, the Kabul police chief in charge at the hotel that February 14, died in a clash with insurgents; and Amin perished at the hands of Soviet invasion forces on the night of December 27, 1979.

AFTERMATH

Washington and Moscow immediately exchanged angry charges and counter-charges regarding the role played by Soviet embassy officials in the assassination of Dubs. Moscow and Kabul claimed that Dubs had been killed as an unfortunate bystander in a shootout with terrorists, a contention that Kabul, and probably Moscow, knew was false.

The United States gradually phased out the Peace Corps and AID programs; within about six months all their personnel were effectively gone from Afghanistan. Later in 1979, Congress reflected the prevailing view in Washington by passing legislation prohibiting assistance to Afghanistan until the Afghan government had "apologized officially and assume[d] responsibility for the death of Ambassador Adolph Dubs." USIS maintained its efforts and enjoyed some success among the general population; but the regime's hostility remained undiminished, and pressures on Afghans not to visit USIS facilities grew. The continuing drawdown in U.S. programs eventually reduced the embassy to a listening and reporting post, an essential function in certain contexts, but not one that had any positive impact on the welfare of the common Afghan.

The hostility in Washington toward the Kabul regime that had been growing since the 1978 coup increased sharply following the Dubs killing. This period marked the onset of significant U.S. military support for the mujahaddin resistance, a program that was to accelerate following the December 1979 Soviet invasion. That military aid program—not to mention the sacrifices of the Afghans themselves—was to lead to one of the most significant Soviet defeats of the Cold War. Moreover, the stresses within Soviet society from a seemingly open-ended participation in an unwinnable war played some role, however small, in Moscow's move toward reform in the mid-1980s and to the eventual breakup of the Soviet Union itself.

COULD THE EMBASSY HAVE DONE MORE?

One always asks oneself after such a tragedy whether anything else could have been done.

The embassy had informed Washington of the potential for an imminent Afghan assault on the room in which Dubs was being held and, at the same time, of Afghan and Soviet assurances of no such intent. Senior Afghan officials deliberately rebuffed our efforts to communicate with them or to convey to them directly Secretary Vance's messages urging patience. Such refusals were clearly part of an effort to prevent any attempts to limit their freedom of action.

One also wonders whether any direct high-level U.S. appeal to the Soviets might have helped in any way. The Soviets always maintained that the Afghans had sole responsibility for handling the Dubs kidnapping. For the Soviets to have intervened to insist the Afghans be patient would have undercut the Soviet argument that the Afghans were managing the crisis and would have violated as well Soviet doctrine on dealing ruthlessly with terrorists.

Soviet KGB advisers in those days were assisting the Afghan security apparatus generally in crushing all domestic opposition, but the Soviets' control over Amin was far from total (hence their invasion months later in which they crushed him). And although Soviet security advisers were assisting the Afghans at the hotel during the assault, it remains impossible to know what advice or help the Soviets gave, or what pressure they may have exerted, beyond providing the critical operational assistance and weapons our embassy officers witnessed.

In any case, time was neither in our control nor on our side and did not permit high-level appeals to the Soviets. (Moreover, two hours after Ambassador Dubs was kidnapped on February 14, Islamic militants took over the U.S. embassy in Tehran, injecting a simultaneous major crisis into Washington.) In the end, I am convinced, the Afghans in charge of the reaction to the kidnapping triggered a denouement so rapid and were so impervious to all our appeals that there was nothing we could have done to avert the tragic outcome.

No one should have been sanguine about the possible behavior of a violent and reckless regime; certainly few of us on the scene believed that the welfare of Spike Dubs was of much concern to the regime in its decision-making process. Our sense of urgency in Kabul, therefore, stemmed mainly from our awareness that the fate of the ambassador depended on decisions by violence-prone people hostile to the United States and determined to destroy all opposition.

In the real world of Kabul on February 14, 1979, I believe, no other outcome was remotely possible. At some point, I assume, Afghan authorities knew, or learned, the identity and objectives of the kidnappers; it would not have taken the Afghan security forces long to extract such information and more from the one they had captured early in the crisis. Whatever Amin knew or feared, he or Taroon apparently decided that no one among the occupants of that hotel room was to survive. Once that decision had been made, there was nothing further either the embassy or Washington could have done to alter the progression of events. Additional appeals to other Afghan officials, demarches by U.N. or religious representatives, even a personal contact by the Soviets with Amin, in my opinion, would have had no impact on Amin's determination to end the matter quickly and, for his purposes, satisfactorily.

The principal lesson of this tragedy, to me at least, is that there are some crises that the United States simply cannot influence, much less control. Regardless of the resources available, determined and brutal leaders in other lands can sometimes defy all efforts, even by a superpower, to sway their actions and decisions. The regime that came to power in Kabul in 1978 and was responsible for the death of Spike Dubs seemed at the time to be one of the last of the leftist revolutionary regimes of the post–World War II world. In retrospect, and given today's headlines, one hopes that it is not instead one of a continuing series of brutal renegade regimes.

A Marine, a soldier, and two Pakistani employees were killed when a mob besieged and burned the U.S. embassy in Islamabad on November 21, 1979. The lightly armed defenders held out for five hours until the rioters dispersed at nightfall. *State Department*

5 | Attack on the U.S. Embassy in Pakistan, 1979

Herbert G. Hagerty

Fall had come—Islamabad's best season—after a long, hot spring and summer. There was a welcome nip in the air that reminded us of football and made a tweed jacket feel good in the mornings, as most members of the American community in Pakistan prepared for Thanksgiving and Christmas. But beneath the surface calm there was growing anxiety within the community about its safety in light of deteriorating relations between Pakistan and the United States, tense conditions in Islamabad, and the turmoil sweeping what news magazines had dubbed the "crescent of crisis" from Marrakesh to Bangladesh.

The chill in the fall air was more than matched by the chill in formal U.S.–Pakistan relations. Administration interest in South Asia had earlier seemed limited to the visit to India by President Jimmy Carter's mother, Lillian, following the restoration of democratic government there. Although the U.S. relationship with Pakistan had had its ups and downs in the years since 1950, a critical barometer of the relationship had been U.S. willingness to be Pakistan's armorer. But Pakistan's plans to seek greater security by matching India's nuclear capability put the U.S. supply relationship in jeopardy. And Islamabad's lurch in the 1970s into authoritarian, then martial-law government, with vague but disturbing Islamization rhetoric, rang additional alarm bells in Washington in view of the new Carter administration's emphasis on heading off nuclear proliferation, reducing arms transfers, and pressing for improvement of human rights.

The slide in relations that began in early 1979 gained momentum after the United States in April suspended all arms sales and assistance to Pakistan because of Islamabad's nuclear policies. The martial-law government increased U.S. unhappiness with Pakistan by its heavy-handed denial of human rights, as dramatized by the long trial (and execution) of former prime minister Zulfikar

71

Bhutto and by images in *Newsweek* and *Time* of Islamic punishments such as public floggings.

These developments in Pakistan should be seen against the rising antiforeign, and especially anti-Western, sentiment throughout the Islamic world following the fall of the shah of Iran in 1978. And on November 4, 1979, this hostility received new focus when our Foreign Service colleagues in Tehran were for the second time taken hostage by a mob run amok with revolutionary Islamic fervor. Acting on cue, the Iranian embassy in Islamabad, in the hands of same-sounding zealots, held nightly bonfire rallies to exhort students in Pakistan to follow the Iranian example in taking direct action against the U.S. official presence. These nightly fireworks violated every "third country" norm of modern diplomacy, leading Ambassador Arthur Hummel and others to protest, on more than one occasion, to the government of Pakistan.

The bucolic atmosphere in Islamabad—it was possible to see from the ambassador's office cows munching in open fields and clothing being washed in nearby streams—gave the circumstances a special air of unreality. Crowds were small, and a traffic jam in Islamabad was several cars and a bicycle. Government officials repeatedly dismissed our concerns about a threat to our security and repeatedly assured us that they took seriously their responsibility for our safety, thus helping to ease some of our anxiety. The decision in mid-November by local authorities to triple (to thirty-two) the handful of armed police normally stationed at the embassy gate was also reassuring, though worrying as well.

Signs of rising anti-Western/anti-U.S. feelings continued to grow throughout the country, especially in bazaars and on campuses, and quickly became a fact of our life. The embassy emergency action committee (EAC) began to meet on an almost daily basis to review and update emergency procedures and to schedule drills. And Ambassador Hummel briefed and reassured the American community at meetings held in the embassy auditorium in the weeks before November 21.

BEFORE THE DELUGE—MORNING, NOVEMBER 21

Sitting in my embassy office late on the morning of November 21—I was counselor for political affairs—I received a hurried phone call from Australian Ambassador Petherbridge, a neighbor in the part of Islamabad where I lived. He was calling to alert me that several busloads of students had just passed his embassy along the road from the university to our part of the diplomatic enclave; he judged from appearances that they were on their way to demonstrate at the U.S. embassy.

We had expected some form of demonstration that day in view of the news from Mecca in Saudi Arabia that had pushed the daily Tehran hostage stories below the fold of local newspapers. The previous day, according to a Saudi government bulletin, "armed renegades to the Islamic religion [had] seized the Holy

Ka'ba," holiest of holy places in Mecca. This alone would have been enough to agitate public opinion throughout the Islamic world (as indeed it did). But the news was coupled in the press with speculation that this action was in some way connected with the announced movement of U.S. naval units into the Indian Ocean and a White House statement threatening the use of force in the Middle East if the Tehran hostages were put on trial.

Most news services, including the BBC World Service, much respected in Pakistan, paired the stories from Mecca and Washington; they were the two major news stories of the day. But carried back to back over the Voice of America (VOA), especially accompanied by on-the-air reporting of press speculation about the identity of the "renegades," they led many in Pakistan to conclude there was a U.S. or U.S.–cum–Zionist hand in the Mecca attack.

The mood in nearby Rawalpindi, according to a special edition of the *Muslim*, an anti-U.S., pro-Shia daily in Islamabad, quickly took on an anti-imperialist, anti-Zionist, *and* anti-American character. VOA's heavy coverage, in fact, fanned the flames of suspicion of an American hand (or prior knowledge), for most Pakistanis saw the Voice of America only as the U.S. government mouthpiece. I drafted an "IMMEDIATE" cable to Washington warning of the sharp rise in public outrage and pointing out the unintended impact of the VOA's implicit linkage of the stories. I had just finished sending this cable when the Australian ambassador's telephone warning came through.

THE FIRST DEMONSTRATION—A TAME AFFAIR

We put our demonstration plan into effect as the student-filled buses pulled up outside our now-locked gates, where a small contingent of police awaited them. As they unfurled banners and chanted slogans, we informed the Pakistan government of their arrival, reminding the government of our repeated expressions of concern about protection. We also telephoned the news to Ambassador Hummel and Deputy Chief of Mission Barry King, both already at their residences for lunch. Hummel had earlier phoned administrative counselor David Fields after noticing the buses on his way to his residence. The ambassador approved our plan to send two officers, Fields and political officer David Welch (an Urdu speaker), to the gate to defuse the demonstration by meeting with the students.

This was our usual tactic in such situations. It enabled us to give the students a hearing, accept their petition, and assure them that their views and petition would be conveyed to the president of the United States. The exchange at the gate this time, too, was calm; and as I watched from my office window, I asked *Time* correspondent Marcia Gauger, waiting to have lunch with me in the embassy cafeteria, to save me a seat, saying I would join her just as soon as the demonstrators dispersed, which they did shortly thereafter.

As their buses roared away in the direction of the university, we breathed a collective sigh of relief, ratcheted down our alert posture a notch, and informed Ambassador Hummel and the Pakistan Foreign Ministry (MFA) that the demonstrators had left after presenting a petition. Now all set for lunch, I phoned Ambassador Petherbridge to let him know that the demonstration had concluded peacefully and the buses were headed his way en route to the university.

THE SECOND DEMONSTRATION—A MOB TAKES OVER

No sooner had I finished this lighthearted exchange and begun drafting a cable reporting the demonstration than Petherbridge phoned back to say that the buses had turned around and were headed back toward us, augmented this time by an even larger convoy of vehicles. I warned Dave Fields, and we battened down again, keeping the ambassador, the DCM, and the MFA apprised by phone of the worsening turn of events and, in the case of the MFA, requesting assistance.

This time when the buses pulled up, the mood had clearly shifted. The crowd was angrier and significantly larger, with even more vehicles apparently on the way. The chants began anew, and the police quickly fell back, overwhelmed, as shots suddenly rang out and a battering ram appeared in the hands of the demonstrators-turned-rioters. I watched from my second-floor office window as they began to pound away at one of the brick columns holding the gates. When it sagged and crumbled, the gate fell, and the mob surged onto the embassy grounds.

Shots continued to be fired, as stones and, we assumed, other missiles, including occasional bullets, began breaking the building's windows. Corporal Steve Crowley, a U.S. Marine security guard on the roof, went down with a head wound and was brought back into the building by two of his colleagues. As the rioters swarmed toward the recently strengthened and now-barred chancery doors, we took cover away from the windows, moving, as called for by our emergency procedures, to the central corridor of the building.

My memory of these moments is a blur of cables to the State Department and telephone exchanges with the ambassador and the DCM, with Dave Fields and Dave Welch, and with the Foreign Ministry's Bashir Khan Babar and Tanvir Ahmad Khan, the directors general, respectively, for the Americas and for Iran. My colleagues responsible for security matters kept up a steady drumbeat of similar phone calls to their opposite numbers on the Pakistan government police and security side, describing the worsening situation and requesting help. From their homes nearby, Ambassador Hummel and DCM King underscored our concerns in separate conversations with Pakistan government officials at senior levels, and the ambassador attempted to contact President Zia in Rawalpindi. We also alerted the acting headmaster of the International School and our families at home by the emergency radio system.

My last look out the window revealed a sea of rioters filling the grounds at the front of the chancery, the gate toppled behind them. I ducked away from the windows as my colleagues and I sought to deal with our personal security and our reporting responsibilities. I recall also signing off on several FLASH cables reporting the results of the earlier demonstration and the start of the second, alerting the Department of State and our consulates elsewhere in Pakistan. We learned later that they were going through their own ordeals.

In accordance with our emergency plan, all employees congregated in the second-floor corridor (the third floor viewed from the back of the building). We continued repeatedly to remind the Pakistan government and local officials—by telephone—of their responsibility to protect us. Our opposite numbers at the MFA responded with sympathy and assurances—even stunned outrage. But nothing tangible was forthcoming as a result either of our entreaties or of Ambassador Hummel's phone calls to Foreign Secretary Shahnawaz and others.

The mob outside continued to grow, and it began to look as if we were in for a long siege. I made one last sweep of the political section, moving on hands and knees to check the safes and spin the dials. And in the corridor, embassy employees, plus the *Time* correspondent, began filing into the embassy records and communications area—actually several rooms in a steel-enclosed area known as "the vault," near the end of the second-floor corridor. A shout from colleagues warned me to hurry. I ran down the hall corridor, and as the heavy vault door closed behind me, I could still hear office windows breaking and shots and shouts reverberating in the air outside.

We numbered 137 in all, and it was about 1:40 P.M. by my watch.

SAFE HAVEN IN THE COMMUNICATIONS VAULT

As I moved to clear working space on top of a piece of machinery, I realized I had left my tweed jacket in my office. To have grabbed it would have required standing. I would not miss the jacket's warmth in the vault—especially after the rioters set fire to the building—until much later that day when we finally got out. As the seriousness of our situation began to sink in, each employee quietly sought sitting space on the floor and the initial excitement gave way to a worried calm.

Dave Fields and I, as the ranking officers in the vault, huddled to plot our next steps.[1] We urged all to stay calm as it began to be clear that we might be in the vault for some time. With us was the Marine security detachment's noncommissioned officer in charge (NCOIC), combat-tested Sergeant Major Loyd Miller, our "gunny," together with most of his Marine security guards (MSGs).[2] At Fields's instance, the assistant Army attaché (a lieutenant colonel), a visiting U.S. Army officer (a Ranger captain), and the Drug Enforcement Agency chief, plus two political officers who were former Marine officers, put themselves under the gunny's authority as part of an expanded security team, largely because of their familiarity and experience with handguns.

Fields was clearly in charge, but our relationship was professionally collegial. We each did what seemed appropriate in terms of our responsibilities and consulted frequently to ensure each knew what the other was doing. He focused on security and administrative matters, even cobbling together a makeshift latrine in a remote cranny of the vault. We both continued our respective efforts to report to the ambassador and to Washington on our situation, while further pressing the Pakistan MFA to take action. We got off several more FLASH reporting cables before our ability to communicate by cable was cut off—around 2:00 P.M., as I recall.

Luckily for us, as we later learned, one of our dedicated Foreign Service Nationals (FSNs) had ensured that our emergency power was protected in another part of the building before he fled the building and we entered the vault. As a result, we retained power and a modest air-conditioning capability through the entire day.

Steve Crowley, our wounded Marine, was in another part of the vault under the care of Fran Fields, Dave's wife, who was the embassy nurse. We did not know how badly he had been hurt, but he had clearly not regained consciousness. Later in the day, we were to organize those with blood types similar to his so that they—and he—would be the first out if we were suddenly rescued and a transfusion was needed.

ATMOSPHERE IN THE VAULT

The mood in the vault was sober as Fields and I made our rounds under the scrutiny of our colleagues, who had little to do but sit on the floor. Most of us were in the vault's single large room, while in one or another of the small rooms a few colleagues carried out various responsibilities such as destroying cryptographic materials or looking after our wounded Marine. We were all worried and not a little frightened by what had happened during the previous two hours, but we were professionals, Americans and Pakistanis alike. We felt safe in the vault, and we believed we would remain safe until such time as we could get out, however long that took—but certainly not longer than a few hours.

Shortly after we had established ourselves in the vault, we learned that our second-ranking Marine security guard, Sergeant Purry, was isolated at Post-2, the barred rear door of the embassy immediately beneath us on the first floor. He reported that he was about to be cut off by rioters who had broken through the lightweight garden grilles on the cafeteria windows. With the ambassador's authority, he was ordered to leave his post and to join us one floor above; the surging mob on all sides of the building by that time rendered too dangerous any attempt to escape via the rear door. He was instructed to disperse tear gas in the corridor as he withdrew to the stairs, adding to that already spread about by other

MSGs when we first entered the vault. And we conveyed to him by phone Ambassador Hummel's explicit authorization to fire his weapon—a shotgun—if needed to save his life.

Gas mask on his face, shouting warnings and waving his shotgun, Purry made his run. He faced down rioters entering the first-floor corridor from the cafeteria, dispersed his tear gas, and climbed the stairs to the second floor. He looked spent but still menacing when we admitted him to the vault, relieved at his safe journey. Instructions or no, I was especially relieved that he had not had to fire his weapon. His passage also emphasized for us how dangerous even the corridors of our chancery had become. I seem to recall that we learned from him, and later from Canadian and British colleagues who had the building under observation from outside the compound, that rioters had set fire to the back of the building, augmenting fluids they had brought with paint supplies presumably stolen from the paint locker beside the rear door. The smell of smoke soon confirmed this.

RIOTERS ON THE ROOF

We also learned from our Canadian colleagues that there were rioters on the roof over our heads. Soon we heard them as they tried to break through the roof hatch and as they fired handguns into the air ducts. Protecting the area under the hatch was difficult, because it was a separate, small room with a higher concentration of tear gas and smoke than the rest of the vault.

Fields and Gunny Loyd Miller organized a rotating watch of groups of three or four men, drawn from our security team. They all took turns in that confined area for periods of fifteen to twenty minutes, sitting in the corners with their shotguns directed upward at the inside of the hatch. With Ambassador Hummel's explicit approval, they had orders to shoot any rioter who succeeded in breaking through the hatch. They suffered great discomfort, since their gas masks did nothing to prevent them from inhaling the smoke. As each group of three or four rotated into other parts of the vault to take a break, another group of three or four would take their places in the area vacated. Luckily the hatch held through the day.

But as the fire spread, the tear gas and smoke spreading through the building began seeping into other parts of the vault, making it difficult for the rest of us to breathe as well. There were not enough gas masks to go around, and we urged all to stay close to the floor, to avoid unnecessary activity, and to breathe through the water-soaked paper towels that we distributed.

We were heartened to know that Ambassador Hummel had opened up a direct phone link to Washington and that he was continuing his effort to discuss our situation with President Zia. Spirits soared briefly when we were told—then heard for ourselves—that a Pakistan army helicopter was overhead and, we understood, was bringing a doctor to help evacuate our wounded Marine. There was considerable confusion about the purpose of the helicopter, and I can recall saying into the phone that what we needed was a helicopter with snipers on board to get the rioters off the roof.

We learned also—I cannot recall the precise sequence of events—that four other colleagues were trapped at the other end of the building, three Foreign Service nationals from the administrative section and a Spanish national who worked for the Foreign Buildings Office. When I spoke to them by phone, they told me they had locked the door of the office in which they had hidden. They reported a lot of smoke and tear gas and asked what they should do. I suggested that they stay put for as long as they felt secure and could breathe; they were safer in the building than if they were to jump from a window into the surrounding mob. I told them there was little we could do for them, given the condition of the corridors between their location and ours.

They phoned again a little while later to say they would not be able to stay much longer where they were and were thinking they would jump to the ground from their second-floor window. I said they had to be the judge of their own safety but noted that since they were all in local *shalwar* dress, they would presumably be able to blend into the mob once they reached the ground. Our phone system broke down shortly thereafter, and it was only the next day that we learned that two of them, a Pakistani and the Spaniard, leaped to safety, suffering between them minor bruises and a broken ankle. The bodies of the other two were discovered the next day in the smoking ruin, dead of asphyxiation.

STAYING THE COURSE

About three hours after entering the vault, Dave Fields and I huddled again, out of sight of the group, and agreed that the situation was grave and prospects poor in terms of our rescue any time soon. But we also agreed that it would be safer to sit tight in the vault rather than attempt any kind of breakout that could risk lives or result in our being taken hostage (as in Tehran). The gunny made a courageous armed reconnaissance out the vault door and along the length of the second-floor corridor. Although there were no rioters on the second floor, he reported, the building was too full of smoke and gas for the corridor to the stairwell and onward to the lobby to be an escape route.

Fields and I agreed that we could hang on until nightfall, if necessary, believing that in the absence of some action by the Pakistan government to break up the riot outside, cooler nighttime temperatures might well lessen the rioters' enthusiasm. We also agreed on the membership of a five-man negotiating team, should we be offered some sort of negotiated end of the siege. Fields had also informed me that Corporal Crowley was dead but that he would not reveal Crowley's passing to the group because of the impact on morale the news was sure to have. In mutual agreement on all these matters, we turned back to our chores, remaining watchful for any sign of panic.

We reported to the group on what Ambassador Hummel was trying to accomplish to get us out and also reported on what had been, up to that point, a safe and serene situation at the International School, where our children were hunkered down. We were to learn later of an abortive effort by a small gang of Pakistanis to raid the school and of the energetic efforts of our colleagues from the diplomatic corps to ensure that our schoolchildren reached home as safely as theirs did.

ON THE EMERGENCY RADIO

After the embassy phone system went out, we had to fall back on the emergency VHF radio system as our only link with the world outside. We found this a painful handicap, because using the radio meant that anyone with a receiver and the appropriate radio channel could hear all of our dealings with the outside world—the ambassador at his residence, the DCM now at the Foreign Ministry, where he had taken up station, the International School, the British and Canadian embassies, and our own homes, where our dependents listened to the drama during the long afternoon. We had nothing to hide from all of those potential listeners, but this also meant that everything said on the emergency radio, incoming or outgoing, was carried over a speaker that all in the vault could hear. There could be no guarded or discreet conversation, no secrets. Dave Fields and I thus had to be circumspect in what we allowed our vault colleagues to hear us say.

Our colleagues outside had the same problem. Descriptions of what the compound looked like from nearby British and Canadian colleagues were the only visual images we had of the situation outside the vault. These were unnerving. When the helicopter that had been hovering earlier went away, news of its departure came on the radio, and morale in the vault went down a notch. Word that the courageous German ambassador, dean of the diplomatic corps, had tried to gain access to our building but had been denied entry by the mob also battered morale in the vault. The repeated news from the outside that our leaders were unable to get the Pakistanis to intervene was also disappointing.

At one of these downturns, the officer then taking a turn at the radio thoughtlessly uttered into the microphone, "Is there no hope?" His voice carried like a prophecy of doom around the vault. I quickly relieved him at the microphone, taking the job myself for most of the rest of our time in the vault. I tried to be as guarded as I could in what I said, and also, as obliquely as possible, to warn those outside to be careful as well.

HEATING UP

The situation in the vault worsened as the afternoon wore on and the air quality in the vault declined. We organized brief visits for small groups to go from the floor to one of the vault's crannies, where a wall air conditioner—meant to keep equipment from overheating—continued to labor, allowing them to catch a few lungfuls

79

of clean air before returning to the floor and the wet paper towels through which we all were breathing.

The sounds from the roof continued, with abundant evidence—from the noise and from the Canadians on their rooftops across the road—that the rioters above our heads had not given up their effort to break through the hatch. Morale went up a bit, and we all laughed, when a scheme by one of our colleagues to electrify the metal hatch fizzled as the four-hundred-volt electric cable he had attached melted, with no visible effect on those pounding on the hatch. The eerie sound of bullets whizzing through the air ducts was punctuated by loud bangs, as colleagues in other parts of the vault physically destroyed pieces of sensitive equipment.

Farsi and Urdu speakers guarding the underside of the hatch told Fields and me that they could hear voices above them shouting in both Urdu and Arabic. We inferred that this meant there were both Pakistanis and possibly Palestinians on the roof (perhaps from among the nearly one thousand Palestinian students known to have been in the Islamabad area at the time). No spoken Farsi (Persian) was heard from the roof, despite the active role of the Iranian embassy in whipping up anti–U.S. feeling in the Islamabad area in the preceding weeks.

Late in the day we caught a glimmer of the situation outside when we heard that the crowd around the burning embassy building in which we were trapped was estimated at between eight thousand and ten thousand. From the radio we also learned that the U.S. Information Service cultural center in nearby Rawalpindi had been razed by a mob, that Pan American Airways and Bank of America offices had been attacked, and that our compatriots in U.S. consulates in Karachi, Lahore, and Peshawar were all having their own difficulties with outraged mobs. (We learned the next day that our cultural centers in Lahore and Rawalpindi and the Convent of Jesus and Mary in Rawalpindi were the only symbolically Western buildings actually attacked; other U.S. facilities had narrowly escaped attack as a result of more vigorous—and experienced—police action than we had seen in Islamabad or Rawalpindi.)

SMOLDERING CARPETS

In the vault, meanwhile, as the clock stood at about 5:00 P.M., we were all hanging on, awaiting an early-autumn sunset and a drop in the outside temperature. Inside, the air quality continued to decline, and, of greater concern, the temperature in the vault had risen above 90 degrees Fahrenheit. The fire beneath and around us was having its effect on the steel in the walls of the vaulted area where most of us sat huddled.

Those on the floor kept up a low buzz of conversation, each helping in his or her own way to lighten the mood, when suddenly one of our American colleagues jumped up to announce that the carpet in the corner near her was beginning to smolder. We quickly moved people away from that corner and used a fire extinguisher on that portion of carpet. But fear noticeably reappeared on people's faces, as each retreated into his or her inner self to cope with this all-too-vivid reminder of flames outside—with still no sign of rescue by Pakistani authorities.

In another corner of the vault, near where I stood at the microphone describing our actions to extinguish the smoldering carpet, a young Pakistani FSN, one of our youngest secretaries, was heard to take a deep, wheezing breath, a possible prelude to hysteria. Quicker than anyone else to react, the senior FSN sitting between us, grandfatherly in appearance and gesture, put his arm around her and his head next to hers to whisper comforting words. She immediately relaxed, and the anxious moment passed. Relieved that panic had been averted, Fields and I made mental notes to ensure that the FSN got an award for his leadership and quick thinking. In a conservative Islamic society like Pakistan, only their age difference, and his demeanor, made such an action on his part possible—and effective.

THE END IN SIGHT?

Although the day dragged on, in retrospect it seems just a short while later that we began to get signs that the rioters on the roof were giving up their attempt to break through the hatch. In the fading daylight outside after five o'clock, our British colleagues suggested that the mob seemed to be thinning, with fewer of them than before on the roof. When all noise on the roof had stopped, Dave Fields organized a scouting party of five—the gunny in the lead, three other members of the security detail, and Imtiaz ul-Haq, a political section FSN—to ensure that the roof was clear. They sought access to the roof via a route undiscovered by the rioters (from the smoke-filled corridor outside the vault), with authorization to shoot, if necessary, to protect the party.

The gunny said afterward that as he broke out onto the roof, he saw the last of the rioters climbing over the parapet on his way down a bicycle rack that the rioters had placed on end to use as a ladder. By radio, the scouting party reported the roof clear and secured, provoking shouts of relief and renewed hope from those now on their feet in the vault. Our optimism that the long day was not going to be our last was not dampened even by the news that the rioters, having failed to break through the hatch, had sought to jam it so it could not be opened.

Working together, those on the inside and those on the roof finally got the hatch open. We all became aware of it before we heard about it on the radio because of the noticeable drop in temperature produced by the venting of the vault into the cool evening air. Another round of cheers and smiles broke the tensions, as we all realized that whatever uncertainties awaited us on the roof, our stay in the vault was about to end.

GETTING OUT

Fields, assisted by Steve Schleiker, an Urdu-speaking consular officer, quickly organized the departure order: women first—FSNs, then Americans—followed by

81

the men, FSNs also going first. I remember someone counting out, five, five, five again, as my colleagues began moving into the area beneath the hatch, no more than five at a time to minimize delay in the smoke-filled environment under the hatch while waiting to climb the ladder to the roof. As I took my turn with Fields in the last group of five to go up the ladder, I can recall my pleasure at looking upward through the hatch to see a clear, star-filled sky above. Once on the roof, I enjoyed the relief of a deep breath of cool fall air.

My delight was quickly tempered by the sight of flames reaching up above the parapet on all sides from the building below. How would we get down through that, I wondered, as I tried to determine where we might be able to land safely if it became necessary to leap off the roof to the ground.

But our male Pakistani colleagues, who were waiting on the roof, quickly propelled me to the part of the roof overlooking the embassy auditorium roof, half a floor below. There on the auditorium roof I saw most of my colleagues. The women were already going down a ladder to the ground at the front of the auditorium, while the male FSNs waited for their American male colleagues before proceeding farther. I was suddenly picked up bodily by two of them and dropped over the edge into the arms of two others standing eight feet below on the auditorium roof. From there, I was led to the ladder at the end of the roof, where, as the women had done before us, the men, Pakistani and American, took turns climbing down the long ladder to the pavement.

I was met at the bottom by Bashir Khan Babar, director general for the Americas at the Foreign Ministry, who had come on his own to the embassy compound to see what he could do to be helpful. On the way, he had commandeered a fire engine, whose crew had been reluctant to approach the burning embassy. (This act, I learned later, cost Bashir his assignment as Pakistan's ambassador to Canada, so rankled was the foreign minister by his actions.) Behind Bashir, I could see the firemen just beginning to pour water on the fire in the vicinity of my office on the second floor; I discovered the following day that the water was too late to save my college diplomas on the wall above my desk and the tweed coat I had left behind (and that I suddenly missed in the cool night air).

At the skewed embassy front gate, I saw *jawans*—troops—of a Pakistan army battalion that had finally arrived on the scene and was making its presence known. There were no rioters in sight, and most of my American colleagues were already on their way, on foot, to the British embassy, which had offered hospitality. Standing at the bottom of the ladder, I felt exhilarated to be safe at last, although I wondered where all of those who had tried to kill us had gone.

As I turned to look back at the building, Gunny Miller came up to say he was not going to leave his dead Marine in the building. The last of us to come down moved as one to steady the ladder as Miller climbed up to the auditorium roof, then to the main roof, and to the hatch. He emerged a few moments later and slowly climbed down the ladder, rung by rung, with the body of Corporal Steve

Crowley over his shoulder in a fireman's carry, still dripping blood. It was the most dramatic moment of the day, and we all wept for the first time. We stood transfixed and unable to move, the scene frozen forever in our memories of that day as the fire continued to devour the building behind us.

AFTERMATH

At Bashir's suggestion, I joined him and DCM Barry King at the Foreign Ministry, where I briefed senior MFA officials and spoke for the first time by phone with the State Department and with my own family members in Islamabad. I was detailed by Barry King to brief the Pakistan army colonel in command of the troops that were deploying in Islamabad on the general locations of our families' homes, so that his *jawans* could patrol those areas during the night.

That finished, I joined my colleagues at the British embassy where Her Majesty's ambassador, Sir Oliver Fraser (whose daughter had dated my older son), met me at the front door with a strong whiskey—the best I had ever tasted. I spoke again on a direct line to Washington, briefed Ambassador Hummel, and then headed home, where my wife and younger teenage son—he was guarding the front door with a baseball bat in his hands—awaited me.

The following day was Thanksgiving, an appropriate holiday for those of us who had survived. We were to learn on that day that all but one of the buildings on the embassy's thirty-one-acre compound had been looted and gutted by the rioters during the previous afternoon. Included was a cluster of embassy staff apartments, where the partly charred body of U.S. Army Warrant Officer Brian Ellis of the embassy's Defense Representative's Office was discovered, dead by a gunshot. With the addition of a rioter apparently killed by the police, this brought to five the number killed on that awful day.

On the day after Thanksgiving, dependents and nonessential staff were evacuated by Pan Am aircraft. We who stayed behind in a tense, often hostile Islamabad proceeded to the building occupied by the diminished USAID mission—a quarter of a mile from the still smoldering embassy compound—to reconstitute the embassy and begin our postmortem. The building would remain our temporary chancery for more than two years while the embassy compound was restored, at Pakistan's expense.

The atmosphere in Pakistan remained tense, although we were relieved some days afterward to learn that Pakistani police confiscated nearly three dozen handguns, plus knives and other weapons, in a surprise raid on a nearby university campus. We continued to receive threats in the weeks thereafter but rather quickly got caught up in developments associated with the Soviet invasion of neighboring Afghanistan the day after Christmas. By the time dependents were permitted to return in late spring and early summer 1980, U.S. cooperation with Pakistan in response to events in Afghanistan had begun to transform our relationship with Pakistan and, indeed, with much of the Islamic world.

POSTMORTEM

In the immediate aftermath of the attack on our embassy, the evacuation of dependents, and the further drawdown of the U.S. mission, we drew a number of conclusions about the events of November 21, 1979. Most, if not all, of these conclusions are still relevant. Among them were the following:

The Culprits

Students were the apparent leaders, and they represented both the left and the right ends of the political spectrum. Those on the right, mostly members of the student wing of Jamaat Islami, were specifically exercised about the perceived threat to Islam as seen in the attack on Mecca; and those on the left, mainly from the student wing of the People's Party, were generally anti–United States. They arrived in large numbers in the second wave, with evidence of having stockpiled weapons and flammables in anticipation of such an occasion, not only in Islamabad, but in Lahore, Karachi, Rawalpindi, and Peshawar as well. From the evidence of Arabic being spoken on the roof, we have to conclude that some Arabs, most likely Palestinians, were also involved.

Students were clearly augmented by nonstudent rabble from Rawalpindi, who arrived through the afternoon by the truckload, reportedly agitated by mullahs proclaiming a threat to Islam. We lament that none were ever formally charged, despite identification of several from pictures taken by onlookers. We concluded that the Zia government was simply not willing to take the lead on this issue if it risked looking as if it were supporting the United States.

The Role of the Government of Pakistan

The attack on our embassy was unprecedented; local authorities in normally bucolic Islamabad had never seen, nor been called upon to deal with, a mob this large or this violent. There were other creditably extenuating circumstances:

- The Islamabad police establishment of the local Punjab province lacked the experience and resources—and the will—to deal with such an unprecedented outbreak of mob violence as it encountered on that date (notwithstanding the courage of the thirty-two policemen on the embassy compound who protected a small group of Americans forced out of the compound's American Club, where they had been lunching).
- The locations of relevant Government of Pakistan offices were split, with the Foreign Ministry in Islamabad, but most others, including the president's office, the Home Ministry, and the Defense Ministry, in Rawalpindi, more than ten miles away.
- Those who were not on the immediate scene were skeptical that what they were being told was as bad, or as serious, as the Americans were claiming. This skepticism was a function in part of the unprecedented nature of the attack, but also of the deterioration in Pakistan–U.S. relations.

• The security elements on the Pakistan side suffered from inadequate communications. This was especially noticeable in the acknowledgment, to me, by the commanding officer of the battalion that eventually appeared that he would have to depend on runners to carry messages to his troops, since very few of his radios were working.

• There were no significant army units available in the area for immediate deployment. None were normally based in the Islamabad area, while the only brigade at hand in the Rawalpindi area had been deployed to the streets of that city to provide security for President Zia, who had been taking one of his bicycle strolls through the town to "meet the people" that morning.

The Role of the Government of the United States

The U.S. government was also slow to react, no doubt immobilized largely by the middle-of-the-night hour in Washington (ten hours behind Islamabad), by the apparently peaceful result of the first demonstration reported, by the suddenness of the violent follow-up, by the unprecedented nature of the violence, and by the assurances—never fulfilled—of the Pakistan government that all would be well.

Although the ambassador, the DCM, the U.S. consul general in Karachi, and others were in direct touch with the State Department on open lines through most of the time we were in the vault, we who were inside the embassy never heard directly from Washington at any time, from the first demonstration until we liberated ourselves six or seven hours later. After transmitting our first five or six FLASH messages, we lost our ability to send and receive cables. Knowing the ambassador was in touch with Washington, we never sought to establish our own telephonic communications with Washington, dealing instead with local authorities and with our own problems of survival.

Once the phones went down, our sole contacts with the outside world—the ambassador, the International School, the British and Canadian embassies, and the rest of the American community—were via the single channel of the emergency VHF radio system. We neither expected nor needed Washington guidance and were content that the ambassador and the DCM, safely outside the embassy, were doing all that was necessary and appropriate to protect our families and get us out.

But let there be no doubt; we got out by ourselves by waiting out the rioters from within a vaulted safehaven that worked remarkably well, despite our problems breathing, our limited communications capability, and our fragile electrical support. Somewhere in the system, however, the White House got the idea that the Pakistanis had rescued us, leading President Carter to thank President Zia. There may have been in this a hope that such a message would actually stimulate the Pakistanis to do so. But from where we sat and stood, having just endured six-plus hours in a burning building, the White House message looked like pandering to the leadership of a government that collectively sat on its hands while we roasted. It suggested that official Washington seemed to know (or care?) as little about our situation as the Pakistanis, and it left a bad taste all around. *Time* magazine's reporter, who was one of us, had to threaten to resign to get her story printed as she wrote it. She got it right; the White House got it wrong.

The Embassy's Organization and Activities

We had an excellent emergency plan for dealing with the crisis that evolved and had been well drilled. It would have been better to abandon the building to the rioters, but the suddenness with which they had enveloped the compound—especially after the false calm following the first demonstration—made an orderly or safe evacuation impossible.

In retrospect, I think we did all that we could from inside the vault; our colleagues in the vault with us kept their cool and gave Dave Fields and me—their cobbled leadership—their full support, aware also that we enjoyed the full confidence of the ambassador, who they knew was doing everything possible to get us out safely. We called our own shots, as we should have, and I doubt we could have gotten out earlier or with fewer casualties.

Evacuation and Thereafter

The nonofficial American community in the Islamabad-Rawalpindi area was minuscule and posed no separate problem for the embassy, either during the attack on the embassy or in the evacuation thereafter. The main nonofficial, permanently assigned people were teachers at the school, plus a very few employees of private voluntary organizations. Evacuation and drawdown of official personnel were smooth and efficient, and the teachers and others joined in. Many helped with dependent children whose parents had been left behind, and a number of them performed above and beyond the call of duty in looking after a party of U.S. teenagers visiting Harappa in rural Sind province.

The State Department's Near East Bureau (NEA) had its share of crises throughout the Islamic world that day. But NEA and the rest of the department came through in a compassionate and professional way in dealing with the myriad problems attendant on caring for our dependents on arrival at the Washington end.

Ambassador Hummel's leadership was superb in handling the drawdown and in getting the rump embassy back in business with minimum delay in the former USAID spaces. He struck a major blow for morale by allowing anyone who chose to leave to do so without prejudice—and a few did. He also converted the guest house adjacent to his residence into an American Club, which became a community center for those who remained. And most important, he ensured that all who had remained got to spend either Christmas or New Year's with their families in the United States, despite our new concern that December with the Soviet rape of neighboring Afghanistan.

Summing Up

Most of these conclusions were put to the Department of State for consideration in developing future policies affecting the security of chanceries and consulates abroad. They were also put to the Congress in hearings during the next two years. In the weeks following the event, some of our conclusions were presented to the Government of Pakistan by those of us authorized by Ambassador Hummel to meet informally with a Pakistan army brigadier assigned personally by President Zia (who was also army chief) to discuss the attack with us. Although Pakistan did beef up security around our temporary chancery, little else came of this effort.

Years later, I continue to believe we did everything we could have done on the scene to protect ourselves and to survive, in view of the swiftness with which the situation unfolded on November 21, 1979. The vault held, but we no doubt would have been better off to have abandoned the chancery and the compound before the mob took it over; Steve Crowley and the others might then still be alive. But that was not to be.

The Pakistan government made good on its commitment to rebuild the embassy compound, at a cost of $21 million. While this was right and proper, it does not compensate for the personnel who died, and it should not be allowed to obscure Pakistan's failure to meet its responsibilities. All foreign diplomats, regardless of nationality, rely for their security on the host governments to which they are accredited. But despite repeated assurances in the weeks before the event and during the event itself, the Government of Pakistan failed to meet its obligation to protect us—whether by design, through ineptitude, or because of the unprecedented nature of the circumstances, or all three.

The news from Mecca and Tehran created a volatile situation throughout the entire Islamic world. The deterioration in U.S.–Pakistan relations in the months preceding November 21, 1979, was real. And the situation in Pakistan was tense, following the storming of the U.S. embassy in Tehran seventeen days earlier. After the event—on the evening of November 21—Zia went on television to urge calm; he was later to apologize to visiting members of Congress, telling them, "We goofed."

But Pakistan's culpability cannot be dismissed so easily. Notwithstanding the courageous efforts (and chagrin) of several senior officers of the Pakistan Ministry of Foreign Affairs and the embarrassment I noted among many Pakistanis, I strongly suspect that more than a few Pakistanis in authority, perhaps all the way to the top, were content to minimize what they were being told and to let the "whining" Americans "sweat it out" a bit. And afterward, they lacked the political courage to apportion blame. There can be no other explanation for the pervasiveness of the Government of Pakistan's passivity on November 21, 1979.

The U.S. Embassy chancery building in Beirut, April 13, 1983. A car bomb that had exploded minutes earlier killed sixty-three people, including fourteen embassy visitors. *Embassy of Canada, Beirut.*

6 | The Bombing of Embassy Beirut, 1983

Richard M. Gannon

The June 1982 Israeli invasion of Lebanon brought the seven-year-old conflict embroiling Lebanon to a new phase. Initially proclaimed as a limited incursion in response to an assassination attempt on the Israeli ambassador in London, the Israeli action resulted in an overwhelming defeat of the Syrian air force and a rapid advance by the Israeli Defence Forces (IDF) to the outskirts of Beirut. Israel demanded the removal of the PLO headquarters and forces from Lebanon and of the Syrian presence from Beirut.

The IDF then subjected Palestinian and Syrian positions in Beirut to a nine-week bombardment. During this period, the U.S. embassy suspended operations in its seaside chancery building housing the embassy's principal offices and moved its personnel and operations to the relative safety of Ambassador Robert S. Dillon's residence in the hills of East Beirut.

ENTER THE UNITED STATES

U.S. Mediation

The United States immediately dispatched Ambassador Philip C. Habib as special negotiator to help arrange a cease-fire and the departure from Lebanon of Palestinian combatants—this despite confusion about U.S. goals in Lebanon fostered by U.S. military and financial support of Israel and dubious Israeli claims of U.S. consent for Israel's Lebanese operation. The agreement finally reached in August 1982 provided for the peaceful departure of PLO forces from Beirut in return for an Israeli commitment that IDF forces would not interfere and a U.S. commitment to the safety of Palestinian residents left behind. On September 1,

1982, the last of nearly fifteen thousand Palestine Liberation Army and Syrian army forces were evacuated from Beirut in fulfillment of the agreement.

Two weeks later on September 14, only four days after the U.S. government had precipitated the withdrawal of U.N.–sponsored multinational peacekeeping forces, Lebanese president-elect Bashir Gemayel was assassinated by a bomb blast while addressing his Phalangist followers in an East Beirut suburb. Gemayel had been closely associated with the Israeli political objectives of reinforcing Maronite domination of the Lebanese government. His assassination, later reported to have been arranged by Syrian agents, set off a new round of bloodletting. IDF forces entered West Beirut on the morning of September 15, in violation of the Habib-brokered agreement. Shortly thereafter, Phalange forces entered the Palestinian refugee camps of Sabra and Shatilla through Israeli lines and massacred hundreds of Palestinian women and children.

Opposition to Growing U.S. Involvement

Throughout 1982 the Islamic fundamentalist movement Hizballah grew in numbers and took increasingly strident anti-American positions. One Islamic cleric from Beirut's southern suburbs had become so alarmed by a fundamentalist mullah's advocacy of violence toward Americans that he quietly reported his concerns to the embassy.

Following the shocking events at Sabra and Shatilla, the United States decided to reinsert a U.S. Marine unit as part of a resumed multinational force (MNF), absent since the departure of the Palestine Liberation Army from Beirut. Desire to help end the crisis in Lebanon led the United States to increase its efforts to help broker a peace treaty between Israel and Lebanon. The perception in some Lebanese quarters of U.S. support for Israeli objectives in Lebanon, including Maronite preeminence, and the growing U.S. government role in training the Lebanese armed forces inevitably drew the United States further into the terribly complicated internal Lebanese conflict.

The United States was enthusiastic about providing its good offices and arranging a peace agreement that would allow for the departure of Israeli troops. Fundamental U.S. objectives included domestic political reconciliation, establishment of law and order, and economic recovery. But U.S. involvement in the extraordinarily complicated, if not insoluble, political dilemma of Lebanon required an increased U.S. presence and concomitant risks.

Western expectations of progress may have been overly optimistic, given the forces working against resolution. Islamic fundamentalists were looking less to participate in the existing government than to establish a new Islamic state. Syria maneuvered to assert political suzerainty over Lebanon, in particular control over the Bekaa Valley, seen as the most likely Israeli avenue of approach to Damascus in any renewal of hostilities. Israel continued to insist on achieving the gains, beyond removal of the Palestine Liberation Army, that it had sought from the invasion, specifically, Maronite preeminence in the Lebanese government and Syrian withdrawal from Lebanon.

The well-intentioned introduction of U.S. military units as part of the multinational peacekeeping efforts was unfortunate. U.S. military assets as configured proved to be too large for hostile elements to ignore yet too small to fight effectively.

In the six months prior to April 1983, the U.S. embassy's chancery building, to which personnel and operations had returned, was not under any direct threat of attack. Although it had been subject to a real but undetermined level of threat from clashes between opposing Muslim factions in West Beirut, there had been no incidents. As peace talks continued in early April 1983, the perception grew that the threat to the embassy from this incidental, intra-Muslim tension was diminishing and the political situation stabilizing.

The embassy had established productive contacts with elected officials, militia commanders, and prominent local religious leaders. Embassy support for a democratic Lebanese political process and Philip Habib's involvement in negotiating an Israeli-Lebanese peace treaty that would lead to Israeli withdrawal compelled Lebanese authorities to provide a small police contingent for minimum security at the chancery. Unfortunately, and despite embassy objections, this squad was steadily drawn upon for reassignment to police duties in other sections of Beirut, thereby diminishing its availability for protection of the chancery building.

THE EMBASSY BOMBING

On April 18, 1983, at 1:06 P.M. (local), as many embassy personnel were finishing lunch, a bomb-laden truck attacked the chancery. The cafeteria, immediately adjacent to the explosion area, was crowded with those lingering over their midday meal. Canadian embassy personnel who had been driving past the U.S. facility later recounted following a heavily loaded pickup truck moving slowly west along the corniche. Witnesses described how the vehicle increased speed, then careened into the embassy driveway, penetrated the wall of an office, and exploded.

The chancery's location on a major thoroughfare and its lack of a setback precluded total protection. But there were other significant vulnerabilities, most obvious of which were the accessible entry and exit points of the facility's semicircular driveway protected only by uniformed Lebanese police. A security survey one month before the attack had recommended installation of heavy wrought-iron gates on the driveway as part of an upgraded security perimeter, but this had yet to be done.

The force of the blast leveled the entrance portico and lobby, gutted much of the ground floor, and collapsed seven floors in the center section of the building. Ambassador Dillon, who was preparing to leave the building for his regular 1:00-P.M. jog on the nearby American University of Beirut (AUB) track, had been delayed in his office on the eighth floor by a telephone call. After he had emerged from the rubble, bodyguards moved quickly to escort him to safety in a nearby embassy-leased apartment, as other staff helped evacuate the injured from the shattered chancery. Many had been seriously injured in the attack, though the final death toll of thirty-two local embassy employees, seventeen Americans, and fourteen embassy visitors and passersby would not be known for another week.

The U.S. military response was immediate and comprehensive; elements of the 24th Marine Amphibious Unit (MAU), under command of Colonel James Meade, were redeployed from positions at Beirut International Airport to the bombing site. They were especially useful in restricting access to the area and searching for classified material in the debris. A platoon of Marines was assigned to the embassy from successive MAUs, deployed as part of the multinational force. At one point in the days after the attack, several U.S. Navy ships steamed close to shore opposite the bombing site in a sign of support for the remaining American presence.

The immediate aftermath of the attack was physically draining, with many either searching for the missing or seeking to establish office functions in new locations. Large floodlights powered by generators were maneuvered into place to facilitate round-the-clock rescue operations, carried on by men and equipment from OGER Liban, a Saudi-linked construction firm. The State Department's support, with few exceptions (one involving the failure of the staff on the newly created Operations Center task force to pass a message to a survivor's family), was consistently excellent.

Coping

The emotional toll was worse for many survivors than the fatigue. Private moments had to be found. One officer made a point of setting aside time each day to walk along the corniche to reflect. These private moments were insurance against further damage to fragile emotions. Some survivors searched for a rationale for why they were spared and close friends, some in the same room, were dead. For some the emotional and physical strain was too great: in two cases post management determined that an immediate transfer was in the employees' best interests.

Lebanese rescue personnel, assisted by American staff members, sifted the rubble for seven days until the last identifiable remains were removed. Even then, relatives of the missing would stand their daily vigil near the site in hopes that a scrap of clothing, piece of jewelry, or some other evidence of a loved one would be discovered. The task of keeping families advised of the search and offering a few words of consolation fell primarily on Consul Diane Dillard. She tried to determine from interviewing surviving staff the location of the missing in the chancery at the time of the attack. Searchers would then reexamine debris in that area in an attempt to locate some sign of the individual. Some of the missing were never located, having presumably been consumed by the blast.

The first few days for the searchers proved especially dangerous as the debris continued to settle. Damaged canisters of crowd-control agents from the demolished Marine security guard post filled the area with tear gas when disturbed. The process was slow, requiring heavy cranes to lift entire slabs of concrete so that lighter debris could be cleared away and a thorough check of underlying areas could be made. Hours were spent clearing away the mound of broken concrete, lifting cement blocks, and restacking the debris for removal. After several days of identifying remains at the American University Hospital, a consular official who was a model of composure and stability quietly asked to be given a one-day reprieve for recuperation before resuming the difficult task.

In early May an elderly Lebanese couple approached the embassy to determine if funds were available for the burial of their only child, a daughter, who had been driving past the chancery when her car was destroyed by the explosion. The woman held tightly to her husband's arm, and tears welled in their eyes as they displayed a picture of an attractive woman in her early twenties.

One month after the attack, Ambassador Dillon spoke at a memorial service held in the AUB chapel. His comments to the victims' families and embassy staff were all that one might expect in such a situation. As he reached the last sentences, he hesitated in his delivery, unable to continue. Blinking back the tears, he gathered his notes and slowly walked back to his place in a front pew.

Picking up the Pieces

The bombing and its aftermath brought out both strengths and weaknesses in those who survived. While there was no formal meeting to discuss how to handle the situation, it was apparent to the chief of mission that there was considerable work to be done before the embassy could again function fully. Essential operations, such as the ambassador's office, communications, and political reporting, were reestablished shortly after the attack in the deputy chief of mission's nearby apartment. These functions would later be relocated in the British chancery less than a quarter of a mile away.

If the adverse impact on the staff was to be minimized, individuals would have to be quickly tasked with specific short-term goals and kept productive. Ambassador Dillon maintained direct contact with Lebanese officials and continually spoke to contacts in Washington by phone. DCM Robert Pugh proposed options for relocating chancery operations, took stock of resources, and set work priorities for the surviving staff. Administrative staff were assigned to reconfigure several nearby American-occupied apartments into office space for nonsensitive functions, such as consular services, public affairs, budget and finance, personnel, the Agency for International Development, and the U.S. Information Service. Security resources were assigned to assist in the search for missing persons, recovery of classified material, and salvage of property.

U.S. Marine units had arrived from their barracks at Beirut International Airport within an hour of the bombing. In addition to restricting access to the area to authorized personnel, they established perimeter security around the site and assisted with the destruction of all classified material. The response of the Marine security guard detachment was reassuring and courageous, as they repeatedly escorted rescue workers into the structure in the search for survivors. They also, as a matter of honor and detachment esprit, unearthed and recovered the remains of the Marine guard who had been on duty at the entrance post.

Some embassy staff did not initially think of the attack in terms of a crisis. It was just one more in a series of such events that Embassy Beirut would survive.

WHAT WENT WRONG?

Although host government protection for the chancery had never been overwhelming, there had been sufficient justification during the previous several years to maintain a twenty-four-hour police force at the facility as well as at the ambassador's residence. Embassy security officers, including the author, held discussions with police officials in the weeks before the bombing regarding appropriate staffing of this small protection squad.

In a city where car bombs were common, the prospect of a car bomb deployed against the embassy had been considered sufficiently real that the task of the Lebanese police posted at the chancery included preventing vehicles from parking near the building. The possibility of a suicide bomb attack on a large building by a moving vehicle, during which the expected death of the perpetrator is key to the attack, was a threat that no one had anticipated. Such an attack provided a new dimension for which the embassy was unprepared.

Arguments can be made that the Lebanese authorities should have assigned a stronger security force, especially at a time when the political process had not entirely succeeded and there remained even the remotest chance of violence directed at the United States. A Lebanese-perceived change in the U.S. role from impartial facilitator to active participant did not seem to increase the threat of a large-scale attack. In any event, the embassy staff, which appeared to accept a certain level of instability and perhaps had even become accustomed to incidents of violence, did not realize that their safety would be linked so directly to subtle shifts in the political climate.

Thus, regardless of any shortcomings in the protection provided by Lebanese authorities, some part of the destruction of the chancery and loss of life resulted from the misreading of indicators, specifically inattention by embassy staff to the significance for embassy security of political unrest in the Islamic community and the changing nature of U.S. involvement. Washington, too, was reluctant to recognize that the political situation was not improving and that, despite extraordinary efforts, the United States might not be able to forge a solution acceptable to all parties.

Contacts between U.S. officials and Lebanese authorities were occurring simultaneously on multiple levels. Some might argue that the complexity of these contacts was compounded by the lack of coordination among U.S. parties in discussing possible courses of action. Embassy officials worked at one level to foster Lebanese government stability and economic recovery, while the Special

Negotiator's Office addressed withdrawal of foreign forces as part of an agreement with Israel.

Personnel of the U.S. Office of Military Cooperation provided Lebanese defense officials with a plan to retrain and equip a Lebanese army capable of meeting Lebanese national objectives, while the U.S. contingent of the multinational peacekeeping force searched for a definable mission. In Washington, military commanders had continuously voiced reservations about U.S. troops acting as a "presence" in a potentially hostile environment simply to enable foreign politicians to reestablish their authority in a volatile situation.

LESSONS LEARNED

The Beirut tragedy, as noted, resulted at least partly from misreading the significance of Islamic fundamentalism in the region. More clearly identified with political changes in Iran, the movement was gaining influence in the Arab world, sparked by a perception of unrestrained U.S. support for Israel. To further complicate matters, both the embassy and Washington also failed to fully appreciate the potentially adverse impact on the embassy of a policy favorable to Israel.

The destruction of the chancery building and subsequent bombing of the Marine barracks in the autumn of 1983 provided the catalyst for a shift in how the United States carried out its policy in Lebanon. Policymakers had to face the reality that political change in Lebanon would not be advanced by the peacekeeping role of U.S. troops—the U.S. military deployment may even have set back the process. No longer was the administration prepared to commit U.S. forces to serve as a presence in an inherently unstable political situation.

The lesson for the United States was clear—good intentions backed up with modern military forces matter little in the political fabric of a region as complex as Lebanon. More immediately, U.S. diplomats would have to pay greater attention to physical security measures when assigned in locations of heightened threat.

In addition to the deaths of many dedicated people, the U.S. lack of appreciation for the complexity of Mideast politics exacted another price—a lost opportunity for the United States in the early 1980s to be a major architect of peace in Lebanon. It would be ten years before the various Lebanese factions reached an accommodation that allowed stability to return—an event brought about more by internal political compromise than by U.S. intervention.

Ambassador William G. Walker meets FMLN commanders following the signing of the peace treaty in the closing minutes of 1991, two years after the final offensive. *U.S. Information Service, San Salvador*

7 | The FMLN'S "Final Offensive," San Salvador, 1989

William G. Walker

In November 1989 the protracted and bitterly contested civil war in El Salvador was one decade old. From the beginning, the policy of the United States had been to provide the Salvadoran government whatever support was necessary, and congressionally possible, to end the war. In the process, the United States also sought to prevent the insurgency of the Farabundo Martí National Liberation Front (FMLN), a coalition of leftist rebel groups, from achieving power through the barrels of its guns.

A second U.S. policy objective was to foster implementation of the political, economic, and social reforms advocated by the coalition that overthrew the military-dominated closed society that had existed prior to 1979. The reformist coup of 1979 had ushered in two civilian-military juntas, which in turn led to a constituent assembly and, in March 1984, to the first election of a Salvadoran president through an honest count of ballots cast. U.S. efforts throughout the 1980s sought to maximize the physical security and legitimacy of each successive round of elections.

DUARTE'S DIFFICULT PRESIDENCY

In 1984, José Napoleon Duarte, the charismatic and combative leader of the Christian Democratic Party (PDC), won the presidential elections. In those elections the U.S. government was thought to have weighed in to prevent the victory of the death squad–tainted Roberto d'Aubuisson, candidate of the right-wing National Republican Alliance (ARENA). Duarte won the 1972 presidential election as well, but the military had branded him a "communist" and forced him into exile.

Duarte's five-year term, 1984–89, earned decidedly mixed reviews. While many applauded his implementation of a politically necessary land reform program, most admitted that its implementation was badly and corruptly administered.

Duarte had entered office a harsher critic of the El Salvador Armed Forces (ESAF) and the private-sector oligarchs than of the FMLN. But when the FMLN kidnapped a favorite daughter in the early months of his tenure, he found himself working with the military leadership from a position of weakness, anxious as he was to secure his daughter's safe release. Duarte never recovered the upper hand of authority vis-à-vis the ESAF, and civilian control of the military, a constant theme and objective of U.S. policy, was barely advanced during the remainder of Duarte's tenure as president.

While some of Duarte's cabinet choices and other nominees were honest and capable, others were not. Appointees at the subministerial level and below in most government agencies, especially those dealing with the economy, were too often ill-suited to their tasks. Corruption and incompetence appeared to be endemic, and Duarte's Christian Democratic Party paid dearly for this perception in loss of public confidence and support. As a result, the PDC lost both the 1988 legislative elections and the March 1989 presidential election to the better-organized, better-financed, and more united ARENA party.

Throughout his tenure, Duarte attempted to entice the FMLN into a negotiation process to end the civil war. Two face-to-face meetings were held, but the result was frustrating and counterproductive public posturing by both sides when the talks led nowhere. In hindsight, Duarte had little if any chance of reaching an agreement with the FMLN that he could have sold to the nation. Given his populist and confrontational style and his long-standing antagonism to the military and the private sector, any Duarte peace accord would have been denounced as a sellout by those critical elements and by the anti-Duarte national press.

President Duarte's final year in office, 1988–89, was particularly disastrous for the Christian Democratic Party and the democratic center, beginning with the discovery that Duarte had terminal cancer. The party split into two warring factions. Corruption and mismanagement of the economy and the war were denounced on all sides. At the end of his term, Duarte was convinced that ARENA's victory meant a return to the worst abuses of authority by the military and to the death squad horrors of the early 1980s. Duarte told me (I was U.S. ambassador) that he was destined to die a political prisoner, his dreams of a democratic El Salvador shattered by an antidemocratic ARENA.

As the June 1, 1989, inauguration of the elected ARENA president, Alfredo Cristiani, approached, U.S. policymakers were deeply concerned that Duarte's predictions, echoed by liberals everywhere, might prove accurate. But the new president's inaugural address surprised his listeners with its moderation. In it, Cristiani solemnly promised that 1989 would be the "Year of Peace" and that his government could and would reach a negotiated settlement with the FMLN.

After several months of discussions on how to begin the negotiation process, the FMLN and the Cristiani government met twice—on September 7 in Mexico

City and October 16 in Costa Rica—with a third meeting scheduled for mid-November in Caracas. As a consequence of the words and actions of the new president and the positive response of the FMLN, a sense of optimism erupted in El Salvador—a return to political stability, economic growth, and even peace seemed attainable at long last. Cristiani's relations with the private sector from which he had come were such that business confidence began to climb, and flight capital was returning. Cristiani was seen to be his own man, gathering internal and external respect for his moderation.

The conventional wisdom became that ARENA and Cristiani could bring the FMLN to the table in much the same way Richard Nixon had been able to open China. At the beginning of November, Washington shared the optimistic perception that a negotiated settlement favorable to the elected government was possible. U.S. policy was to do whatever was necessary to encourage a successful conclusion to the United Nations–sponsored negotiations.

U.S. RELATIONS WITH THE CRISTIANI GOVERNMENT

By November 1989 the United States had for ten years been the principal, virtually sole, foreign power supportive of the beleaguered government of El Salvador. U.S. support had been massive, to the tune of over $3 billion in economic and military assistance. With the Salvadoran government dependent on the United States for nearly 50 percent of its budget, one would expect the bilateral relationship to have been close and mutually supportive.

Although that was partially the case, there were tensions in the relationship. Duarte's illness and his conviction that the United States had lost confidence in his regime and party had loosened the bonds of cooperation throughout his last year in office. By November 1989, after five months in office, the Cristiani government remained tentative in dealing with its U.S. ally.

For many in the president's ARENA party, the United States had been shamelessly entwined throughout ARENA's history with their archenemy, Napoleon Duarte. Party militants could not forget or forgive what they interpreted as U.S. intervention that blocked the 1984 election of the party's founder and idol, Roberto d'Aubuisson. Even the party's moderate wing, represented by Cristiani and his philosophical backers in the private sector, suspected U.S. motives. Misunderstandings, missed and mixed signals over the years on the subject of human rights, and highly critical U.S. congressional and editorial comment on the dark nature of the ARENA government contributed further to defensiveness and resentment on the part of the Cristiani regime in its early relationship with the United States.

The president and his closest advisers entered office influenced by what the party's military experts, former major d'Aubuisson and former colonel Sigfrido Ochoa, were telling them—that the Salvadoran armed forces were fighting with one hand behind their backs in deference to the "gringos'" insistence on experimenting with U.S. low-intensity-conflict (LIC) doctrine. Neither the president nor his civilian advisers were knowledgeable about military matters. They accepted the jingoistic view of Ochoa and d'Aubuisson, who claimed that, unhindered by U.S. restrictions and given free rein to pursue a military solution under air force chief General Bustillo, the armed forces could and would win the war in a matter of months. ARENA backers endlessly repeated among themselves, and occasionally to outsiders, that although this might be low-intensity conflict for the gringos, it was total war for Salvadorans, with the Pentagon testing its LIC theories while Salvadorans were paying the tab with the lives of their soldiers.

On assuming office, many of Cristiani's cabinet ministers were surprised at the magnitude of the U.S. Agency for International Development (USAID) involvement in the day-to-day management of the ministers' portfolios. They greatly resented this micromanagment and initially denied the necessity of deferring to the dictates of U.S. advisers. The resentment only deepened when it had to be masked during face-to-face encounters with USAID counterparts.

On the U.S. side, there was uncertainty as to exactly what it was dealing with in the Salvadoran government. Was Cristiani in charge? Or, as virtually all the pundits were saying, was he a pleasant face covering a darker but truer visage of ARENA? Washington questioned whether ARENA's constituencies were prepared to accept anything short of total surrender by the FMLN. Was Cristiani in any position to accept the concessions that would have to be made to achieve a negotiated settlement?

The Bush administration's ability to maintain congressional backing for continued assistance was increasingly problematic. With pressing demands elsewhere for ever scarcer assistance funds and the apparently diminishing relative importance and intensity of the Salvadoran conflict, convincing the policy's congressional critics became increasingly difficult. Some in the U.S. government also harbored fears that the Salvadoran Armed Forces, under new leaders chosen by d'Aubuisson and his reactionary wing of the party, might revert to the discredited early 1980s variety of total war against the Salvadoran insurgency.

In sum, as El Salvador entered the second half of November 1989, what outwardly appeared to be a firm U.S.–Salvadoran alliance, with common goals and objectives and with each partner confident of the other's abilities, motives, and methods, was far different. Historical suspicions and irritants existed on both sides. Brought together by the unpredictability of a free election, the partners had not yet faced a common crisis. As mid-November approached, they were about to do so.

THE CRISIS

All indications that peace in El Salvador was around the corner were upended during the late evening of November 11–12, when the FMLN launched a totally unexpected and unwelcome (even to many of its friends) "final offensive." Deploying some 2,500 to 3,500 heavily armed urban commandos into San Salvador and similar forces into the nation's other major population centers, the FMLN had decided on one last military effort to defeat the Salvadoran Armed Forces, rally and arm the populace, and bring down the Cristiani government. In the first hours of the offensive an attempt was made to assassinate Cristiani in his residence.

The guerrillas tried initially to drive the government's security forces out of the capital's working-class suburbs, assuming that the proletariat, once free of government forces, would rush to its cause. Instead of creating public support for the rebels, however, the sudden dashing of expectations of peace and normalcy had a devastating impact on the public's state of mind.

Given the unexpectedness and ferocity of the initial attack, the government and its armed forces responded in confusion, frustration, and anger. Several key military officers were out of the country, including the air force commander and the spokesman for the high command. The government imposed a sundown-to-sunup curfew. Fighting was minimal during daylight hours, but the nights belonged to the guerrilla and armed forces units as they battled it out in pockets of intense combat throughout the city. The nature of the FMLN's tactics, attacking at the time and place of their choosing, required the government's units to sit in fixed positions until nightfall and wait for the enemy to attack. The FMLN held the military initiative throughout the offensive.

Media Frenzy

The arrival of an avalanche of media representatives added to the confusion. While a few were veterans of earlier assignments in El Salvador, the majority were not. In most cases, the experienced journalists who reported on the horrors of the first bloody years of the war had moved on in the mid-1980s, when the spotlight of world attention shifted to other hot spots. Many of the recent arrivals readily accepted the atrocity and repression stories circulated by the FMLN during the 1989 "final offensive." Virtually all, veterans and newcomers alike, lost sight of the fact that it was the FMLN that had made the decision to abandon the peace process and return to all-out military confrontation.

Reports of "indiscriminate aerial attack" by air force helicopter and C-47 gunships, of wholesale invasion and intimidation of religious communities by security services, and of massacres of innocent civilians in areas dominated during the night by FMLN units were the grist of journalists' on-the-spot reporting. Many of the first reports by CNN and the network anchormen spoke of "tens of thousands" of government-caused civilian deaths inflicted by ESAF attacks on working-class neighborhoods where the FMLN maintained control. These hasty and grossly exaggerated journalistic judgments colored world opinion of the offensive.

The U.S. embassy's public affairs officer, Barry Jacobs, in an effort to balance this speculative and all-too-often exaggerated reporting and to fill the void caused by the absence of an official Salvadoran government voice, asked me to bring the facts as the embassy knew them into more general circulation by briefing those in the media who were demanding embassy reaction to and interpretation of what was happening. My first such effort involved talking with some two dozen print and television reporters for thirty minutes on the afternoon of November 12.

That briefing was so to the liking of the press corps, and the absence of an official Salvadoran voice so damaging, that I continued these on-the-record briefings each afternoon for the next eight days. By the end, each session had well over a hundred aggressive print journalists and some dozen Salvadoran, European, and U.S. television crews demanding their afternoon feed. The final briefings were closer to two hours long, with each more confrontational than the previous, each event on the battlefield provoking greater sharpness in the reporters' questioning.

The "Final Offensive" Unfolds

And many were the events in those first two weeks. During the initial attack on the night of November 11–12, the FMLN had emerged from a complex system of ravines that honeycombs the capital. They attacked the presidential residence, bombarded the Estado Mayor (the armed forces' headquarters) and police stations, and attempted to establish themselves in concentrations throughout the city. These pockets, not by accident, were nestled in the midst of tightly packed civilian populations.

The following night was relatively free from the sounds of battle, causing some to believe that this had been a one-shot attack and that the worst was over. The night of November 13–14 proved how wrong that analysis had been. Again the commandos used darkness to cover their descent from the neighboring volcano and popped out via the ravine network to attack in many corners of the metropolitan area.

When daylight came, the guerrilla concentrations evaporated, attempting to hold only scattered sections of the poorer suburbs during the day. It was the government ground and air force units' attempts to dislodge these pockets that resulted in journalists' descriptions of excessive use of force by ground troops and indiscriminate aerial bombardment of civilian neighborhoods.

The hours of darkness of November 14–15 were again surprisingly calm, perhaps used by the guerrillas to regroup and rearm. Throughout the offensive, the FMLN's ability to handle the logistics of their widely scattered attacks and reequip their dispersed units was nothing short of spectacular. Not appreciated at the time, this interlude on the 14th–15th was to be the last until offensive military operations ended in the latter part of December.

The hours of darkness of November 15–16 were the most memorable of the offensive, perhaps of the war itself, both in terms of the intensity of combat that night and the occurrence of the single most shocking episode in a decade of unspeakable violence. Six Jesuit leaders of the capital's Catholic university, together with two servants, were pulled from their beds and gunned down. From this point to the end, events tumbled one upon the other, ensuring that the battle for San Salvador was never far from the front pages of the *Washington Post* and the *New York Times* and a lead item in nightly newscasts. What follows is an abbreviated list of such events.

The FMLN Seizes Affluent Homes and a Hotel.   In the early-morning hours of November 21, an FMLN urban commando team seized control of the Sheraton Hotel, situated in one of the city's more affluent suburbs. The takeover caught everyone by surprise, most emphatically the secretary-general of the Organization of American States, João Baena Soares and his delegation, who were in El Salvador to promote an end to the conflict and were staying in the hotel. While Baena Soares was able to escape with minimal damage to his dignity, twenty-two U.S. Special Forces advisers, overnighting in the hotel while on a mobile-training-team mission, ended up barricading themselves in their rooms. The result was a standoff between extremely well-armed, nervous, but professional units of the FMLN and U.S. militaries. Luckily no shots were fired. In addition, a small number of other U.S. citizens connected with the embassy were taken captive in their rooms.

Within the same week, several U.S. citizens were trapped in their homes as FMLN units began to penetrate the wealthier suburbs. At least two had their residences occupied by FMLN fighters. The embassy's administrative counselor spent part of the day talking his way through FMLN roadblocks to extract mission families from perilous situations.

The Government Arrests a U.S. Religious Worker.   On November 26 another incident exploded. Salvadoran authorities arrested Jennifer Casolo, a young woman from the United States resident in El Salvador under the sponsorship of a humanitarian Christian organization. A raid of her residence had revealed a massive cache of weapons buried in the backyard, evidently intended for the FMLN. The arrest on such charges of a U.S. citizen, especially a woman and a self-proclaimed pacifist, generated front-page coverage around the world and provoked instant efforts by U.S. members of Congress, congressional staffers, and religious and human rights leaders to obtain her release.

President Cristiani was pressed on all sides: by his military and outraged citizens, who demanded prosecution of this foreigner for contributing to the violence, and by a spectrum of friends and critics, mostly foreign, who insisted that she be released immediately. Former U.S. attorney general Ramsey Clark flew in to argue the latter case, as did innumerable religious figures. After days of frenzied activity, President Cristiani yielded to those advocating release and ordered the young woman deported on December 13. Immediately upon her return to the United States, Casolo undertook a nationwide public speaking tour to declare her innocence and denounce the Government of El Salvador and its U.S. patron.

The Embassy Takes On the Challenges.   The embassy had no sooner waved goodbye to the deportee than those on its staff considered "essential" waved goodbye to their dependents, fellow employees, and a few private citizens. I had called for a voluntary evacuation of all "nonessential" elements of the mission. A heavily overburdened administrative staff was tasked with arranging the departure of over 250 persons on twenty-four-hours' notice.

Adding to the burdens was the ever-increasing presence of visitors, official and otherwise, some of them sympathetic to the FMLN cause and hostile to any and all U.S. assistance to the Salvadoran regime. Members of Congress and their staffers came to see for themselves what was going on. The U.S. military increased its numbers as one after another element from the Pentagon, the U.S. Southern Command in Panama, and Fort Bragg arrived to evaluate one or another aspect of their assistance programs under battlefield conditions. Even Washington's efforts to assist in managing crises added to the embassy's burdens by sending more people and equipment to an already overburdened mission.

By mid-December the shooting had greatly diminished, and the battle shifted to the political and public affairs fronts. The Jesuit killings, the deported Casolo's campaign to denigrate the Cristiani government, tales of repression and wanton massacres, charges of indiscriminate bombing, questions as to who had won militarily, what effect the offensive might have on the interrupted quest for a negotiated settlement, and inquiries about the U.S. government's policies and actions of the past decade emerged as the issues to be addressed in the days and weeks after the shooting subsided.

HOW THE EMBASSY ORGANIZED ITS CRISIS RESPONSE

From the opening shot and throughout the first confusing days of the offensive—perhaps until conclusion of the Sheraton Hotel takeover—the embassy had to assume that it would be a primary military target of the FMLN and that both diplomatic and military staff were at risk. Nonofficial U.S. citizens were assumed to be similarly in harm's way, the consequence either of deliberate targeting by one or the other side or of being in the wrong place at the wrong time, injured or killed inadvertently in the heavy fog of war. Indeed, one of the first fatalities had been a schoolteacher from the United States, out for drinks and heading home in the wee hours of November 12, who caught a round as he pulled up to his quarters—a shot quite clearly not meant for him.

Among the more frightening possibilities the embassy faced was that some element of the Salvadoran military, in a panicky response to what it interpreted as a Pearl Harbor attack by the FMLN in the midst of peace talks, might decide to vent its anger on the many resident foreigners, mostly from the United States, whose sympathies were thought to be with the FMLN. The thought that either a rogue among the military or a member of a right-wing paramilitary gang might attempt to teach the human rights community a lesson was never far from the embassy country team's collective mind. Unfortunately, occasional intelligence tidbits, among the avalanche of rumors that passed for fact during those first days, reinforced this concern.

The most serious such threat would clearly have been against representatives of those humanitarian organizations the military viewed as actively supportive of the insurgency, but the list of potential targets was much broader. It might have included foreign journalists, representatives of the various churches critical of the government, and assorted others working to improve the lot of the Salvadoran underclasses. While the welfare of U.S. citizens and those with resident alien status in the United States was the embassy's primary and legally mandated responsibility, the country team was cognizant that armed forces' anger and violence directed toward other nationalities in the same categories would also damage U.S. policy objectives. Any such incident, whatever the circumstances, would have had an immediate and devastating impact on Washington's ability to provide further support to the Salvadoran government.

One difficulty in addressing this danger was the wide geographic dispersion of possible targets. Moreover, few U.S. citizens sympathetic to the guerrillas' cause bothered to register with the consulate. Many were extremely hostile to the U.S. government and anything it might be involved in, even outreach to ensure their well-being. In short, El Salvador was teeming with scattered U.S. citizens and residents, doing who knew what, for whom the embassy had compulsory consular responsibility. And these were only a fraction of a larger population whose safety was of concern for humanitarian and policy reasons.

Initial Embassy Actions

What did the embassy do in response to the outbreak of the FMLN offensive? In the first hours the answer was simple: it went by the book. The country team immediately convened and remained in session as a permanent crisis management committee. The Emergency Action Plan was taken off the shelf and opened to page one.

Since Embassy San Salvador had lived under FMLN guns for more than a decade, the plan was as current and applicable as these massive compendiums can be. Embassy staff had conducted regular exercises on the plan's component parts, and players were familiar with their assigned tasks. The embassy was also secure in the knowledge that offshore participants in executing the plan, namely the United States Southern Command in Panama and a score of agencies in Washington, had up-to-date familiarity with their roles.

The initial embassy response was thus of the textbook variety—establish a dedicated telephonic line with the State Department's Operations Center, agree to the setting up of a Salvador Crisis Task Force in Washington, activate and recheck the U.S. citizen warden system, and notify the official and private local American community to remain at home and await further instructions. I appointed officers to keep logs, both a master chronicle of events and chronologies of individual issues.

Dealing with Real or Potential Dangers

As the offensive intensified and the pattern of guerrilla operations became more evident, the combination of human intelligence and the evidence of the unfolding scenario revealed that the FMLN was not only not attempting to target Americans, official or otherwise, but was doing everything possible to avoid putting them in harm's way. In an early broadcast on Radio Venceremos, the official voice of the FMLN, the political-military command announced that its commandos were under orders not to target embassy personnel, with the exception of members of the Military Assistance Group.

Though the caveat concerning MILGROUP members was worrisome, events surrounding the takeover of the Sheraton Hotel indicated that not even U.S. military personnel would be intentionally harmed by the urban commandos. The best evidence was the guerrillas' handling of their unexpected encounter with the twenty-two Special Forces soldiers who had barricaded themselves in their rooms; both sides did everything possible to avoid a shooting confrontation. Similarly, when FMLN units in separate incidents in other parts of the city forcefully occupied the residences of a MILGROUP-attached technician and a State Department officer, they treated the hostages with the utmost courtesy and released them unharmed at the first opportunity.

Confirmation that the FMLN's leaders were attempting to minimize risk to U.S. citizens, even those previously identified as "military targets," derived from conversations in Washington between working-level elements of the State Department and U.S.-based FMLN representatives. At the opening of the offensive, several raw intelligence reports had indicated that voices in the FMLN leadership were advocating the targeting of U.S. officials and installations. The embassy asked the department to use discreet channels available either in Washington, where the FMLN maintained a lobbying presence, or in Mexico City, where the collective leadership was directing the attack, to head off implementation of any such plan. When contact was made in Washington, the FMLN response was emphatic: "Our rules of engagement order that everything be done to avoid harm to American persons and properties."

It was not the FMLN alone that understood how damaging it would be to be seen as threatening foreigners, even those suspected of causing harm to its side. The government and the armed forces also absorbed the lesson that aggressive action against a foreigner, however rationalized and explained, was in the long run counterproductive. Although many officers and nationalistic civilians were adamant that a foreigner caught flagrantly abetting FMLN violence must not be immune from prosecution, the president and others of a more pragmatic mind accepted that there were other priorities. While not relishing the criticism of colleagues who denounced their succumbing to foreign pressures, Cristiani and those calling the shots saw that release and expulsion of such foreign collaborators stood the best chance of minimizing problems with the external world. All but the most xenophobic ARENA politicians eventually accepted this approach as wise.

This view, first acted upon in the case of the young woman with the backyard cache of weapons, was even more evident in a second nasty incident involving a woman from the United States. No sooner had one U.S. citizen been put on an airplane than the International Committee of the Red Cross (ICRC) was contacted by the FMLN and told that another American woman, this one with a serious wound, could be found at a specified location in the bush. The ICRC picked up the woman, whose jaw had been destroyed by a bullet, and transported her to a San Salvador hospital. She had evidently been moving with an FMLN unit when it clashed with an army patrol. Clearly the government could have held and prosecuted this foreigner for taking up arms against it. Nevertheless, with the first experience vividly in mind, the government did not hesitate to patch the young lady up and deport her into her parents' care as soon as she could travel.

Analyzing the Crisis and the Embassy's Performance

The realization dawned on the United States that the FMLN attitude toward it had undergone a transformation from that of earlier years. In 1985, for example, a guerrilla assassination squad had massacred five U.S. embassy Marine security guards in a San Salvador sidewalk café.

In the post-offensive period this realization was a significant factor in my deciding that I could safely visit the FMLN refugee community of Santa Marta. That visit was cited in turn by the FMLN as the signal it needed to conclude that U.S. policy no longer insisted on a government military victory and that the negotiation process was serious on all sides.

The activities that emanated from embassy involvement in the events of the offensive were so diverse, so spontaneous, and so unforeseen in the context of emergency action planning that the mission's Emergency Action Plan was quickly overtaken by the complexity of the real-world situation. Who could have foreseen or planned a rational response to the mindless assassination of the Jesuits? And yet virtually nothing that the embassy did in the aftermath of that singular event was unaffected by it. Within days of the killings, I convened a special embassy task force under the direction of Deputy Chief of Mission William Dieterich. Meeting once or more a day, the task force coordinated embassy efforts to see justice done and produced a situation report series devoted exclusively to the Jesuit matter.

As event piled upon event, it was also apparent that embassy responses would likely be the subject of postcrisis examination and critique. Embassy San Salvador had long experience with having to explain and document its actions. Without question this was among the most inspected, evaluated, and investigated of embassies. Given the partisan, politicized nature of the issues it dealt with for more than a decade, the embassy was seldom without an inspector general or Government Accounting Office presence. Hence my insistence on detailed logs and copious reporting.

The embassy's performance during the November 1989 "Final Offensive" was, as foreseen, subjected to such after-action analysis and critique. Though short of unrelieved praise, the results were certainly encouraging. Many things had gone well; a few had not.

After the accidental death of the schoolteacher in the first minutes of the shooting, as far as is known no other U.S. citizens were killed, despite the ferocity of the fighting and the presence and involvement, active or passive, of so many U.S. citizens. The emergency evacuation of dependents and others went off without a hitch. Support from the State Department, the United States Southern Command, and other U.S. government agencies was constant and effective throughout. As often occurs in such situations, embassy morale and cohesion soared, as did embassy relations with the broader U.S. community.

AFTERMATH

Of special importance, U.S. policy made it through the offensive relatively unscathed. In some respects, the United States saw its hand in the negotiation process strengthened. While it was not immediately apparent, both the FMLN and the United States saw mutual perceptions undergo significant change, virtually all on the positive side. Though they were to continue as antagonists until the signing of a final peace accord on December 31, 1990, a subtle and important evolution in the relationship had occurred during the dark days of November– December 1989.

In a similar vein, the Cristiani government ascended a number of learning curves. The president and his party discovered that the FMLN was not on its last legs, that it had superlative military and logistical skills, and that the Salvadoran Armed Forces were both better and worse than previously thought. The FMLN had dramatically demonstrated the will and wherewithal to carry the battle to the affluent suburbs of the capital, wherein resided ARENA's most ardent supporters, previously untouched by the war. The offensive also revealed both that the FMLN had the capability to veto a return to normalcy and that the economic aspirations and promises of the Cristiani presidency were unachievable as long as the FMLN chose to continue the fight.

The guerrilla leadership also absorbed painful but highly useful lessons. Its long-trumpeted popular support had not materialized, as would have been necessary to bring down the Cristiani regime. There was no single incident during the offensive in which local inhabitants accepted the guerrillas' offer of arms and joined the fight.

The FMLN's carefully cultivated ideological support in Western Europe, the United States, and Latin America began to erode with the difficulty of defending such an irrational attack in the midst of the U.N.–sponsored peace initiative. The patience of the Mexicans, the Spanish, the Scandinavians, even the Russians was sorely tested. The FMLN learned that not only the Salvadoran populace and the U.S. Congress were weary of this conflict; so was the world at large.

The offensive thus set the stage for what was to come two years later—FMLN and government signatures on a final peace agreement. It was an outcome that one would hardly have thought possible during the violence itself.

LESSONS LEARNED

The crisis engendered by the FMLN's 1989 "final offensive" contained learning experiences for all involved. For the embassy, many were of the nuts-and-bolts "what to do when it hits the fan" variety, while others related more to policy and its implementation. Following are some of the lessons absorbed by the United States.

Nuts and Bolts

Communications. During a crisis, especially one involving threat to the lives and possessions of U.S. citizens caught unprotected, an embassy's maintenance of open communication to those it serves is among the most essential tasks it will perform. This proved true in the Salvador case for both practical and psychological reasons.

For an emergency and evacuation plan to work as it must, the broadest possible dispersal of timely and factual information is an imperative. On the first day of the offensive, the embassy activated its radio communication network, with the regional security officer proffering practical advice to the local American community regarding immediate response and protection. He warned them all to remain in their homes, check their radios, and implement the warden system. With a radio and telephone in every official's residence and an extensive warden net pulling in virtually every U.S. citizen known to be in the country, the embassy had the needed access. When it became clear that rumor and fear could overwhelm the U.S. enclave, the embassy broadcast summaries of the situation as known to the country team two or three times daily. On most occasions, I delivered the assessments.

Feedback was uniformly positive. When the U.S. citizens being evacuated bid me farewell at the aircraft stairs on departure, fully half felt the need to tell me how reassuring and appreciated these radio messages had been. Whether the news had been good or bad, the importance of hearing the authoritative voice of the embassy was clear. Despite difficult and dangerous moments, the U.S. community kept its bearings through the worst of the violence, no small feat.

Help from Outside. When a crisis is in full bloom and the embassy involved appears stretched to the point of breaking, the arrival of outside assistance too often adds to the burden rather than relieves it. During this offensive there were instances when the embassy identified a need that could be met only by bringing in an outside expert. During the early effort to investigate the Jesuits' deaths, for example, I asked the Drug Enforcement Agency for the temporary assistance of an agent with unique qualifications to do police work in the Salvadoran environment. In another instance, the embassy legal officer requested dispatch of an FBI polygrapher for a mission-specific task. Both requests were honored, and the embassy took on board human resources it lacked in its normal complement.

Contrast that with Washington's sending of a team it thought would have application in the Salvador situation. Some came with country-specific knowledge, others without. Their arrival only compounded the embassy's workload.

The lesson learned should be to let the mission identify its own shortcomings and not ask the country team to accept or reject an offer of Washington expertise. The response will almost always be acceptance, because the embassy would not want to be accused of rejecting assistance—and will probably not grasp that some of the visitors will require more assistance than they will dispense.

Record-keeping. Keep logs of everything the embassy does.

Managing the Media. Work the press and the public relations side of the event as much as you can handle locally and as much as headquarters permits. Handling an excited, often frightened press corps—which assuredly contains some who are antagonistic to what the embassy is trying to do—can be frustrating and often career-damaging, but it must be done and done well.

In the midst of a crisis of the magnitude of the FMLN offensive, an embassy spokesperson will inevitably share information and opinions that are later found to be incorrect. This will almost certainly be interpreted as purposeful and malevolent on the mission's part, but the downsides of not being open and informative with the press are even worse.

On the other hand, Embassy San Salvador also learned that attempting to inform the "news-entertainment" programs of the *60 Minutes* variety of what was happening and why was a futile exercise. A ninety-minute on-camera interview will be reduced to a microscopic bite, included only to enhance the entertainment value of the carefully crafted final product. That bite will most assuredly portray any government official as hopelessly incompetent, insensitive, or worse. The lesson learned: let Washington handle this brand of "journalist."

Policy Lessons

A protagonist in a war, even one of the duration and bitterness of an El Salvador, must establish channels of communication with the enemy and maintain them, even during the worst of the fighting. The existence of links between the State Department and spokespersons for the FMLN was of critical importance throughout the offensive, and later in the peace talks, in avoiding actions and misunderstandings that could have put at risk the longer-term objectives of peace and reconciliation.

As it is said to be darkest just before the dawn, so it may often be the case in war that the violence reaches its greatest intensity just prior to the outbreak of peace. The bloodiest and most intense battles of World War I were those that immediately preceded the Armistice, as both sides went with everything they had left to maximize their hand at the peace table. Similarly, when the history of the

Salvadoran civil war is written, the question will be asked: What impact did the 1989 "final offensive" have in what turned out to be the closing days of that bitter struggle?

Prior to the offensive, the perception had been of a tentative peace process underway, likely to meander through many meetings and innumerable difficult issues. When the FMLN launched its attack, instant wisdom held that it could only retard, if not derail, this promising but delicate process. What happened was just the opposite. Neither the FMLN's last desperate effort to achieve its initial goal of bringing down the system nor the government's momentary dream that it could achieve a military victory significantly changed the correlation of military forces.

What did change, though, were the perceptions and mind-sets of virtually all the players. The leaders on all sides of the conflict learned lessons that may have been prerequisite to any realistic chance of success in the peace talks. The horrors of the offensive, and there were many, served to focus attention on a few simple realities. As long as the FMLN remained outside the system, its military strengths were such that it could effectively thwart implementation of any decision to which it was not a party. The government was not about to fall, nor the armed forces collapse, as the FMLN predicted. The war-weary Salvadoran people generally blamed the FMLN for prolonging the instability and agony, but also craved many of the political, economic, and social reforms the FMLN claimed to stand for.

The external players—the United States, the Soviet Union, Cuba, Nicaragua, Mexico, and the other Central American nations—shared that weariness, and were increasingly turning their attention and resources to other problems. The realization that time was running out for both sides only sank in as a result of the final offensive. Late in coming, perhaps, and extremely costly in terms of lives and resources, that lesson was a major ingredient in achieving the peace accord thirteen months later.

The U.S. embassy's "final five" on the day of their evacuation from Iraqi-occupied Kuwait, December 12, 1990. From left: Wayne Logsden, Barbara Bodine, Nathaniel Howell, Connie Parrish, and Jeffrey Jugar. *B. Bodine*.

8 | Saddam's Siege of Embassy Kuwait: A Personal Journal, 1990

Barbara K. Bodine

There Are Many Reasons to Build a Bridge

It may very well be that history, at least literary and cinematic history, has judged Colonel Nicholson too harshly. Colonel Nicholson may be neither the unmitigated villain nor the consummate British dolt William Holden would have us believe. The good colonel does set out, with ever-increasing obsessiveness, to build the perfect bridge, the "Bridge on the River Kwai." We will never fully know Nicholson's motivations, for we will only know William Holden's side of the story. What saves Nicholson from utter vileness or the stupidity of his ultimate obsession, and what our narrator will not concede, is that Nicholson recognized (or stumbled onto) a basic truth of survival: the grimmer the situation, the greater the sense of hopelessness and helplessness, the greater the need for order, structure, and, above all, purpose.

I did not read Boulle's classic until several months after the end of the siege of Embassy Kuwait. I doubt I would have read it the same way before the siege.

THE STAY-BEHINDS

At dawn the oppressive heat of the August day was already evident. It had been a long night after endless bad days. After hours of pointless, Iraqi-manipulated delays, the convoy rolled out of the compound.

Over a hundred embassy dependents, nonessential personnel, basic baggage, and pets were on their way, we had been assured, to Baghdad, to Amman, and home. For them, an end to three weeks of life confined by Inman-standard

113

embassy walls[1] and the increasing brutality of the Iraqi occupation of Kuwait seemed near. The Department of State had negotiated safe passage with Baghdad, gaining an Iraqi assurance that our people would travel unharassed and unimpeded.

This is not a story about that convoy and those broken assurances but one about those of us who stood in the parking lot watching them leave.

On December 9, 1990—nearly four months later—three of the remaining eight diplomats were able to leave, followed four days later by the last five. None of us in our wildest dreams or darkest nightmares could have foreseen that the siege would last that long. Even more remote was the hope that we would be able to accomplish anything while so trapped.

No one who stayed behind that August morning envied those heading north, nor they us. On August 9, Saddam Hussein, unable to form an even minimally credible puppet government in Kuwait, had announced the "return" of the nineteenth province of Iraq to the motherland. At the same time he had announced, with impeccable logic, that since Kuwait was no longer a sovereign state, embassies and diplomats were no longer appropriate.

All diplomatic missions in Kuwait were given two weeks to either close, convert to consulates, or face being forced out, at gunpoint if necessary. Missions were to be stripped of their status unilaterally, personnel were to be denied their privileges and immunities, and all utilities for and access to and from the embassies were to be cut. The Iraqis made clear that any mission personnel remaining in Kuwait, no longer protected persons, would be subject to seizure and to the "human shield" program.[2] Local occupation authorities made ominously clear that they would not guarantee our safety from "spontaneous" actions against us by either troops or rent-a-mobs.

From each embassy, and from each of our capitals, there was the same reply— we were staying. We were staying to demonstrate that we did not, individually or collectively, accept the annexation or sanction the invasion. We were staying to keep faith with our citizens trapped and, in some cases, hunted throughout the city-state. We were staying because, perhaps for once, there was meaning in that old cliché about the need to show the flag. At the time, proud and angry words had been spoken in many capitals denouncing the invasion and the occupation, but neither Desert Shield nor later Desert Storm had made manifest those words of defiance. That was left to the embassies in Kuwait—and their personnel.

NEW PRIORITIES: NEW COUNTRY TEAM

At the time of Saddam's annexation of Kuwait and the threatened siege, there were over a hundred Americans living on a compound that normally supported half a dozen.[3] More Americans, official and unofficial, would bring the final population to nearly two hundred at the time of the convoy. About fifty were private citizens, primarily businessmen passing through Kuwait; but they also included the local Protestant minister and his family, a research physician at the local university, civilian and military contractors with various elements of the Kuwaiti government, and a schoolteacher.

The crisis had begun just after midnight, August 2, 1990. Fifteen hours after Iraq had abruptly, probably premeditatedly, broken off its Saudi-brokered talks with Kuwait in Jeddah, Iraqi forces—representing the fourth-largest army in the world—invaded Kuwait. Iraq's forces were twice the size of the native Kuwaiti population of half a million. In contrast, the total manpower of the combined Kuwaiti armed forces was no more than twenty thousand. There was never any question as to the outcome of the invasion, with or without the element of surprise.

By early dawn, the invading forces had reached the amir's residence and the U.S. embassy, having already passed most government ministries, the Parliament building, and the British embassy. The invasion slowed at perhaps only one juncture as it made its way down the Gulf Road: the gold *suq* (or market) was cleaned to the bone.

Like a cold front passing through, the invading forces moved relentlessly south. One European diplomat, returning north to Kuwait from Dhahran that morning, drove undisturbed past columns of Iraqi tanks and support vehicles heading south toward the Saudi border. It was not until he was well up the column that he noticed that neither the tanks' markings nor the troops' insignias and uniforms were Kuwaiti.

A relative calm settled over neighborhoods that were now behind Iraqi lines but not yet under occupation control. An American family, relocating to Kuwait, landed at 4:00 A.M. on board the ill-fated British Air flight.[4] They passed through customs and immigration and proceeded by taxi to their midtown hotel, now behind the lines. It was only the absence of desk or other hotel personnel that told them something was amiss. An American businessman, staying at a hotel down the coast and arriving at its coffee shop at 8:00 A.M. for breakfast, was irritated that the normally slow service seemed totally nonexistent. It was.

The embassy in the meantime was trying to satisfy the State Department's insatiable need for information, to locate all our employees, and to attend to the American community. Embassy staffing was at its typical summer low, with the political section chief absent on vacation (and the economic counselor trapped across town with his family). The head of the consular section, Gale Rogers, had arrived only a week before the invasion; the administrative chief, Wayne Logsden, filling a five-month-old vacancy, had arrived only thirty-six hours before the Iraqis. To backfill during the summer gaps, the post was relying on three summer interns. ("Don't worry, folks, I'm not going to *that* part of the Middle East. . . . I'll be home safe in time for the fall semester.")

For a time, the embassy continued to function normally. Information was gathered from any source we could locate—our diplomatic colleagues, the business community, and Kuwaiti and other friends around town, albeit no longer those with the civilian or military elements of the Kuwaiti government. There was a vast upsurge in "welfare and whereabouts" cases to attend to, and there were sitreps to produce.[5]

As time went on, though, the emphasis shifted toward caring for the increasing population on the compound and for our citizens in the city. News repeatedly brought to the front office told of yet another American, with or without family, with or without bedding, food, or pets, who had come to the embassy seeking sanctuary. There was never a question of not accepting them, only of where to put them and what sort of work to find for them. The focus for us became communications, food, medicine, housing, and the development of various contingency plans for evacuation, each dependent on how (and if) we were able to leave.

With this shift in priorities came a shift in embassy organization. The traditional "country team" no longer represented the new issues or divisions of responsibility.[6] A new country team evolved representing the new priorities: housing (the wife of the noncommissioned officer in charge of the Marine security guards, the "gunny"); food (the general manager of a local hotel); provisions (a chief warrant officer and the commercial attaché); evacuations (a logistician from the military assistance group); medical (the security officer's wife). The embassy security officer and others continued on the country team in their traditional roles, but this was not true of all country team members.

The redivision of labor did not, however, mean that people were left to fend for themselves. Maintaining our burgeoning village was a full-time job. If a particular job was not full-time, we made it so. As one example, pet owners brought their pets to the compound along with their family members and valuables. Given the precarious state of some of the children (and some adults), it would have been unreasonable to expect them to abandon these virtual family members. It was also unnecessary.

Serendipitously, the nearly forty cats and dogs (and one gerbil) provided much-needed employment. Carpenters were needed to build first a kennel and a cattery and then, for the convoy, travel cages. Teenagers, a particularly fragile and vulnerable group, were tasked with feeding, walking, and otherwise caring for the critters. The goal, beyond the immediate need of caring for the animals, was to give purpose and direction to people who had at that point little else but worry on their minds.

DARK IMAGININGS AND REAL FEARS

Another major element was to keep the information flowing and the front office accessible—and thus the rampant rumors reasonably under control—without distracting the embassy leadership from its other responsibilities. This was a tough balance, especially when hard information was in short supply, but rumors and dark imaginings appeared to be limitless, and an even tougher task when there were grounds enough for real fear.

The embassy was not a military target of the Iraqis, and at no time were we under direct fire. But these truths were known only in retrospect, not at the time. The threat of a stray round, however, was very real and prevented or badly constrained our ability to allow the young children to venture outside within the compound at all to run off their pent-up frustrations and fears. One evening I stood helplessly at the chancery door, restraining frantic fathers, as young Marine guards ferried small children across the dark compound to safety when a firefight erupted around the compound.

The sound of artillery was too close to allow sleep. It seemed to start every morning at 4:00 A.M., as if it were a premeditated Iraqi sleep-deprivation program. Emergency procedures were instituted on what to do in case of incoming artillery or automatic-weapons fire. Iraqi hints that all of us on the compound might be forcibly removed could not be dismissed and only heightened the fear within the compound.

So accustomed did I become to the sound of artillery that I could stand in an open parking lot chatting with a British colleague while subconsciously calibrating the distance and direction of the rounds, as well as their number. A week earlier the same sound would have sent me under the nearest shelter in a cold panic.

Caught outside as the Kuwaiti Air Force pounded Iraqi positions throughout the city, expending their last ordnance before deploying to Bahrain, I realized in slow motion that this "air show" was for real, and that I was directly under it.

A wrenching quandary—having to decide the fate of embassy families without knowing where the greater danger lay. Should they be left in their homes, risking seizure as part of the human shield program, or brought to the embassy, risking arrest en route? Several families, unable to make it to the compound but unable to stay in their homes, had to be moved to the basement of a friendly embassy, for God knew how long. Was this embassy any safer than our own?

In the face of the oppressive weight of the Iraqi occupation and its callous use of civilians as human shields, heroes began to emerge. One hero was my Japanese colleague Chargé d'Affaires Akio Shirota, who took fifteen American embassy staffers and their families into his own beleaguered embassy, already bursting with over three hundred private Japanese citizens, and sheltered them for two weeks.

Vowing not to allow "another Tehran," the Canadian chargé, William Bowden, also stepped forward to help. Bowden offered Canada's embassy and residences to any U.S. citizen needing shelter but unable to get to our embassy, though they turned out not to be needed. In the weeks ahead, however, the Canadian hand of friendship would again be extended and would become an instrumental part of our operations and of the survival of the American community in Kuwait City.[7]

DETERMINING DRAWDOWN NUMBERS

By the third week in August, with the assistance of the Kuwaitis, we had gathered provisions for 180 people for several months—including a remarkable collection of baby and toddler food and diapers. At the same time, the Department of State sought assurances from Baghdad that we could safely evacuate our embassy dependents and nonessential personnel, even as we made ready to defy the closure order and maintain our embassy.

Why choose to maintain an embassy and leave staff behind under such circumstances and under such a credible threat? The lesson of Tehran and elsewhere might have been to remove all staff as soon as possible.

The answer came down to the fundamental reasons we have embassies around the world: to project U.S. policy, to act as the eyes and ears for policymakers in Washington, and to protect U.S. citizens, who in this case were literally caught in the cross fires of war. To leave would have been unprofessional—and immoral.

The question then becomes how large (or small) a staff to leave at post. Normal staffing at embassy Kuwait was between sixty and seventy direct-hire Americans, with perhaps a hundred local or third-country employees. Ambassador Nathaniel Howell and I—as DCM—considered a number of criteria in determining who should be asked to stay.

Function. Some positions were obvious choices: administration and general services, consular, communications, language skills. Others were perhaps less so. Were secretaries useful if there was no electricity? Should the security officer or Marine guards stay if they would be powerless to resist a direct Iraqi challenge to our presence? Were the order and discipline the Marines could bring to a situation, in addition to their youthful enthusiasm and energy, worth the risk that they might become POWs? What would be the role of a computer systems manager if power was cut, as threatened, and virtually all computer systems had fallen victim (as they did) to a sledgehammer to keep their technology from falling into Iraqi hands? Were his technical skills and talents transferrable to other problems that might arise and that would be beyond the competence of your average liberal arts diplomat?

Performance to Date. This was a more difficult question. There were no major breakdowns or failures within the difficult first three weeks of August. There were, however, the inevitable and understandable burnouts and stress-outs. Too many of the staff were working days on end with no relief and considerable pressure. Some had reached the end of their ropes. They could and would bounce back, but to have them stay to face a siege of indeterminate length and severity was unreasonable and unfair.

Family Situation. This was the most important criterion. Given the stresses to date, and the uncertainties ahead, including the threat of forcible removal from the compound, if at all possible we would avoid splitting up families in staffing the core stay-behind group.

In the end, we were able to create a group that met all three criteria. There were more who were willing and able to stay than we could keep. We spoke to each individually and in total confidence, giving assurances that a disinclination to stay, for whatever reason, would never be shared with anyone. All who were asked to stay agreed.

The problem was not in finding volunteers; it was in explaining to those who would be in the convoy but felt a commitment and a duty to stay why they could not. In all those cases, the determining factor was family considerations, not ability. (The Iraqis had no such compunctions. They culled from the convoy in Baghdad all adult men, including college students, and the embassy secretaries, allowing only dependent wives and children to continue on.)

When we first talked with the Department of State about drawing down to a core staff, the goal set by Washington was fifteen. We believed we could accomplish our goals with between twelve and fifteen.

At the last minute, the department reduced the number to eight. One of the great mysteries is why. Perhaps fewer people in the compound meant fewer to worry about—or fewer to lift out by helicopter if all went badly. Or fewer names for State's green marble memorial plaque if it all went very badly indeed.

But there is a point beyond which a staff can no longer function. There is no guarantee that twelve or fifteen could have managed; it was certain that eight could not, whoever they were and whatever their mix of talents. By dictating this unrealistic number, the Department of State set up the embassy for failure. Alone, a staff of eight could have neither supported and assisted the American community in the city nor even maintained the compound to keep the flag flying as a symbolic defiance. Worse, Washington ran the risk of an embarrassing failure if the U.S. embassy was forced to close early and its personnel were to leave without having helped the American community one whit. Our staying under those conditions would have become a hollow gesture.

The British embassy was a negative model of draconian drawdowns. It began the siege with four—the ambassador, a consul, and two others—then dropped to just the first two. They provided few support services to their community—we arranged the evacuation of most British subjects and their dependents—nor did the British embassy support their Commonwealth and European Community partners and their communities as those embassies were forced to close. Again, much of this responsibility was taken on by the U.S. embassy, which provided communications and evacuation support, as well as informal protective power functions for about twenty other governments.

What the British embassy in Kuwait was able to do was hang on. Full stop. It is perhaps a difference in philosophy. If we had had to cope with only eight, it is highly questionable we would have achieved much more than the British embassy did, which was virtually nothing.

In essence, the British embassy and we represented two aspects of an embassy's mission. There was a shared realization that we were both to stay as a symbolic challenge to Saddam Hussein. Where we parted company was in the apparent British decision that providing a symbolic "pole" for its community was sufficient. The American approach was to provide a practical "pole" as well. The former was worthy and important. The question was whether it was enough.

THE INGATHERING OF THE AMCITS

What to do about the oil executive who lay in a local hospital, having suffered a heart attack just days before the invasion—was it better to leave him where he could get professional care but be subject to arrest by the Iraqis, or bring him to the embassy, where, though safer, he could not get the medical care he needed?

The reason the U.S. embassy in Kuwait was able to hold out as long as it did and accomplish all that it did against the odds is simple: we did not do it alone.

First, we were not alone on the compound. With us after the convoy departed on the morning of August 22 were upward of fifty private U.S. citizens (Amcits in the jargon), including a number of women and children. They came to the compound for protection and could not safely leave with the convoy. The risk of roundup was too great. As the gate closed behind the last car, we turned and looked at each other with sinking feelings of "What now?" and, more critically, "Who on earth are you?" This was not a cohesive group well known to one another and used to working together.

With exceptions, the private American citizens knew neither the embassy staff nor each other. The embassy staff, for that matter, did not know one another all that well. The core group included three who had arrived at post within the week (Consul Gale Rogers, Administrative Counselor Wayne Logsden, and his wife, Mildred Logsden, a secretary) and two communicators who had spent every waking and most sleeping hours since the beginning of the crisis buried in their windowless vault keeping us in touch with Washington.

The Amcits, a collection of residents and transients, had scrambled from their homes and hotels, some tossing luggage from second-story windows with others below running to catch it as it came down. The Meridian Hotel bus arrived with a load of American businessmen and the American manager of the hotel with his family in tow. An American consul who arrived at the SAS Hotel one step ahead of the Iraqis crammed too many people and too much luggage into a car too small. There would be no second trip this time. Unloading at the embassy, they were like endless clowns coming out of a circus Volkswagen.

And what had we collected? If there had been a computer printout of what sort of talents and what sort of people we needed, it would have been strikingly close to what we got. Fortuitously, the citizens represented nearly every talent needed for the business at hand—maintaining the compound and serving our community on the outside.

120

Like a toss of the dice, if the invasion had been even a day later, the mix would have been entirely different. Most of the visiting businessmen were scheduled to depart the morning of August 2. If the invasion had occurred a week earlier or later, even the mix at the embassy would have been different because of transfers, vacations, and the like. The ambassador had been due to leave post at the end of the week.

The mix, as the fates would have it, included a banker, engineers of all sorts—hydraulic, chemical, civil, and electrical—a teacher, a preacher, a doctor, a native Arabic speaker, a computer programmer, and a landscape architect (a skill that proved surprisingly important).[8]

STARTING OVER

The Navigator is not a long book nor Morris West's most famous. It is the simple story of a Noah's ark of characters shipwrecked on an uncharted island. Each had been selected for a scientific specialty (they were searching for a legendary island of great Polynesian navigators), and they must re-create society—some sort of society—in order to survive.

At Embassy Kuwait, we lived on an island 5.7 acres small, surrounded by a sea of hostile Iraqis. Within those walls we had to re-create a society. We had lost all the basics of life—water, electricity, plumbing, freedom of movement, and access to the outside world, including access to fresh food and medicines. In a very real sense we had lost an element of who we were. Much of what we possessed and did in the outside world became increasingly irrelevant. What was important was who and what we were on our island, and what we were able and willing to contribute to the whole.

Sitting on a second-floor balcony within the compound, overlooking the Iraqis and the gulf, with the lights curving down the coast ultimately to Saudi Arabia, it is the quiet that comes from no motors, no voices, no cars, no movement or signs of life anywhere—an unchanging scene. Was this the latest from the Twilight Zone, or Stephen King? The world beyond the walls does not exist. The voices on the phone and heard over the walls do not exist. The sky that moves from day to night is an illusion. We are on the ultimate island.

The enemy was not the Iraqi invasion force, nor the collection of absurd and pitiful conscripts charged with "guarding" our compound. It was not even the Mukhabarat, the Iraqi secret police charged with and presumably delighting in making our lives miserable, while entertaining themselves by spectating on life in the compound from the balconies of the adjoining hotel. The enemy was Time, Boredom, and Uncertainty. It was the fear of being helpless, literally without help beyond the walls, without the ability to help oneself.

From some press reports there is the impression that for 134 days this random sample of humanity did nothing more than twiddle its collective thumbs and wait passively for something to happen, although there may have been some recognition that conditions were not up to snuff—the mythology of our drinking swimming-pool water, or the fact of eating tuna fish every day, twice a day, for almost five months. The opposite end of the spectrum was equally inaccurate, portraying us, as it did, as starving, helpless victims. The common denominator in both versions, however, was that we were passive.

In truth, there was an inherent challenge to be met. The Iraqis banked on the assumption that we were too fat, too lazy—too Western—to put up with the level of inconvenience they set upon us. And inconvenient they made it.

As promised, the siege began at 11:00 A.M. on August 24 (noon, Baghdad time, the official start of the siege). The following day as we sat at an enclosed guard shack and watched our water line dug up and severed, the Iraqis cut off our phones, which they had been doing episodically for the past three weeks, and the electricity. The Iraqi occupation authorities also made it clear that there would be no one and nothing allowed either in or out. It was 130 degrees Fahrenheit (50+ Celsius), and we had no lights, no electricity, no air conditioning (a necessity, not a luxury, in that part of the world), no plumbing, only the food that had been stockpiled, and virtually no medicines.

The Iraqis bet that we would ultimately succumb and "voluntarily" close the embassy—that we would choose to make our principled stand from some more comfortable location and seek to help our citizens from some other post. The odds were on the Iraqis' side. One after another of the embassies equally committed to staying had to close because of broken generators without spare parts, ruptured water tanks, or, for some, a loss of will. By early October only the British, American, French, and Canadian embassies remained open, and the last two were forced to close by month's end.

It would have been quicker to haul us off at gunpoint, something we were repeatedly threatened with. But, as the Iraqis seemingly understood, that risked unpleasant retaliation by the growing U.S. and coalition troop concentrations just across the border in Saudi Arabia. So the game was to persuade us, albeit not that gently, to leave of our own accord.

We, to the contrary, figured we were a whole lot smarter and tougher than the Iraqis imagined—and we had the time to prove it.

Tinker, Tailor, Candlestick Maker

We also knew that we had real business to attend to. Trapped within the city were nearly three thousand U.S. citizens and their families, primarily American women and their dual-national children but a sizable community of other American residents as well. Another consideration was the chilling realization that we had no alternative: if we could not keep the compound functioning and ourselves healthy and sane, we would be forced to shut down the embassy. The private citizens would become human shields; we would have failed in our mission.

Each person on the compound took responsibility for a specific task, a responsibility that was his own. Or her own, for there were four women in the mix, all embassy staff—the DCM (myself), the consul, one of the two communicators, and the secretary-wife of the administrative counselor.

The engineers tinkered with the aged generator, monitored the water both potable and nonpotable stored in large tanks, rewired the embassy to ensure that essentials, primarily communications equipment, were supported, and pulled up dormant local phone lines.[9] A chemical engineer maintained the pool—no, not as a source of drinking water, but as a critical water reserve nonetheless.

There was food to be prepared, the kitchen to be cleaned, and trash to be collected and burned. Weekend carpenters built an outhouse, cleverly placed over a sewer maintenance grate. There was also security to be maintained, if only by rotating shifts at our guard posts to let the Iraqis know that we were still watching them watch us.

The computer programmer tailored a program for tracking the Americans in Kuwait, a program made of whole cloth, as all records had been destroyed in the initial days of the invasion. And the teacher, once his last charges had left in the middle of September, took on, among others, the task of melting candle butts to make new candles.

Following the debacle of Saddam's fatherly chat with a clearly terrified British youngster and his subsequent relaxation of the human shield program to allow women and children to leave, endless hours were spent on the phone making manifests of Americans for what would finally total thirteen U.S.–sponsored evacuation flights. Equally long hours were spent on the phone with the American men left behind who were in self-imposed deep hiding from the Iraqis. The doctor and the minister, trained and experienced in dealing with people in crisis, assisted Consul Gale Rogers in her outreach program to the American community.

Everyone had a role, a purpose, a new identity within the evolving community known as "Camp Kuwait."

Digging a Well, Planting a Garden, Building a Bridge

And then there was Paul Brown's well. Paul was a landscape architect from Ohio on contract to the Kuwaiti government. One day Paul decided he would dig a well. A water well. In Kuwait. Absurd, silly, and obviously futile. But it was a project. It provided focus and a lot of hard work, and it was a "no hurt." So we provided a shovel and advised only that he not dig too close to the buried rotted food.

From time to time, others would wander by to lend a hand, but few gave this enterprise much chance for success. This was, after all, Kuwait, the desert. If there were any springs around, it could be assumed they would have been discovered decades if not centuries before.

Paul's well hit water on October 15 at a depth of fifteen feet, just about as far as he could go given that a corrugated garage door was being used to shore up the sandy walls. Not a ruptured water main but groundwater, slightly brackish, but clean, safe, and usable, it came in at a respectable two hundred gallons a minute.

Using a jerry-rigged pump and fire hoses, we were able to reconnect the pool showers, heated by plastic pipes coiled over the tin roof, a marked improvement over a tepid sponge bath from a bucket. And we were able to start a garden that ultimately provided fresh vegetables and green salads of a sort, divine after weeks of canned food, most notably tuna fish. With the well we also replenished the pool and were able to flush toilets (using buckets of water) and do laundry.

The well also did something far more important. It gave all of us the sense that we could outlast the Iraqis after all. We were back in control. Objectively, little had changed. We were still, miserably, without any electricity or other basics. Our food supply was finite, as was the fuel for our generator, our true Achilles heel. And, although we did not know it, we still had a long way to go. The well came in in mid-October, less than halfway through the siege.

The objective facts did not matter. Before the showers were connected, before the garden was planted, before anything practical was done with our new treasure, we washed the cars—the derelict, rotting cars stranded with us on the compound, cannibalized for any number of nonautomotive purposes and nowhere to go, ever. In bathing suits and muddy feet, we washed the cars under the noses of our Iraqi minders, gleefully squandering that which is most valued in the Middle East. It was a declaration of nondependence.[10]

We made it through Halloween and a costume party with a heavy emphasis on the creative use of found art. We made it through Thanksgiving with a strong sense of fellowship and a Thanksgiving service for Jew and Muslim, Catholic and Protestant, believer and nonbeliever. We made plans for Christmas, and for New Year's.

Hostages R Us

As the weeks went by, there emerged a gallows-humor idea that we all had a future on The Outside as professional hostages. We had finally figured out how to do this and, rather than have some poor amateurs struggle through what we went through, we would simply rent ourselves out to the next crisis—"Hostages R Us." As bizarre as that sounds, there was truth to it. We had figured out how to make the best of our situation, and it seemed a shame to let all that hard-won experience go to waste.

Siesta time, between lunch and our afternoon "séance" with Washington, with the high heat of the day still on us, the compound is stone quiet—except for the frantic, increasingly plaintive cries for help coming from beyond the walls of the compound.

In late November, for reasons known only to God and Saddam, the Iraqi Mukhabarat asked what we on the compound needed. After listing the obvious—water, electricity, and freedom—we then asked for nonessentials—fruit, vegetables, soda, and cigarettes. This was partly tactical—we did not want to ask for anything that would lead the Iraqis to believe we were desperate; but it was also partly pragmatic—without electricity and with dwindling cooking fuel, we could neither store nor prepare meat, eggs, butter, and the like. It also never occurred to us that anything would come of the conversation.

At one o'clock that afternoon a Chevy Caprice, white and probably stolen, pulled up to the embassy's pedestrian gate. In its trunk were bags of bruised apples, oranges, and cucumbers, and a case of Iraqi cigarettes. In the excitement of unloading these treasures, two of us (one of the Amcits and I) forgot to prop open the security door. The Amcit had not been outside the compound since the siege began and had no way of knowing the door would lock behind us—as it did, locking us out. After months of dreaming about freedom outside the walls, we found ourselves in the surrealistic position of pleading to be let back in! The Iraqi secret police, showing uncharacteristic grace, refrained from commenting on the absurdity of the situation.

The Pepsis were delivered the next day.

THE OTHER COALITION

In John le Carré's Russia House *there's a line that goes something like this: Heroic deeds are ordinary men simply doing the decent thing.*

From the first days of the Iraqi invasion of Kuwait until the end of Desert Storm, there was a coalition of coalitions that organized to defeat Iraqi brutality against Kuwait. There was, first, the unprecedented array of military might in the Saudi desert, armies of upward of thirty nations, under the command of General Norman Schwarzkopf. There was the diplomatic coalition, crafted by Secretary of State James Baker and U.S. Ambassador to the United Nations Thomas Pickering, that reflected the international outrage and opposition to the invasion and gave legitimacy to the Desert Shield/Desert Storm response.

But there was also a third coalition, less mighty, less organized, less publicized, but equally dedicated and international. Those caught in Kuwait on the morning of August 2 confronted in the most direct way the dilemma of how to respond to the invasion—not the strategic or legal issues, but the moral and personal ones.

Simply surviving was not the point for those of us within the embassy. The point was to help our citizens on the outside. Saddam's decision in early September to cease using women and children as human shields allowed us, at last, to start evacuating our community on the outside. Using the reconnected phone lines and the computer program for tracking citizens, we launched twelve flights over a two-month period that evacuated all American women and children and their family members who wanted to leave.[11] (The thirteenth flight was in December 1990, when the remaining "human shields" went home.)

Despite our constraints, we were the only embassy able to mount evacuation flights. In addition to the U.S. citizens and family members, nearly a thousand nationals from thirty countries were flown to safety on our planes—an early thank-you to our Desert Storm coalition partners.

But just as we could not have maintained the embassy alone, we could not have accomplished this air evacuation alone. Trapped within the embassy compound, we could not handle the on-ground logistics of such flights. Some of the planes chartered were 747s with almost five hundred seats; some weeks we would run several separate flights using smaller planes.

It was at this point that Canadian Chargé Bill Bowden, similarly trapped within his embassy, offered the services of his community, trapped in an Iraqi-imposed limbo. While not subject to detention as human shields, the Canadians and some other Westerners were not permitted to leave Kuwait or Iraq. Rather than hunker down and wait out the invasion, these men, at first individually and then with increasing organization and structure, became our foot soldiers on the outside. Enduring searing heat well over 100 degrees, they worked long hours organizing the several hundred frightened and confused evacuees for the flights home and ran interference with the Iraqi soldiers who inevitably showed up to throw spanners into the works. These Canadians made our twelve flights work.

Beginning in mid-September when women and children were allowed to leave, we made sure they did; but adult American men remained under threat of detention. Those who escaped being picked up in the early weeks of August went into deep hiding around Kuwait. They gathered in small groups, laid in supplies, and prepared themselves to wait it out. But few anticipated living that way for months on end.

The role of the International Wardens, as the collection of Canadians, Australians, New Zealanders, Irish, Danes, and others ultimately styled themselves, was to keep these men physically alive and mentally together. Working in close coordination with the embassy, the wardens organized food runs and an underground mail system, found doctors willing to pay clandestine house calls, and established and distributed a highly satirical bootleg newspaper. Those in vulnerable locations were moved to safe houses, often provided by Kuwaitis.

For the wardens it meant eighteen-hour days and seven-day weeks for an indefinite period of time. It demanded a sense of operational security and discretion of the highest order. Food runs, mail runs, and phone calls could not compromise the location of those in hiding.

To help break the crushing sense of isolation, the embassy and the State Department communications network were used to pass messages between these men in deep hiding and home. Those on the compound spent hours phoning out messages and transcribing messages to be sent home.[12] One man sent the loveliest, corniest poems to his wife every week for four months. Voice of America, breaking its tradition of serving only foreign audiences, began "Postcards from Home"—taped messages from family members broadcast to Iraq and Kuwait repeatedly throughout the day on various VOA frequencies. As was only right, this system was shared with our European friends who were doing so much for our men. It was the least we could do in return.

There were no shades of gray in Kuwait. Everything was in stark black and white. One Irish warden, explaining later why he had done what he did, said simply that he got mad. He could not allow Iraqi atrocities and cruelty to go unchallenged, whatever the cost to himself. Another warden, a Kiwi, given the opportunity to leave early, refused, believing that his responsibility to those in deep hiding outweighed other commitments, including those to his own family safe at home in New Zealand. The private citizens on the embassy compound, too, rose above their anxiety for their own perilous situation to work for those on the outside and to support each other.

AND THEN, IT WAS OVER

A wish for which most dared not pray at that ecumenical Thanksgiving Day service was answered on December 6, when Saddam revised his "travel restrictions" on foreigners, thus ending the human shield and deep-hiding ordeals for the Americans and the others in Kuwait and in Iraq. The last U.S. evacuation flight, the thirteenth, left Kuwait City on Sunday, December 9, 1990.

Men in deep hiding had to be contacted and reassured that the release was genuine and not some cruel hoax by Saddam to flush them out. Transportation to the airport had to be arranged. Again, the wardens were instrumental in reaching all the Americans in deep hiding. The wardens' commitment was such that few were able to make their own arrangements to take the flight.[13]

With those who had been in deep hiding went the nineteen private citizens who had shared our compound with us and three of our own. After months of assuring the private citizens that we would not abandon them to the Iraqis, when it came time for them to leave on December 9, many of them balked at the prospect of leaving five of us behind.

With all the U.S. citizens who wished to leave Kuwait now on their way home, and with the full force of Desert Shield about to be unleashed (as Desert Storm) on the Iraqis, the twin missions of the embassy had been fulfilled.[14] The last five remaining U.S. embassy staff closed the compound and left for home on December 13, 1990.[15] We left with the flag still flying over the compound, where it remained until the city was liberated ten weeks later.

LOOKING BACK OVER TIME

A Few Factors in Our Favor

• The Iraqis, for all their threats, saw merit in not moving against the embassy with force. We were utterly defenseless, except for the promise of retaliation that was building as Desert Shield.

• The compound was large enough that we could to some degree avoid a stifling claustrophobia. You could not go far, but you could find your own quiet, private corner.

• At the same time, there was remarkable tolerance and mutual support, for the most part and at most times. No one needed to feel totally cut off, abandoned, or alone. With very few exceptions, we understood there was no margin for selfishness.

Lessons Learned, Lessons Shared

• Order is essential. It need not, should not, be some mindless reproduction of a traditional embassy staffing pattern; but roles, responsibilities, functions, and purpose, once agreed upon, need to be maintained. This is not a call for dictatorial powers but for real leadership.

• At the same time, the society within the embassy must be as classless as possible, based on a new meritocracy. Relative position, status, and wealth on the outside are of little importance compared to talents, contributions, and efforts within.

• It is vital that there be no walls between the official embassy personnel and the private American citizens. In Kuwait a strong sense of shared dependency and shared support forged the necessary partnership.

• Life need not be unremittingly serious. One of us was a natural social director. Early on he organized a talent night (we discovered we had none), then a Halloween costume party, tennis tournaments, and a host of other silly diversions. Another took on the most dangerous and thankless job of all—he became the resident Siskel and Ebert for our one luxury, a nightly video powered by our baby generator. (As Dr. Sidney said on *M*A*S*H*, "Anger turned inward is depression; anger turned sideways is Hawkeye.")

• There should be a free exchange of information, and as consultative a decision-making process as possible. This was particularly true in the first three weeks of our siege—before the convoy—when rumors were rampant and insidious. It was important in keeping information flowing and rumors under control within the confines of the embassy, both before and during the siege. It was equally important in maintaining the embassy's accessibility and its credibility with its community—and with others, as became the case in Kuwait.

• The importance of the embassy's role as a community manager should not be underestimated. In Kuwait, the U.S. embassy played a critical role as both a symbolic and a practical pole for the captive community outside. This role was thrust on all embassies in the beginning, ex officio, with some able to assume the role more effectively than others. Ultimately, in the words of a warden leader, the U.S. embassy became the only effective "pole." (This same warden gives due credit to the British embassy for the symbolic role it played throughout, but concedes it was "shamelessly lacking as a practical pole.")

• When it is all over, and while it is still fresh in everyone's mind, "after-action reports" or "lessons learned" or other such debriefings should be required. Every situation is unique, but some truths are transferable. That is, after all, the raison d'être of this book. There were, alas, no debriefings of the Embassy Kuwait personnel—ever. A few memoranda were produced by support players in Washington with no reference to or consultation with those who had been on the spot in Kuwait.

• We found the real-world value of crisis management exercises marginal. CMEs conducted at embassies around the world by State Department contractors at considerable expense to the U.S. taxpayer were designed to train embassy personnel on how to manage a range of crises. At best, they offered useful insight into staff members and embassy leadership and who would work well in a real crisis. In late 1994, CMEs were in abeyance; retoooling efforts were under way, perhaps to result in a more relevant approach.

• Emergency action plans (EAPs), the bibles for posts in crisis, present at best an outline of the optimum. To borrow from General Eisenhower, the value of a plan is in the planning. As anyone who has been in a crisis knows, the first thing in the shredder is the EAP. Work is distributed according to expertise, to be sure, but also according to common sense, judgment, and ability, emotional as well as substantive. Formal staffing patterns sometimes fit and sometimes don't. If it is a choice between bruised egos and dead people, there should be no question.

At the Department—A Single Voice

State Department support was critical on a number of fronts: freezing credit card accounts, notifying mortgage companies, intercepting mail, and especially stabilizing points of contact between the State Department and family members and friends. By dealing with the same people, our families and friends developed a sense of confidence and trust. It made the department human to those important to us—and perhaps made us human to some in the department.

Restricting the channel of communications was most critical. The embassy had a finite and inadequate amount of fuel with which to run our communications generator. As a result, we were able to power up only three hours a day for the first few months, and only nine hours a week for the last six weeks. We would have run out of communications fuel around Christmas Eve. Communications thus had to be sharp and concise, focused and unduplicated.

For virtually the entire time there was one voice and only one voice on each end of the line between the State Department and the embassy. In the beginning, Ambassador Ryan Crocker was the point of contact; at the end, Ambassadors Mary Ryan and Mark Johnson. Clearly there had to be backups, but even they were constant and known. Whoever is to be the department's point of contact should be already known to the post and to the person on the embassy end of the phone. The middle of a crisis is not the time to be building confidence and trust.

Such a requirement for restricted communication demands tough discipline on the part of the department. There is a natural urge for superiors to involve themselves, and for myriad bureaus and offices to demand what they consider their fair share of access. That this was effectively resisted in this case was a lifesaver.

Drawing Down vs. Going Under

The size and certainly the composition of any presence left behind in a drawdown, even one less dramatic than this one, should be deferred to the embassy—the ambassador, the chargé, the DCM. Once the department has defined the fundamental purpose and goals of the residual embassy, the chief of mission will (or should) know who can perform the essential functions and how many it would take to do so. If the mission cannot be accomplished with the prescribed numbers, the department and the embassy should either adjust the numbers up or adjust the mission down. The core staff should not be left in an untenable position; too small a staff to accomplish what is required imperils not only the mission but the staff's personal safety as well.

The State Department, in the course of the discussions on the size of the core group, cut our numbers from fifteen to eight. Had we not had the private citizens with us, and had they not had both the right talents and the proper attitude, we could not have stayed as long as we did nor have accomplished what we did. There would not have been thirteen evacuation flights that rescued not only the American community but many nationals of other countries as well. There may not have been a focal point for the support and supply efforts undertaken by those on the outside for the American men in deep hiding. And the flag would not have flown over that compound throughout Desert Shield and Desert Storm.

CRASH LANDING—ONE LAST LESSON

During one of many late-night conversations in Kuwait, about the time we realized we had not only learned to cope, but had adapted to our new lives, the obverse confronted us. If we had adapted so well to this new world of ours, would we be able to readapt to our old worlds? If this was now normal and "real," how would we handle the world we left behind?

Here, then, is one more major lesson. For those at ground zero, a crisis of whatever shape will continue well beyond its formal resolution. That is a fact that must be dealt with.

The siege of embassy Kuwait did not end with the last evacuation flight on December 9, 1990. Nor did it end at 9:20 A.M. on Thursday, December 13, with the last of us walking out the compound gate and onto the Iraqi bus for our ride to the airport. Nor did it end with our arrival the next day at Andrews Air Force Base in Washington, D.C. The siege of Embassy Kuwait did not just stop for those—both embassy staff and private citizens—who had spent four and a half months together on that small compound.

Against the advice of a number of people at the National Security Council and the State Department, and perhaps elsewhere, someone somewhere decided to bring the Embassy Kuwait hostages straight back to the United States. There was no Wiesbaden AFB,[16] no transition out of the world to which we had adapted, no easing out of the sensory deprivation. There were no physical examinations, nor personal counseling sessions for us or for our families. (The last five out did have an hour-long breakfast at Frankfurt Airport on Friday morning with a State Department psychiatrist, but that hardly counts.)

There was no time or place for a transition from the community that had become our world back to our families, our friends, and our jobs. There was no opportunity for those of us who had become friends, who had become dependent upon each other, who had become nearly family, to say goodbye. There was no time for what the professionals call "closure." There was no effort to help us answer the question that had so troubled us: Would we be able to readjust to our old worlds? There was no apparent interest even in the existence of such a question, nor any now in what the answer might have been.

There has never been an explanation for that decision. Perhaps it was because we were not, by some accounts, "hostages," or had not, quite candidly, gone through an experience comparable to that of our colleagues in Tehran a decade before or to that of the men held so long in Beirut. Perhaps it was out of a compassionate desire to get us all home to our families as quickly as possible, something we all wanted very much. There were any number of positive motivations.

Whatever the reasons, the decision was wrong. Anyone caught up in a prolonged crisis, whether an official or a private citizen, should be not only afforded but required to go through the sort of decompression and professional assistance Wiesbaden has come to represent. The euphoria of release is heady, and some may resist, but decompression should not be waived. Terry Anderson, when released by his captors in December 1992 and flown to Wiesbaden, apparently chafed at the confinement of a military hospital and said in his early public statements that he was anxious to get on with his life. In another public statement a few days later, while jogging at dawn, he conceded that he needed the transition time. This lesson must be learned and remembered.

We arrived at Andrews at 4:00 p.m. on a Friday afternoon—just in time for the evening news.

Ambassador Peter Jon de Vos welcomes Brig. Gen. Granville R. Amos to Embassy Monrovia, along with a few hundred Marines under his command, as civil war engulfs Liberia's capital in early August 1990. *State Magazine*

9 | Evacuation During Civil War, Liberia, 1990

Dennis C. Jett

When the news of the rebel attack on the border post at Butuo first reached Monrovia the day after Christmas 1989, it was initially considered an insignificant and probably isolated event. Several men with guns had crossed into Liberia from Côte d'Ivoire and shot things up. A couple of customs officials were killed, or perhaps they were just missing. Reports were sketchy, and such stories always became more dramatic each time they were retold as they traveled by word of mouth from up-country. There was no reason to think that this was any more serious than previous incidents.

While no one realized it at the time, the attack at Butuo marked the beginning of a protracted civil war that engulfed Liberia for years to come. It affected everyone in the country and left tens of thousands of Liberians dead. The vast majority of those who died were innocent noncombatants, and the killing may not yet be finished.

It also permanently changed U.S. interests and representation in Liberia. When the war finally reached Monrovia, the effect on the American embassy was swift and dramatic. The official community shrank by 95 percent in just a few weeks, then months later swelled by two hundred or so in minutes, as Marines landed by helicopter and fanned out to protect the compound. It was the only embassy, and virtually the only institution of any kind, that operated continuously throughout the war.

It was an embassy in the midst of a sustained, long-term crisis, and some of what it experienced may hold lessons that could be applied elsewhere. To understand what happened—and to assess its possible relevance in a future crisis situation—requires an explanation starting at the beginning and briefly recapping Liberian history.

THE ROOTS OF THE CRISIS

Liberia was founded by the descendants of freed American slaves who first landed in the Monrovia area in 1822. While their numbers were greatly diminished by tropical diseases and conflict with the natives, some of the settlers nevertheless hung on and declared Liberia's independence in 1847. They were known as Americo-Liberians, and they set up a replica of the only society they knew, only this time they were the privileged class. Although they never numbered more than 5 percent of Liberia's population, the Americos controlled the country. The government was handed down from one Americo president to another. Under this system, "indigenous" Liberians had virtually no chance of success in politics or business unless they were adopted by an Americo family.

Americo domination continued until 1980, when a master sergeant named Samuel Doe and sixteen other noncommissioned officers, including Thomas Quiwonkpa, seized power. They did it by sneaking into the Executive Mansion late one night and killing twenty-six people—including President Tolbert, who was still in his pajamas when he died. There was dancing in the streets the next day as many people welcomed Tolbert's demise and the end of a century and a half of Americo-Liberian rule.

The non-Americo majority, after so many years of second-class citizenship, were glad to see one of their own take over. The fact that he was a sergeant with at best a high school education was lost amid the inflated expectations and sense of liberation. Besides, there were early promises of a rapid return to civilian rule and true democracy. Hopes were high, and U.S. aid increased to help the economy develop and the military become more professional. While Monrovia was tense for a time and the army uncontrolled, the situation stabilized in short order—not however, before Doe had ordered most of Tolbert's cabinet tied to telephone poles and shot. The festive atmosphere of the executions, performed before crowds of onlookers and invited journalists, was marred somewhat by the drunken firing squad's needing several volleys to finish the job.

By 1985 the early promises remained unfulfilled, the election was stolen, and most hopes had been dashed. Doe's remaining popularity was limited mostly to his fellow Krahn tribesmen and to those few who took advantage of the pervasive corruption of his government. With such narrow support, the country was ready for another coup, and those Americos in exile who hated Doe for ending their privileged status were ready to back one.

It came in the person of Doe's former colleague Thomas Quiwonkpa, who returned from exile and launched a rebellion that took over most of Monrovia. The revolt was declared a success on the radio and people poured into the streets to celebrate.

While many people "jubilated" in response to Doe's supposed downfall, Quiwonkpa and his men rushed about trying to consolidate their victory. They knew the informal rules for a successful overthrow dictate that the rebels have to take the airport, the radio station, and the presidential mansion before they are considered the winners. But the mansion was still held by Doe and some of his men.

Using a hand-held radio, Doe went up to the roof and called in reinforcements from a base forty kilometers away. Doe's radio call, relayed by a repeater the rebels had neglected to knock out, quickly brought help from loyal troops. They ended the coup attempt before it had done anything more than spark the spontaneous and premature victory celebration.

The local television station had videotaped the revelers for that evening's news. Doe's men carefully reviewed the tapes, and those revelers who could be identified were picked up and reportedly executed. In addition, Doe's soldiers went on a rampage in Nimba County, since that was the home of Quiwonkpa's ethnic group, the Gios. Within a few weeks, however, life was back to normal, except for those who had lost it and those who waited for the chance to avenge them.

There was much to avenge. For despite the military aid the United States had poured in, the Armed Forces of Liberia (AFL) were best known for lack of discipline and for extorting money from those who passed through the numerous checkpoints around the country. To ensure the army's support, Doe had seen to it that promotions were based on tribe and loyalty to him rather than competence. Attempts to improve the quality of the army therefore only provided a thin veneer of professionalism.

When the AFL went north in response to the 1989 attack at Butuo, they were returning to Nimba County, where the loyalty of the local population remained suspect. Not surprisingly, reports of attacks on civilians quickly started to filter back. The traditional rivalry between Doe's Krahn tribe and Quiwonkpa's Gios and the legacy of the failed coup of 1985 thus contributed to the cycle of violence unleashed in early 1990.

The war grew very slowly at first, in fits and starts. Rebels would make a major advance and then seemingly melt back into the bush with another lull in the action. They would eventually reappear and each time bring more territory under their control. Army reinforcements would be dispatched, but the only result was new reports of attacks on innocent villagers by the soldiers.

While the initial incident was hundreds of kilometers away, a much more proximate threat to Doe's regime also emerged—other rebels had been infiltrated into Monrovia. But before they could regroup, they were captured and paraded before the press. They described in detail how they had been trained in Libya and commanded by someone named Charles Taylor. They called themselves the National Patriotic Front of Liberia (NPFL), and their goal was simple—to overthrow Doe.

Even though any fighting was still far to the east in Nimba, the fear of rebel operations in the capital caused the level of tension to rise immediately. New checkpoints began to appear, and bodies started turning up all over town. At the Omega station, a navigation beacon funded by the U.S. Coast Guard, a Liberian employee was found dead. He had not been a political activist of any kind. He was, however, a Gio.

Another ethnic dimension to the war soon emerged with the entry into the conflict of the Mandingos, a Muslim tribe residing in both Liberia and Guinea. Many Mandingos were successful small merchants, and they were believed to have remained loyal to Doe throughout the 1985 coup. Whether it was the identification with Doe's regime or their traditional animosity with the Gios, reports from the front indicated the rebels were killing anyone associated with the government and all Krahns and Mandingos. As the war came closer to Monrovia, the Mandingos decided to depart en masse for Freetown, Sierra Leone. The next day Monrovia's streets, normally jammed with taxis and trucks, were virtually empty as the Mandingo drivers used their vehicles to escape.

Despite the growing rebel gains, Doe remained confident and determined. He repeatedly tried to reassure his supporters that the insurgents were on the run. One police official, apparently unconvinced, invested in a new bulletproofing potion. After several beers, he handed his revolver to a colleague and insisted the potion would protect him. It failed the test, and the officer became a victim of the war without ever having been close to it.

In a press conference, Doe demanded the rebels surrender and set a deadline for them to do so. He suggested they turn themselves in at several sites, including a town already under rebel control. Though he refused to step down, Doe attempted to be conciliatory by saying he would not run for reelection. At the same time, however, he also urged all citizens to take up arms against the rebels.

Doe's speech did nothing to diminish the fighting up-country and only caused greater attacks on civilians in Monrovia. People all over Monrovia who had reason to fear they would be considered rebel supporters sought shelter by moving onto any diplomatic compound or into any church or school that would take them. One night, men in military uniforms dragged two dozen Gios from the grounds of the U.N. Development Programme offices, took them to a nearby beach, and executed them. The next day, the government denied that the "men in military uniforms" were soldiers and blamed the rebels. One man, however, who had only been wounded in the attack, crawled two miles down the beach to a missionary hospital. He identified the killers as soldiers from the Executive Mansion guard. The United Nations evacuated its entire staff that day.

THE WAR REACHES THE CAPITAL

By the end of April 1990, the rebels were within a two-hour drive of Monrovia, and the international airport, an hour out of town, was next in their line of advance. After numerous consultations with Washington and among the members of the embassy's emergency action committee, the embassy requested to go to "authorized departure status." This meant that any employee or dependent who wanted to evacuate would be returned to the United States at government expense and maintained there for the duration of the crisis.

With the Voice of America (VOA) and diplomatic communications relay personnel, Peace Corps volunteers, U.S. Agency for International Development (USAID) and embassy staff, and dependents, the official community numbered over six hundred. Within two weeks only a few dozen essential staff members remained. Most left thinking they would be back in a few weeks, and many welcomed the break from the growing tension. Others wanted to stay, but were convinced they should depart with their children, or that someone else could carry on the most essential work of the embassy.

Those who departed feeling they would soon be back were not just trying to rationalize being separated from those who stayed behind. The experience in 1980 and 1985 suggested that whether coups were successful or not, they ended quickly and conclusively. After a brief period of uncertainty and turmoil, life returned to normal. With the rebels now making steady progress toward the capital, everyone believed the war would not go on for much longer. This optimism was offset by the realization that if Doe decided to fight to the end, his last stand would likely take place at the Executive Mansion, in the heart of downtown Monrovia a mere mile from the embassy.

Flights from the international airport ceased in May as the rebels closed in. The in-town airport and the road to Freetown remained open and many continued to flee, including all but one or two of Doe's cabinet. One departing minister implored an embassy officer to send in the Marines to save Liberia and then excused himself to get on a plane departing for Freetown. As the rebels closed in on the city, water and power supplies were cut off. Eventually, international phone service was also lost when the satellite earth station on the outskirts of town was attacked. Embassy generators began running around the clock, and tank trucks had to run a gauntlet of hostile checkpoints each day to draw water from nearby wells to keep the compound supplied.

By early June the Firestone rubber plantation, a few miles from the international airport, fell to the rebels. One plantation executive, a British citizen married to an American, watched for weeks as the rebels drew closer. Then when the plantation was finally overrun by a mob of unruly rebels, he got on the radio and demanded a Marine helicopter be sent to extract him from their midst. When it was not sent, his wife went on the Cable News Network (CNN) to criticize U.S. policy and the failure to rescue her husband.

With the rebels now only an hour's drive away, the embassy went from a voluntary to an "ordered" departure. This meant that any remaining dependents and all but the most essential employees had to leave the country immediately. With great difficulty, the embassy struggled to draw down staff to an irreducible minimum. What had been an official community of over six hundred, counting dependents and Peace Corps Volunteers, was down to less than fifty.

Partially offsetting these departures, a military planning team and additional security officers were sent in because of the crisis. A task force of four U.S. Navy ships ordered to the area added an advance team of military officers to the embassy total in late May. Within a few days the task force, with 2,500 Marines on board, arrived off the coast and stood by to evacuate U.S. citizens if necessary. Although most private U.S. citizens had departed, a couple of hundred remained. They were about to be left with no way out.

By early July the task force had been on station for over a month, and embassy relations with our military were beginning to fray. The advance team had been brought into the country without the normal formality of informing the local authorities to avoid the inevitable misinterpretations of their mission. The commander of the team, however, suddenly requested permission for his men to wear their uniforms, which could not have gone unnoticed by many Liberians. He also asked that Liberian visas be obtained for himself and his men, although it was never clear why he thought them necessary.

Both requests were turned down, because they would call attention to this new military presence and raise the suspicions of the few officials in Doe's government who had not fled. There was considerable mistrust of American intentions and, at the same time, demands for military aid to help combat the rebels. Both grew as Taylor's forces closed in on the capital.

The team commander then insisted that an underwater survey be performed by a group of frogmen to determine if the evacuation beaches were safe for landing craft, but Washington canceled the exercise before it could take place. Since it would have to have been conducted within sight of the Executive Mansion and the army's main base, an armed confrontation was entirely possible.

Command and control also proved to be a problem. Numerous meetings were held in Washington on rules of engagement and other issues as the possibility of conflict involving U.S. forces and any of the various Liberian combatants became more likely. Seemingly mundane questions, such as what weapons the troops would carry when put ashore, went as far as cabinet level before being decided.

By mid-June, heavy fighting was taking place on the outskirts of Monrovia. Doe's soldiers roamed the capital looting and killing virtually at will. Despite the incident at the U.N. compound, many people continued to camp out at churches, schools, and embassies, hoping their numbers would provide safety from the marauding troops. Before dawn one morning, "men in military uniforms" entered a church holding Gio refugees and killed an estimated six hundred men, women, and children. The bodies remained in the church until October, when the United Nations could finally reach the area safely and organize the burial of what remained.

Despite repeated attempts by the embassy and others to get the government and the rebels to negotiate, the war continued. With virtually all economic activity having ceased, malnutrition became common and widespread starvation likely.

Thomas White, the embassy's economic counselor, and Colonel David Staley, head of the military mission, tried valiantly along with relief workers to keep emergency food supplies flowing from the port to feeding centers throughout the city. Each convoy became more dangerous than the last as the soldiers grew more desperate and aggressive. Finally the growing chaos in the streets made such efforts impossible and food distributions came to a halt.

The embassy's relations with Doe and his government were also deteriorating as fast as the overall climate in the city. The situation rapidly went from serious to bizarre as accusations began to fly that would have been laughable in other circumstances. When rebels fired a rocket-propelled grenade at the mansion from a boat, Doe accused the United States of having attacked his residence with the deck gun of a submarine. He claimed he knew it was an American sub because he saw the U.S. flag flying on it. A few days later, he ordered Colonel Staley out of the country within twenty-four hours, claiming he had been seen leading a rebel attack. Staley left that afternoon on one of the last small charter planes to get out of Monrovia.

In addition to being bizarre, the situation was getting more confused, as Taylor's forces split into two. A small faction led by Prince Johnson began marching on Monrovia, attacking both the AFL and Taylor's men. By mid-July, the capital was totally cut off. Johnson's rebels were only a kilometer north of downtown, in control of the port and astride the road to Sierra Leone. To the east, Taylor's forces were almost as close and had shut down the remaining airport.

With the Atlantic Ocean to the west and south, the embassy staff and everyone else still in Monrovia could only sit and wait for the final battle. Supplies of food, fuel, and water rapidly began to run out all over the city. The embassy had only a few weeks' worth of food and fuel and was collecting rainwater to drink and bathe in.

The streets in front of the embassy became a battleground as Johnson's forces fought the government's AFL troops for each square block of downtown. With their backs to the wall, the AFL finally fought back, but still took the quieter moments to continue looting. The territory under Doe's control shrank to a dozen blocks as the two rebel forces raced to be first to take the mansion.

The situation became stalemated, however, and the decisive battle never came. Prince Johnson, deciding that the war was not getting enough international attention, announced he was going to start taking Americans and other foreigners hostage and seized several. With supplies getting critically low and the embassy now in the part of Monrovia controlled by Johnson, U.S. Ambassador Peter Jon de Vos, who had replaced Ambassador James K. Bishop in late June, decided it was time to call in the Marines.

Early the next morning, the ships of the task force that had been steaming in circles just over the horizon for two months drew closer to shore. Simultaneously, from their decks, helicopters flew off to three sites. The largest group landed 237 combat-ready Marines on what had been the embassy's basketball court, overlooking the sea. They immediately fanned out to defend the compound, and for the first time in weeks there was no small-arms fire to be heard or armed men in view on the streets outside.

The other helicopters descended on two communications relay stations, one several miles to the north, in Johnson's territory, and the other in the suburbs to the east, in the area under Taylor's control. They were on the ground only long enough to quickly extract the eighteen American communications technicians that had been isolated there. At all three locations, these operations were carried out swiftly and without incident.

Not knowing how the AFL would react to seeing the Marines land, de Vos called President Doe on the radio to tell him about the operation a few minutes before it started. Doe initially had no comment, but then called back to offer to send his troops over to assist. Since this would have set off another firefight in front of the embassy with Johnson's troops, the ambassador declined the offer.

The helicopters then began shuttling between the task force and the basketball court. Several hundred Americans and thousands of third-country nationals who had succeeded in reaching the embassy compound were evacuated in the next few days. A week later, these same helicopters evacuated about a hundred expatriates from the port of Buchanan, about one hundred miles down the coast, and took them out to the waiting ships. In addition, the helicopters brought in much-needed food and fuel. For several weeks, they were our only link to the outside world.

On August 24, the Economic Community of West African States (ECOWAS) dispatched a cease-fire monitoring group (ECOMOG), a peacekeeping force made up of soldiers from five West African countries. ECOMOG landed in Monrovia's port and pushed Taylor's people back to the outskirts of town. On September 9, Doe left the Executive Mansion and visited the port, which was under ECOMOG's control but still in territory held by Johnson. A gun battle with Johnson's forces ensued, and Doe was captured. He died the next day from the wounds inflicted before and after his capture.

ECOMOG went on the offensive in October and pushed the NPFL out of rocket and mortar range of Monrovia. A semblance of normality returned, as the port and the in-town airport were then able to resume operations. Militarily, however, the situation became a stalemate that remained unchanged for two years.

In October 1992, Taylor, who had rejected numerous efforts to disarm all the parties and hold elections, decided to attack both ECOMOG and Johnson's remaining forces. His men initially gained ground and came within mortar range of downtown Monrovia. ECOMOG quickly regrouped, however, repulsed Taylor's forces, and, going on the offensive, continued to push him back well beyond the original battle lines. Taylor's October assault destroyed what was left of Johnson's forces, and Johnson left the country.

In the ensuing months, new armed groups joined the fray. One, the United Liberation Movement for Democracy in Liberia (ULIMO), consisting mainly of Krahns and Mandingos, launched an attack on Taylor's NPFL forces and succeeded in capturing a significant part of western Liberia. To the north in Lofa County, the Lofa Defense Force (LDF) sprang up and began cooperating with the NPFL against ULIMO. In the southeast, the Liberian Peace Council (LPC), another Krahn group with links to the AFL, started attacking the NPFL.

As in the past with each new outbreak of fighting among this alphabet soup of guerrilla groups, it was often innocent civilians who suffered. A group of armed men entered a refugee camp near the Firestone plantation the night of June 6,

1993, and killed nearly six hundred men, women, and children. The motive for the attack was unclear, and initially the blame was placed on Taylor's forces. NPFL spokesmen vigorously denied any responsibility. A thorough U.N. investigation subsequently determined that AFL soldiers were responsible. Predictably, senior AFL officers claimed no AFL personnel were involved.

Thus, what had started as a minor border incident at the end of 1989 sparked a full-scale civil war, which continued to devastate the country as this was written in mid-1994. While the level of fighting, some of the players, and the number of guerrilla groups had changed somewhat, the conflict continued to grip the entire country and to spill over into neighboring countries, with lasting peace a distant hope. Of Liberia's 2.5 million people, 700,000 were refugees, and up to a million of those who remained in the country had been forced from their homes.

After a long series of political negotiations, with the assistance of ECOWAS, and a number of failures and false starts, a peace agreement was signed in July 1993 in Cotonou, in Benin. It provided for a cease-fire, which took effect in August 1993, and a 360-person force of U.N. observers, disarmament and demobilization of the combatants, a transitional government (LNTG) composed of the three groups that signed the agreement, and national elections.

The parties subsequently agreed they would seat the LNTG and simultaneously begin disarmament on March 7, 1994, with elections to be held by September 7, 1994. Disarmament began slowly, picked up steam, and then faltered. In the first three months less than 10 percent of the estimated 35,000 combatants had been processed for demobilization. The guns they surrendered made it clear that none were turning in their best weapons. The LNTG was eventually formed, but only after protracted squabbles between the parties over control of the most powerful cabinet positions and the most lucrative government-owned companies.

The cease-fire was not universally observed, however. The Krahn-Mandingo alliance within ULIMO shattered, and the two factions began attacking each other and carrying out ethnic retribution against civilians. The LPC neither signed the Cotonou Accord nor accepted the cease-fire, and it continued to attack the NPFL in several southeastern counties.

Despite these localized conflicts, the agreement did permit humanitarian aid to reach more people than before. As of mid-1994, two-thirds of Liberia's inhabitants require humanitarian assistance. The U.S. government alone had spent $326 million aiding them since the beginning of the war.

The formula called for in the Cotonou Accord—U.N. observers and multinational peacekeepers, disarmament and demobilization of the combatants, and general elections—is not unique to Liberia. "Peacekeeping force" has become a phrase as easily uttered as "multiparty democracy," "human rights," "market economy," and "free and fair elections." For many, however, these are only expressions they think the outside world wants to hear. The political schemes and military maneuvers continue; when those fail, a peacekeeping force can be summoned to provide a respite and time to regroup. The only thing the various Liberian groups have in common is their distrust of one another. In such an environment outside assistance can feed the hungry, but not heal the wounds or instill the political will to achieve lasting peace.

AMERICAN INTERESTS

From the very beginning of the war the embassy had several priorities: to limit human rights abuses by both sides, to encourage a cease-fire and negotiated settlement, and to protect U.S. citizens and U.S. government facilities. Given the ethnic hatred and brutality that had been unleashed, little could be done toward achieving the first two goals without introducing outside forces to try to separate the combatants. When U.S. forces were finally used, it was strictly to achieve the third goal.

Despite public statements by the embassy and the State Department explaining this limited mission, many Liberians hoped and believed the Marines would be used to bring an end to the fighting. Given the historical linkages between the two countries, they felt the United States had an obligation to intervene and stop the civil war, even though no one could agree on a political solution that would address the war's causes.

But the embassy was able to do little more than appeal for an end to the killing and a beginning of dialogue. Such efforts had little effect. Soon after the very first reports of attacks on innocent villagers in early January 1990, the embassy issued a statement of concern about civilian casualties. Ambassador Bishop issued a second statement a few days later noting the AFL's lack of discipline, but neither pronouncement did anything other than irritate the government.

The rebels had just as little concern for human rights considerations as did the government. Charles Taylor began his uprising with a small group trained in Libya. His forces quickly grew as many, mainly Gios, joined to help bring down Doe. As the number of men under arms increased, any suggestion of discipline disappeared. Many of the insurgents would go into battle wearing women's dresses and underwear and other paraphernalia such as goggles and wigs. The air of insanity they affected may have succeeded in unnerving their enemies, but did nothing to add to their discipline.

The group led by Prince Johnson that split from the NPFL was more orderly, but equally vicious. Johnson's numbers never got very large, and his method of discipline was simple. If he found one of his men disobeying orders, he usually killed him on the spot. He was as ruthless with noncombatants as the others. He once arrested and handcuffed together a French relief official and a Liberian Red Cross worker. Accusing them before a crowd of onlookers of making a profit on the sale of relief rice, he shot the Liberian several times, killing him.

This lack of discipline and training made for forces that were rarely effective when faced with any serious opposition. Ethnic hatred therefore became a means to encourage the men to fight, with the result that civilians quickly became the targets of choice and any considerations of human rights the first victims. Civilians were easy objects on which to take out revenge, and they did not shoot back.

Thus our words urging respect for human rights did little to lessen the brutality on which both the government and the rebel forces relied. Taylor's forces set up checkpoints to screen the streams of people fleeing the fighting in Monrovia. Any man, woman, or child believed to be Krahn, Mandingo, in the army, or in the government was frequently executed immediately. At these killing fields the bodies were generally left where they fell. Spent cartridges, bones, and bits of clothing littered the ground for many months afterward. The AFL roamed the ever-shrinking territory under their control and dealt the same way with whomever they suspected of supporting Taylor.

Attempts to encourage a political settlement were equally fruitless. Taylor was intent on taking power and saw things going his way. Doe could not accept the possibility that he could lose power. He argued, in the face of all evidence to the contrary, that once the rebels were near Monrovia they would have to cease their guerrilla tactics and come out in the open. His forces would then, he confidently predicted, engage them and defeat them. Any attempt to suggest he was losing was brushed aside. His only response would be to sweep the streets of Monrovia for more young Krahns and other loyalists who could be given a gun and added to the ranks of his ragged army.

There were attempts at negotiations. Talks were begun in Freetown, and efforts made to begin them in Washington. Both sides saw it only as an opportunity to negotiate their way to victory, and little was accomplished. Given the failure of any political process to resolve the conflict, there was some debate as to what could have been done, including whether the U.S. government should have urged Doe to step down. For a number of weeks, the embassy had air transportation standing by and a country that had agreed to accept him in the event he decided to flee. We never directly urged him to go, however, although the offer to get him out was made on more than one occasion.

Some argued that Doe would have gone if the United States had pressured him to leave, and had found someone he respected to deliver a blunt message that his situation was hopeless. But his faith in his own military abilities and judgment never appeared to waver. In any event, the policy was that we would not urge him to go; this would have made the United States responsible for what resulted, and the alternatives at the time were leaders of no higher quality. What his followers, who remained trapped in Monrovia, would have done if he had fled and what would have happened to them when the rebels took over were also scenarios not pleasant to contemplate.

American efforts to protect American lives were largely successful, but not totally. As the conflict heated up, the embassy issued travel advisories that covered more and more of the country and became increasingly emphatic as time went on. A series of community meetings were held both in Monrovia and wherever embassy officers traveled up-country to brief groups of Americans on the situation. Americans were assisted in departing as commercial flights filled up.

143

When scheduled flights ceased, the embassy arranged for charter flights to take people out.

Some Americans ignored the embassy's warnings, however. An American missionary just back from leave early in the war insisted on returning to his home in Nimba County, where he had lived for decades. He and his British wife were killed a few days later in a rebel ambush.

An American aircraft mechanic driving home from a bar in Monrovia late one evening passed a checkpoint that had not been there a few hours earlier. When he failed to obey a stop sign propped up on a tree by the side of the road, soldiers fired at his car. Although only hit in the leg, he died on the operating table the next day.

Another missionary who stayed to protect church property in Monrovia was hit by a ricocheting bullet when soldiers tried to shoot the lock off the gate to his compound so they could loot the place. He died a few hours later from shock and loss of blood.

After the resurgence in fighting in October 1992, five American nuns were killed by the rebels. The nuns had left when the war was at its worst, but had returned to conduct relief efforts. Though Taylor denied all responsibility for the murders, eyewitnesses clearly identified his forces as the killers.

When the Marines came ashore, the number of official Americans stood at fifty-eight. Forty were at the embassy compound downtown. Fifteen others were evacuated by helicopter from a communications site in an area controlled by Johnson, and three were lifted from a communications site in an area controlled by Taylor.

The nonofficial American community had shrunk from several thousand to an estimated three hundred persons. Estimating how many were left at any given time was essential for evacuation planning, but impossible to do accurately. Some, but by no means all, Americans will register at the embassy when they arrive in a country. Precise information about who has left is much harder to obtain and usually secondhand, unless they were on a charter flight arranged by the embassy.

Deciding who would be assisted in leaving, or evacuated when it came to that, was also not straightforward. As the community shrank, many of the Americans left were infants born to Liberian mothers visiting the United States. With only one infant American citizen among an extended family of Liberians, one of the more difficult decisions was how many Liberian family members in addition to the infant American the embassy had a responsibility to evacuate. In the end, it was decided that each minor American citizen could be accompanied by one adult. If the American was an adult, he or she could be accompanied by both spouse and children, regardless of nationality.

There were thousands of third-country nationals in the capital whose governments had asked for evacuation in the event U.S. forces came ashore. Another dilemma was who would be taken out by Marine helicopter and who would not. After much discussion, it was decided that any citizen of another country who made it to the embassy compound would be lifted out by helicopter to the ships offshore. Over 2,500 were eventually taken out, of whom fewer than 10 percent were Americans.

There was continuing debate over whether to keep the embassy open at all. Those in favor of closing it said the risk to our personnel was too great and we should write off what was left of official property not already destroyed or looted.

Keeping the embassy open made it possible for relief efforts to continue longer and resume much sooner once the worst of the fighting was over. As a result, many Liberians survived the war who otherwise would not have. That the embassy was able to keep functioning was due not only to the dedication of its reduced staff, but also to the efforts of thousands of sailors and Marines.

Efforts to protect official U.S. property were of limited success. The embassy compound and the staff housing in the immediate neighborhood stayed largely intact, but the farther away something was from the compound the more likely it was to be looted. The VOA relay complex, the offices for the Peace Corps, USAID, and the U.S. Information Service (USIS), and a large number of embassy houses were looted. Even those left untouched were damaged by mildew as dehumidifiers went for months without electricity. Although instructions were given on several occasions to bring any sensitive documents or valuables to the embassy compound, classified material was found in the ruins of both the USAID and USIS offices and money was taken from both. A stack of blank forms that could have been exchanged for plane tickets was recovered from what was left of the Peace Corps offices.

LESSONS FROM MONROVIA

What are the lessons to be learned from the Monrovia experience? There are some that cannot or should not be very instructive. The Liberian crisis took months to develop fully. It kept several ships and thousands of sailors and Marines committed for months. Most crises are not so likely to take the pace of a slow-motion train wreck. With a downsized, post–Cold War military likely to be committed elsewhere, one cannot always count on having a small armada readily at hand.

Some conclusions can be drawn, however, that might be of use in future situations:

- *You can never do too much contingency planning, and no matter how much you do, things will always develop in unexpected ways.* Plans should be flexible and alternative scenarios considered. They should be worked out and reviewed frequently with all of the official community and with as much of the unofficial community and as many of the other embassies as possible and practical.
- *History never repeats itself.* Using past coup attempts as a guide, everyone thought, or at least hoped, that this one would be quick and decisive. It was neither. It is easy to learn from the past; it is harder not to be trapped by it. We

145

thought that the men at the two outlying communications sites would be able to keep functioning and that the coup would pass them by as it continued down the road to Monrovia. We did not foresee the battle becoming protracted, and their situation soon became untenable and dangerous. When the Marines landed on the embassy compound on August 5, they simultaneously had to extract the remaining personnel from these two communications sites.

• *There will always be at least one American citizen who did not get the message that the embassy said it was time to leave, or who was unhappy with the arrangements after doing so*. That person (or a close relative) will be the one interviewed by the media. To lessen that possibility, warden systems and other means of contacting private U.S. citizens have to be constantly updated and exercised.

• *The host government will never like some elements of U.S. policy, but on the other hand, neither will the government's opponents*. Both will see ulterior motives where our goals seem straightforward to us. Each time we changed the travel advisory to warn U.S. citizens of the worsening situation, the Foreign Ministry complained. In one meeting three Foreign Ministry officials accused the embassy of exaggerating the seriousness of the situation in one breath and of abandoning Liberia in the next. Of the three, one was killed by rebels a few weeks later. About the same time, the wife of one of the other two officials was killed by Doe's soldiers for being an Americo.

• *When communications with Washington are needed the most, they will fail*. Our cable communications worked consistently, but voice is vital in a crisis situation when time is essential. Our phone service depended on the local phone company, which had its earth station well out of town. When that fell to the rebels, we were not entirely cut off, but frequently felt like it. One tactical satellite phone link was an exercise in frustration reminiscent of a scene from the old television spy comedy *Get Smart*. A commercial satellite telephone we finally obtained was great, but incredibly expensive and frequently broken. Repairs or replacements took forever and there were no user-serviceable parts.

• *Communications systems for reaching the unofficial community will also fail or be compromised when needed the most*. Telephone service within the city, which was sporadic even before the war, often failed during the worst periods. Embassy radio networks were compromised quickly, as soldiers and rebels alike rarely pass up the opportunity to seize and use a radio. Only depleted batteries saved us from many a tirade by an angry combatant. Listening to radio chatter from different points in the city was a source of information as well as anxiety. It was a "party line" to which many had access. Conversations included a discussion of whether to burn down the church with the six hundred bodies in it, as a way of dealing with the health threat created by the remains, and many calls for help from people who could not be reached.

• *The only communications systems in overabundance will be those of the military, and it will be difficult to track those and to know who is reporting what to whom*. It is essential to try to coordinate, or at least be aware of, what is being reported. Nothing brings the bureaucracy in Washington to a halt more quickly than the befuddlement that arises from conflicting information from the scene of a crisis. No two observers will provide identical impressions, and the advocates of inaction, of whom there will always be some, will exploit the inconsistencies.

• *Whatever is most vital will run out first.* Because, in the best of times, Monrovia's municipal services were poor to nonexistent, the embassy had a well-developed ability to be self-sufficient, at least for a time. We were able to supply our own water, food, fuel, and electricity, because we were able to accumulate and store quantities of what was needed. This nevertheless required some amazing and courageous feats by our administrative and security personnel. Our biggest limiting factor was water. In order to gather rainwater for drinking and washing, a catchment system to collect runoff from rooftops was constructed that Rube Goldberg would have been proud of. Our doctor had extended discussions with Washington about the health implications of bathing in unclean water and decided that, on balance, it was safer than doing nothing at all.

• *While the embassy and Washington will be talking about the same crisis, they won't see it the same way.* With today's means of communications, Washington responds to CNN at least as much as to embassy reporting. If CNN is not carrying your story, this could translate to a lack of urgency on the other end. If CNN is reporting it heavily, though, Washington will seem far more concerned than the embassy.

• *But being on the ground is not necessarily the best vantage point.* There is a certain amount of denial by the people on the scene, in part motivated by a desire not to see their loved ones and colleagues whisked away for an indeterminate length of time. There is also the tendency to want to stay at your post and do your duty, long after you should have left.

• *Stress has many symptoms, and before the crisis ends you will exhibit all of them.* People react differently, but all showed some signs of the strain we were under. One of the most popular was weight gain or loss. Unfortunately, there will be no Monrovia diet plan, for the effect was perversely opposite to what most would have desired. Those who were overweight to begin with gained, and those who were thin lost.

• *It is harder on those who leave than on those who stay.* Evacuations are not easy; their indefinite length and the lack of communication make them all the more difficult. If you want to test your marriage, go home tonight and tell your spouse to pack one suitcase of summer clothes because she (or he) and the kids are getting on a plane tomorrow to stay with her (or his) folks. Add that you don't know how long it will be or when you will be able to let her (or him) know, because there will be no phone communication and no point in writing either, since it will either never get through or be out of date by the time it does.

With a C-130 gunship covering them from above, Marines and SEALs on the Mogadishu rescue mission exit a CH-53 helicopter and take up defensive positions. *Marine Corps Gazette*.

10 | Escape from Mogadishu, 1991

James K. Bishop

The illuminated tips of their rotors described five phosphorescent circles above the swirling sand as the first wave of helicopters was loaded with evacuees. Bob Noble, who managed the U.S. embassy's contract guard force, radioed that Major Sayed, the local police commander, had appeared at Gate 1. With a grenade in one hand and a radio in the other, Sayed was threatening to signal prepositioned Somali troops to open fire on the choppers if they tried to take off. Thinking to myself that reality seemed patterned on a State Department crisis management exercise, I told Noble to bring the major to the front of the chancery, where I would talk to him.

It had been a full day since two CH-53 helicopters had dropped over the compound wall at dawn on January 5, 1991, and disgorged sixty very welcome Marines and SEALs. Their presence would presumably deter the armed looters at whom we had been obliged to shoot the previous morning. Indeed, as they were deployed, the Marines had pulled down ladders that looters had used to scramble back over the compound wall when they saw the helicopters approaching.

Soon after their colleagues stationed themselves around the compound, a team of Marines and SEALs had driven the quarter mile to the military mission compound. Colonel David Staley, chief of the Office of Military Cooperation (OMC), and other officers safe-havened with him, as well as a badly abused Kenyan ambassador and his wife and staff, were waiting there in lightly armored vehicles. The two miniconvoys had emerged and sped back to the compound's Gate 1, as our lookouts signaled the absence of Somali military traffic on Afgoy Road outside the gate.

As the sun rose higher in the sky, the volume of fire around the embassy compound had picked up more slowly than it had on the several mornings since December 30. That was the day when the Somali government's attempt to disarm residents of eastern Mogadishu provoked a spontaneous popular uprising. Nor had we yet heard that day any sound of the artillery and armor fire the army had been employing indiscriminately against rebellious neighborhoods, after having first tried to subdue them with mortars and rockets.

WIDENING CHAOS

Violence had been endemic in Mogadishu for many months. During the summer of 1990, embassies and government buildings had been bombed by the regime's opponents, and senior police officials had been assassinated. Westerners, including one of our Marines, had been injured, and several others had been killed in criminal attacks.

My family and I had returned to Washington from Monrovia, Liberia, in March of that year, departing as rebel forces inched toward the coast. They had moved slowly since entering Liberia the previous Christmas, and Washington thought it more important for me to prepare to set up shop in Mogadishu than to remain in the Liberian capital. However, well before confirmation hearings on my nomination as ambassador to Somalia could be arranged, the rebel forces neared Monrovia. Instead of boarding a plane for Somalia, I found myself chairing the task force formed by the State Department to handle what became a full-blown crisis. Throughout the late spring and summer my task force colleagues and I helped coordinate the dispatch of a naval task force to Liberian waters, set up abortive peace talks between the Liberian protagonists, and facilitated the evacuation of most Americans from the country. Lessons learned there would prove valuable in the Horn of Africa.

On August 1, my Somali consultations began with a visit to General Norman Schwarzkopf in his Tampa, Florida, Central Command (CENTCOM) headquarters. Given the extensive violence in Somalia, my first priority was to be sure that the general and his staff had current plans for the possible evacuation of Mogadishu. It was reassuring to learn that they indeed had this contingency in mind, and two staff officers and I reviewed CENTCOM's relevant data holdings.

In early September 1990 my wife, our youngest daughter, and I finally reached the Somali capital. There had been no letup in the violence. Bombs exploded at three government buildings downtown the day we deplaned, killing several people. We had our first personal encounter with Somali mayhem within ten days of our arrival. At a supposedly safe beach just south of town, a handful of young brigands leaped over a wall and rushed up the steps to the beach-house porch from which my wife and two other women were watching my daughter and me wade in the salt water fifty yards away. Wildly waving a pistol, one of the Somalis fired a bullet just to the side of my wife's head from a few feet in front of her and then lunged at her with a knife after she kicked her handbag toward him. A hysterical child and a frightened, angry wife left the Somali seashore, never to return.

The American presence in Somalia reflected several U.S. national interests. Among these the most prominent was military access to the ports and airfields at Mogadishu and Berbera, provided under the terms of a bilateral accord reached in 1981. Negotiated in the wake of the Soviet invasion of Afghanistan and the revolution in Iran, the access agreement was an important element of the strategy developed to protect the oil fields of the Middle East from Soviet or Iranian adventurism. The airfield at Berbera, built, ironically, by the Soviets, would permit the stationing of combat aircraft that could help defend the Arabian Peninsula and U.S. naval forces operating in the Red Sea. Jet fuel was prepositioned there and in Mogadishu, and bunker fuel was stored at Berbera.

Three American companies prospecting for petroleum were our only economic interests in the desperately poor country. From the humanitarian perspective, Somalia was a substantial concern. Not only were its people terribly impoverished, but an estimated 700,000 refugees remained from the Somali-Ethiopian conflict of the mid-seventies. The U.S. Agency for International Development (AID) was running a number of programs providing them relief and trying to encourage economic development.

On the political level, we had two interests. After Iraq's invasion of Kuwait on August 2, 1990, our first concern was keeping Somalia on the coalition's side in the runup to Desert Storm. Desperate for cash, fuel, and arms, the regime of President Mohammed Siad Barre was flirting with both camps. Our second objective was to try to keep the country from coming apart violently.

There were three rebel armies in the field, one operating within a hundred miles of the capital; but without an air force, armored corps, or much artillery, they had not been able to take any provincial administrative centers from government troops relatively well equipped with modern arms. The Egyptian and Italian governments were the primary sponsors of a peace process designed to bring all armies and political movements to a conference table in Cairo. In Mogadishu, we and the Italians were promoting dialogue between the regime and its political opponents, extracting promises of government reform as part of this process.

My paramount responsibility as U.S. ambassador was the welfare of the American community. Warfare in the countryside had required the withdrawal of most Americans working on assistance projects outside Mogadishu, and the terrorist bombings were a reminder that political violence was not limited to the rural areas. But the gravest threat to inhabitants of Mogadishu, including Americans, was criminal violence. Car thefts were commonplace, street robberies rampant, and break-ins a daily occurrence.

As I made my introductory calls on senior officials, including the president, I insisted that armed guards be assigned to protect our installations. Within the official American community, additional restrictions were placed on movements inside Mogadishu. We began a series of drills made as lifelike as possible to prepare everyone, including the schoolchildren, to cope with sudden emergencies. We improved our physical defenses. We stockpiled medicine, food, and water in the buildings we would use as safe havens, and a new safe haven was established in the chancery basement, below the line of fire of rockets and artillery, one hoped. Radio equipment was moved to the OMC compound to enable us to communicate with Washington if the principal compound was overrun.

In my early calls on my Soviet and Western colleagues, I quizzed them about their evacuation plans. Several messages were then sent to Washington asking that steps be taken to coordinate evacuation contingency planning with the British, French, and Italian governments, all of which had military forces in the area participating in Desert Shield. No action apparently was taken on that recommendation. The French, Italian, and U.S. naval vessels eventually sent to the Somali coast could not even communicate with one another.

We did receive a visit from a special messenger sent by a senior State Department official with instructions to ask me to make plans to relocate the Marines off the compound if the chancery was attacked, in order to avoid embarrassment should Marine lives be lost. I made no attempt to disguise my amazement at the stupidity of the suggestion that there could be somewhere else in Mogadishu where the Marines could be safer than on the compound and my fury that avoiding embarrassment could take precedence over use of the Marines to protect the American community in extremis.

During November 1990, the war drew closer to Mogadishu as the rebels operating in the center of the country established positions within thirty miles of the capital. We were in direct contact, however, with both their military and political leaders, who assured us no battle for Mogadishu was planned. The rebels were members of the tribe that formed most of the capital's population, and their political leaders were wealthy merchants. It therefore made sense for them to avoid a battle in Mogadishu, which would jeopardize the lives of their relatives and their leaders' investments.

A strategy that ruled out a full-scale assault on the capital did not, however, preclude either fighting between rival tribesmen living in the city or the assassination of government officials by rebel hit squads. By threatening to withhold assistance from any group that came to power after engaging in indiscriminate terrorist attacks against buildings or embassies, we were able to reach an understanding that there would be no further such activity.

The pace of criminal activity picked up, and the suspects included both rebels and off-duty military and police. Four-wheel-drive vehicles became too dangerous to operate, with drivers of nine such vehicles killed during one mid-November night. Shootouts between the police and robbers and between rival tribal groups kept our people awake many evenings. Diplomatic immunity was violated increasingly by the thieves, who stole U.N., Red Cross, and embassy vehicles and even invaded the compounds of the United Nations and of other embassies in search of cars and trucks.

On the local political level, movement toward reconciliation was fitful. The government issued a new constitution and then promptly violated it by arresting and detaining oppositionists without due process. One of the main rebel groups said it would not attend the proposed Cairo peace conference, and the participation of other key groups remained problematic.

As war in the Persian Gulf became more likely, the Somalis rallied to the coalition and even offered to contribute troops in the hope of financial rewards from the Saudis and ourselves. For the same motive, the government indicated it wanted to renegotiate our military access agreement. However, the willingness of the Saudis to permit our forces to use air bases in Saudi Arabia itself made the airfields at Berbera and Mogadishu redundant as far as our war planners were concerned. The bunker fuel at Berbera was uplifted and transferred to the gulf, and the U.S. Air Force stopped permitting its aircraft to overnight in Mogadishu because of security concerns.

By late November, the extent of criminal violence in parts of the city where our aid personnel normally worked, the associated need to warehouse all of our four-wheel-drive vehicles, and the banditry and warfare just outside Mogadishu made it impossible for our aid projects to function without unacceptable risk to American staff. We therefore began sending AID contract personnel home. We also began to relocate AID's offices to the main compound. Movement of members of the official community was restricted to an area within two kilometers of the compound flagpole. Only those of us with armored cars and armed guards were authorized to travel beyond that radius.

For several months there had been frank discussion of the security situation at the community meetings open to both official and private Americans. Everyone familiar with the embassy knew that improving our physical security and our ability to cope with emergencies had become our top priority. Few Americans, therefore, seemed surprised when, at a standing-room-only special community meeting on December 5, following two nights of tribal fighting in downtown Mogadishu during which rocket-propelled grenades and mortars were used, I announced that I had recommended to Washington the voluntary departure of U.S. government dependents and nonessential employees.

To underline to private Americans the seriousness of the situation, the vice consul read the text of the ominous travel advisory we proposed that Washington issue. I also volunteered that my wife and daughter would be among the early departees. In subsequent telephone calls to parents with children at post, I emphasized the desirability of the children's early departure.

Well before those leaving voluntarily had flown off, we passed several of the benchmarks we had set to identify the time when ordered—that is, compulsory—departure for U.S. government employees should begin. The tide of violence was swelling. Another of our drivers, the second in three weeks, was shot, and his vehicle stolen. The daily light-arms fire around the embassy became more worrisome when a firefight on the road outside Gate 1 sent bullets flying through the air and into our vice consul's home just as our employees left for the day. The roundtable talks in Cairo aborted when the Somali government arrested two of the prospective participants.

Then the United Nations moved to an ordered departure of its own employees and dependents. I recommended to Washington that we do the same, and Washington readily agreed. With our own people instructed to go by December 19, our official community had shrunk from 147 to 37 by that date, and we believed that half of the 90 private Americans still in Mogadishu in early December had also left by that date.

Between the 19th and the 30th we were busy packing up the belongings of those who had departed, rehearsing our emergency procedures, and trying to encourage both cabinet members and opposition leaders to curb the violent activities of their followers. But the situation only became more acute as even more intense intertribal fighting in the capital added to the lawlessness. Sensational international press reports claiming that one of the rebel armies was poised to attack Mogadishu rang alarm bells in Washington.

In meetings with the prime minister and several key cabinet members, I could identify no government game plan for stemming the growing chaos. Somewhat desperate, they asked my advice. I counseled redoubled effort to engage the opposition in good-faith negotiations. The same message was given to opposition leaders. When I finally succeeded in obtaining an appointment with President Siad Barre, after trying for several days, we met on December 27 with only one aide at his side. Siad Barre appeared tired and resigned to resolving his differences with his tribal enemies by force of arms.

Siad Barre's son-in-law General Morgan, who commanded the army, likewise seemed committed to further military struggle when we talked. After moving a considerable force outside the capital to attack rebel formations, Morgan and his men had returned, apparently without inflicting any serious injury to opponents, who largely moved out of the way of the regime's forces.

We experienced some alarm when a friend at the Pentagon sent me a cable warning that the military were so busy preparing for Desert Storm that they might not help us evacuate if so requested. We subsequently prepared vehicles and supplies for a possible overland evacuation to Kenya, which would have involved driving long distances through territory controlled by rebels and bandits. Leaders of the rebel forces outside Mogadishu tried to allay our anxiety with renewed assurances that they did not intend an early assault on the capital, and they pledged that by the time they did enter the city they would have a trained force of a thousand men dedicated to protecting foreign embassies and economic installations.

Given these ominous indicators, we began organizing a further drawdown. But our plans to again reduce our numbers were overtaken by the December 30 uprising. Its nature and extent were not clear for several days, but the firing that broke out throughout much of the city made it evident that we were dealing with violence on a new order of magnitude.

The greater danger was personalized the next morning when our defense attaché, Colonel Ken Culwell, arrived at my residence with several bullet holes in his car. The previous evening one of the rounds fired by a belligerent soldier had found a gap in the vehicle's armor and cut across the driver's seat an inch behind Culwell's backbone. A bullet hole in the roof of another defense attaché office vehicle parked beside the chancery reminded us of the damage that the stray rounds flying into the compound could do to less resistant surfaces. That evening an impatient soldier at an impromptu roadblock sprayed with his AK-47 a carry-all driven by Lieutenant Colonel Neil Youngman, deputy chief of the Office of Military Cooperation. Youngman rode it back to the OMC compound on the front rims, thankful that only the tires had received fatal punctures.

CIRCLING THE WAGONS

Over December 30–31, we moved almost all American employees into either our residence, the Marine house, or the kilometer-7 (K-7) compound across Afgoy Road. Because both the government and the political leadership of the tribe fighting the government's troops in the city seemed receptive to Italian efforts to promote a cease-fire, we thought this a likely outcome. If not, government forces, already making unrestricted use of their greater firepower, presumably would extinguish the uprising. By staying within the high walls of our compounds, we hoped to keep out of the fray.

The insurgents, however, would not negotiate or be cowed. They held their own in the eastern neighborhoods and attacked government strongholds at the presidential compound and the airport. In other parts of the capital, including our own, soldiers became the targets of armed youth. The military responded by indiscriminate use of mortars and heavy machine guns, as well as rocket-propelled grenades. What proved to be my last early-morning jog around the chancery compound was cut short New Year's Day, when small-arms fire around the embassy forced me to take cover three times in twenty minutes. Nervous soldiers made Afgoy Road a shooting gallery that same morning, cutting off from the embassy those in safe havens outside its walls.

Unfortunately, I had allowed the New Year's party to be held in the K-7 compound provided those attending remained there for the night. The participants included our communicators, without whose help I could not inform Washington of the worsening situation. I have seldom felt as impotent as I did listening to the increasing gunfire outside a chancery left mute by my failure to keep at least one communicator within the compound walls. As would become the case until the K-7 compound was invaded four days later, we began opening our gate to send armored vehicles to pick up people or to receive evacuees, but only when lookouts posted on the roof of the K-7 apartment building radioed that no armed personnel were on the road. The communicators were among the first brought back to the compound in this fashion, and with their assistance Washington was informed of the spreading violence.

Among the thousands of Somalis who began streaming past our gate on their way out of the embattled city were members of our employees' families. Many of

155

our Somali colleagues, as well as numerous contract guards, were staying in the compound overnight, because their homes were beyond government lines.

The new year brought the first requests from private Americans for refuge within the compound. AID director Mike Rugh was asked to put his considerable organizational skills to work providing food, shelter, and public order for them and a compound population that ultimately exceeded five hundred. AID contractor Peggy O'Rourke, who had been preparing meals for fifty Foreign Service Nationals (FSNs) and guards at the now-vacated AID compound, took over the embassy snack bar kitchen. There she was ultimately to prepare hot meals for some 350 evacuees, FSNs, and guards.

At the OMC compound, Colonel Staley, whose family had run a restaurant while he was growing up, was preparing more than a hundred meals a day, many of them for his local guards and the armed policemen assigned to his compound, who were chasing away the soldiers looting elsewhere in the neighborhood. Somali officers ducking in to see Staley provided some not always reliable information on the fighting around town.

My executive assistant, Lynda Walker, nurse practitioner Karen McGuire Rugh, and public affairs officer Karen Aguillar took over direction of the embassy kitchens and began providing gourmet meals for their embassy colleagues. Several of Aguillar's faithful Somali employees brought or sent word about conditions elsewhere in the city. Political officer John Fox and I shared the task of drafting the telegrams that kept Washington and other diplomatic and military posts aware of what we could learn from all sources about the political and military situation.

By January 2, the government was employing heavy artillery against the dissidents, whose strength nonetheless appeared to be increasing. Low-altitude overflights by government warplanes suggested the regime might bomb the rebels, as it had done two years earlier in similar circumstances in the northern city of Hargeisa, destroying much of that town. Looting was becoming commonplace, and the nervous behavior of the soldiers calling at a supply depot set up across Afgoy Road inspired little confidence in their discipline. Already, uniformed men had broken into several AID compounds to steal vehicles, and they were beginning to loot homes vacated by embassy personnel.

Although we saw the Somali Airline's Airbus occasionally use the airport, the firing all around us precluded any movement in that direction. The insurgents in the city were reported to have been joined by soldiers from the rebel army outside Mogadishu, and together they were capturing artillery pieces and armored vehicles from government forces. Should the latter be forced out of the city, our compound would be on their line of march, creating the possibility that the tide of battle and accompanying artillery fire could sweep across our vulnerable and crowded compound.

On December 31, the second day of the uprising, I had cabled Washington that the threat level had reached the point where it would be prudent to begin contingency planning for an evacuation using helicopters to lift us out of the compound at night, in case departure by commercial airlines became impossible. The following day, January 1, we had received word via radio from the Italian embassy that Rome was not only sending ships and planes to evacuate the European community but had granted my informal request that Americans be taken out as well. I promptly requested Washington's permission to exit with the Italians. That possible escape route closed on January 2, however, when the Italians decided there was too much fighting going on around the airfield to use it for any purpose.

With soldiers being killed on the road outside our gate, small-arms fire coming regularly into the compound, plumes of smoke rising downtown from the impact of heavy artillery shells, and Somali fighters making occasional low-level passes overhead, I cabled the department January 2 asking that it put into operation the contingency plans for a nighttime evacuation by U.S. military helicopter that I had recommended be prepared two days earlier.

In Washington, an urgent meeting took place soon after our message was received, and a task force under Deputy Assistant Secretary of State Jeff Davidow's capable and sympathetic leadership was established at the State Department. Later the same day we were told that President Bush had ordered C-130s to fly immediately to Mombassa, Kenya. They would be prepared to fly into Mogadishu as soon as flight clearances could be obtained and arrangements made for us to proceed safely to the airport. In addition, the USS *Guam* and the USS *Trenton* had been instructed to set course for Mogadishu from their positions in the Gulf of Oman. By January 7, they would be able to evacuate us by helicopter from the compound itself, should that be necessary.

Although Mogadishu's phones were out, we were able to communicate with most Western European embassies by radio. They reported that the Italians, whom we could no longer contact directly, were negotiating a cease-fire with the government and rebels. Indeed, several cease-fires were announced by the government radio. Our efforts to obtain landing clearance for the C-130s at Mogadishu were frustrated, however, by our inability to communicate with anyone in the government. A runner we sent to the Foreign Ministry found its gates chained and the building vacant. We then passed word to the Italians to ask the government for the landing permission we needed. The response we received from the Italians was that the president had agreed in principle that foreign governments could evacuate their nationals. Details, he had told the Italians, were to be worked out with the Foreign Ministry

More significant than Siad Barre's evasiveness was the fact that combatants in both camps were ignoring the cease-fires accepted by their nominal leaders. It became increasingly evident that the rebels had no command-and-control structure. They were fighting as individuals and small groups. It had also become apparent that command-and-control within government forces was eroding fast, and that guns were being distributed to undisciplined young members of the president's Marehan tribe. We also began receiving reports that soldiers had shot officers of tribes other than their own when given orders to which they objected.

On January 3, the Italians, Soviets, and Germans all tried to land aircraft in Mogadishu to evacuate their communities, but aborted these efforts because of violence at the airport. A French naval vessel approached the coast, but Paris decided to postpone an evacuation attempt when the commander of the Somali navy threatened to attack the ship with combat aircraft for having violated his country's territorial waters. In these circumstances I advised Washington that the C-130 option was impractical and that evacuation indeed would have to be in a nonpermissive mode by helicopters, as soon as the *Guam* and the *Trenton* could launch their aircraft. I also suggested that specially trained military personnel, some of whom had visited us in November, be parachuted into the 160-acre compound to assist in its defense.

As fighting and looting in Mogadishu became still more widespread, the population of our compound swelled. Almost the entire official American community was shoehorned into our residence and the Marine house. Two embassy officers were holed up at the K-7 apartment building across the street, still using its roof as a lookout post. Colonel Staley and three other members of our community remained a quarter mile away at the OMC compound, where the backup radio was positioned. Three other embassy members were cut off by the fighting in their private residences two kilometers away.

GOLF COURSE GUN BATTLE

With artillery thundering, plumes of smoke marking impacts downtown, small-arms fire everywhere, and looting becoming still more widespread, I received notes from several diplomatic colleagues asking for rescue and refuge. The response to each was that while they were welcome to join us, we could not mount any rescue operations. Some took advantage of lulls in the firing to make their way to us. Eventually the heads of ten diplomatic missions, most of those in Mogadishu, were among the evacuees. Several chiefs of mission, including the Kenyan and the Sudanese, had been beaten and robbed by uniformed looters. Walt Fleming, our tireless and courageous Foreign Buildings Office facilities manager, helped Mike Rugh accommodate them, ducking at one point an AK-47 burst that drew an arc through the wall just over his head. Fleming, a former Seabee and racecar driver, also took the wheel each time we sent a vehicle outside the gate to pick up an embassy officer cut off at his residence.

January 4 was our worst day. Half of our compound was a primitive eighty-acre golf course. Like the wall on Afgoy Road, the wall within the compound separating the recreation area from the chancery, Marine house, residence, and Joint Administrative Office (JAO) complex was perforated every twenty yards by two-foot gaps blocked by thin bars. Normally we did not have to worry about anything more lethal than wild dogs coming through the gaps. But early on January 4 we learned that looters armed with AK-47s were trashing the golf club and terrifying the FSN families given refuge there. From the golf course they would be able to fire through the gaps in the internal wall at anyone moving on the embassy half of the compound.

Local guard force supervisor Bob Noble, a Scot and a former Special Air Services trooper who had spent much of the previous few days facing down well-armed Somali soldiers as they tried to bully their way into the compound to obtain vehicles, fuel, and other goods, went to deal with the intruders. He was accompanied by Elaine York. On her first tour abroad as a security officer, York had come from Abidjan to assist us and demonstrated remarkable stamina and physical courage. She and Noble fired over the heads of the looters when more subtle means of chasing them off proved unsuccessful. The looters returned fire, directed at York and Noble, who defended themselves, hitting at least one looter. Both sides then withdrew.

While Noble and a nearby militia commander he had befriended negotiated for the militia's armed help in fighting off the golf course looters, soldiers broke into the K-7 compound and seized lookout Bill Mueller. They released him only when he gave them the keys to one of the vehicles in the courtyard. Mueller and fellow lookout Chris Swenson then retreated to a safe haven, while the soldiers helped themselves to our vehicles.

Back at the chancery compound, commercial officer Mike Shanklin, a retired Marine major, armed himself and took an armored van to evacuate to the chancery everyone in our glass-walled ambassadorial residence. It was now in the line of fire of looters on the golf course. We then buttoned up the chancery and the JAO headquarters, the compound's two safe havens, and in a series of FLASH messages alerted Washington to our situation.

Noble's militiamen came to our rescue, chasing the looters off the golf course in a brisk exchange of fire. Mueller and Swenson made it back to the embassy compound once the soldiers had departed the K-7 area and Noble had identified a gap in the military traffic on Afgoy Road that permitted him to open the gate. Mueller and Swenson were then replaced as lookouts by communicator Matt Kula, who kept watch from a trapdoor on top of the compound water tower, until it came under fire later in the day. In addition to small-arms impacts, a rocket-propelled grenade, probably aimed at the water tower, went through the wall of the warehouse next to the JAO safe haven.

We could not predict how long Bob Noble's militiamen would stand guard at the golf course, and the army's violation of the K-7 compound clearly put us in great jeopardy. We certainly could not count on remaining unmolested until the scheduled arrival of the Marines three days later. I therefore asked Washington for two platoons of parachutists from Saudi Arabia to hold the compound until the vessels approaching us could launch their helicopters.

After high-level meetings in Washington, we were informed that parachutists were not available, an unconvincing response given the presence of 400,000 U.S. troops in Saudi Arabia. At the same time, however, we were told that advance elements of the Marines would reach the compound at dawn the following day. Moreover, as the *Guam* and the *Trenton* had been proceeding at top speed, they would be ready to evacuate us a day earlier than scheduled.

During the afternoon our "combat consuls," Brian Phipps, Mark Manning, and John Fox, dressed in flak jackets, ducked bullets at Gate 1 as they decided whom to admit to the compound for evacuation. These were painful decisions, made in a tense and emotional environment, and all three performed superbly. In addition to Americans and foreign national members of their immediate families, we had decided to evacuate all foreign diplomats, all third-country nationals working for the embassy, and private citizens of NATO countries. Given their numbers, we could not assist members of the Ethiopian or Yemeni private communities, which were the largest expatriate groups in the city. We also would be taking one special Somali national, a four-week-old orphan girl that Mike and Karen Rugh planned to adopt. Knowing her inclusion in our plans would provoke endless questions from State and Defense, I decided to let Washington know she was along if and when we made it to the *Guam*.

An American woman, shot two days earlier, turned up at the gate. Together with a Sudanese diplomat's wife nine months pregnant and a Sudanese diplomat who had been knifed, the wounded American was treated by Karen Rugh and our Indian contract physician, who was among the evacuees.

When we were informed that the C-130s and naval vessels had been ordered to position themselves to evacuate us, I had asked Ken Culwell to take responsibility for dealing with the flood of inquiries I knew from my Liberian experience soon would hit the communications unit from various military commands. "Don't lose your patience when you are asked the same question a dozen times or are expected to provide a level of detail a Ph.D candidate might have difficulty furnishing," I counseled him. The *Guam* was under instructions not to communicate directly with us, but when our ex-Navy communicator Mike Ingram picked up the vessel's radio, we persisted in talking to it until a link was established. As the military became more involved, we were able to gain access to frequencies otherwise reserved by the military for Desert Shield. Using these it became possible to maintain a reliably audible voice link with Davidow and his task force colleagues in Washington.

Very much concerned that looters might enter the compound after dark, I authorized the purchase of several AK-47s. These were issued to American embassy colleagues who had received appropriate training. Anxious to avoid fire-fights, I gave instructions that everyone on the compound was to retreat within the chancery or JAO compound if armed strangers scaled the walls. The Turkish ambassador's offer to have his bodyguards supplement our defenses was declined and their weapons were taken from them, as I did not want anyone armed who might initiate firing without my authorization.

Keys were put in the locks of the vehicles brought by the evacuees to the compound, in the belief that there would be less risk to the owners if looters did not have to go looking for keys. Vice Consul Mark Manning, a hunter and marksman, was stationed inside the JAO safe-haven door with instructions to fire only if authorized or confronted by an attempt to break through the door. The Marine security guards, several of whom had been posted in battle dress at the JAO compound during the afternoon to reassure those in that safe haven and to intimidate would-be troublemakers, were withdrawn to the chancery. Other armed Americans joined Bob Noble and his local guards at the gates.

During the afternoon we had received reports that a .50-caliber machine gun had been brought into the K-7 apartment building, from which it would be able to fire on the ground we had cleared of camels and other obstacles to serve as a helicopter landing pad. However, after tracing the reports back to their sources within the compound, I found no one who had actually seen the machine gun carried in. As there undoubtedly were armed looters in the building, and we had been told that a C-130 configured as a gunship would cover the helicopters' arrival and would be able to knock down the K-7 apartment tower with its cannon, I decided not to risk sending anyone into the building.

THE MILITARY AND THE FOREIGN SERVICE GETTING IT RIGHT, TOGETHER

While some of us tried to recharge our batteries with a few hours' sleep, the Marines and SEALs were boarding CH-53 helicopters for the 450-mile flight to us. The planners aboard the *Guam* had been severely handicapped by the lack of intelligence available elsewhere in the military establishment. Not only was information collected by the special team that had visited us not forwarded to them; they were not sent any of the material in the emergency and evacuation plan held by CENTCOM. Moreover, our ability to discuss tactical information with the *Guam* was inhibited by the fact that the radiotelephone link we were using was not secure and therefore was vulnerable to Somali interception.

In fact, the plan first worked up aboard the *Guam* on the basis of a ten-year-old road map would have sent the rescue force to a location both five miles away from us and at the epicenter of the carnage downtown. Only when an NCO on the *Guam* who had served as a Marine security guard in Mogadishu informed the Marine commander that the embassy had been scheduled to move to a new location could the planners correct their mistake.

Heavily armed with personal and antiarmor weapons, the Marines and SEALs were in for an uncomfortable and very dangerous experience. The helicopters' Omega navigation system failed soon after takeoff, leaving the pilots to locate by dead reckoning the C-130 refuelers waiting for them. To do so they took the helicopters up to an altitude that badly chilled the aircraft, crews, and passengers. When the first of two refuelings was initiated, a leak in the lines aboard one helicopter sprayed many of the Marines with jet fuel before contact could be broken. Fortunately for us, a crew member quickly repaired the broken seal, refueling was completed, and the mission was not aborted.

Dropping low as they approached the coast to avoid the potential threat posed by Somali antiaircraft missiles, the pilots looked for our golf course as their landmark. No one had thought to explain that our sand, cow dung, and scrub course did not resemble the well-watered greens usually associated with the game. Consequently, the pilots missed us and went back out over the sea to orient themselves for a second, and successful, attempt.

It is doubtful any of the evacuees will forget the welcome chatter of helicopter blades as two CH-53s came over the compound wall soon after dawn. Our rescuers had flown for three and a half hours on a mission that reduced safety margins to a razor-thin edge. Despite their ordeal, the Marines and SEALs were on top of the situation as they exited the choppers.

From the start, coordination between military and diplomatic authorities could not have been smoother. Another of the lessons I had learned from the Liberian task force was to avoid a predeployment debate over command of military forces within the compound. I relied on good sense prevailing and was not disappointed. Marine and SEAL officers decided where to deploy their men, and responsibility for use of lethal fire remained mine. While a shot or two was fired as the Marines and SEALs took up their positions, the .50-caliber machine gun report proved bogus, and the C-130 gunship flying overhead held its fire.

As soon as the Marines and SEALs had their gear out of the helicopters, we boarded sixty evacuees. These included all of the private Americans who had reached the compound and those chiefs of diplomatic missions who had so far arrived, as well as U.S. Deputy Chief of Mission Joe Borich and three other U.S. mission officers, who went out to the *Guam* to coordinate the evacuation with the naval and Marine commanders aboard.

Repeated Rescues

Later in the morning, once the recovery of the group at the OMC compound had reunited our ranks, we focused on what help we could provide to other diplomatic missions. The Soviets had made contact with us by radio the previous day, informing us that they had been attacked and lost vehicles to looters the day before. Their ambassador had seen the helicopters fly in from the sea, and by radio he asked if I would send someone to escort his staff and their dependents to our embassy. Bob Noble persuaded a then cooperative Major Sayed to provide an escort for a fee, and an hour later we had thirty-eight Soviet guests.

A similar operation, at a significantly higher per capita fee, brought us fifteen British nationals from their embassy, which was in a more dangerous area. Unfortunately, the South Koreans did not trust the bona fides of the escort we sent them and refused to leave their embassy. Special arrangements made with a senior Somali resulted in the recovery of the British ambassador and the German chargé, who had spent five days under intense fire across from the president's headquarters—brave men both.

During the morning two Marine sharpshooters, who had replaced Matt Kula as lookouts on the embassy water tower, reported that they were taking fire from Somalis they could see through the cross hairs of their scopes. They requested permission to shoot the Somalis. Given the number of armed Somalis around us and the hundreds of unarmed evacuees within the compound, my approach was to avoid gunfire if at all possible. To limit misinterpretation of the object of the rescue mission, we had asked that in their coverage the VOA and BBC emphasize that the Marines and SEALs were not in Mogadishu to take sides in the ongoing conflict, but were in the compound only to protect its occupants.

I denied permission to return fire and had the lookouts come down. I figured that return fire, while almost sure to be successful in eliminating the Marines' tormentors, would tempt other Somalis to play the same game and possibly escalate into a more general and dangerous exchange of rounds.

Leaving our FSN employees was an extremely painful experience for many, particularly for personnel officer Sharon Nichols, Bill Mueller, and Walt Fleming, who had strong bonds with those who worked directly for them. Everyone was troubled by having had to leave household employees, especially after Mike Shanklin's manservant turned up brutally beaten by looters who had confronted him within Mike's home. Washington had turned down our request that the *Guam*'s helicopters carry the compound's Somalis twenty miles out of town, to move them away from the looters and undisciplined soldiers. We did not have sufficient cash even to pay the FSNs and household staff their wages due.

During an afternoon break in the firing around us, I met with many of the FSNs under a tree and explained that we would leave what cash we had and the commissary keys with the FSN committee leaders, who would distribute money and food among them. They were also promised that everything possible would be done from Nairobi to send funds to them. The FSNs agreed that fate gave us few options, and only a handful made futile requests to be evacuated.

During the afternoon, .50-caliber machine-gun fire struck the chancery and a rocket-propelled grenade hit the nearby compound wall. From their command post on the chancery roof, the Marines requested authorization to return fire. In response I asked if they could identify the source of the incoming rounds. As they could not, and the rounds could have been strays, I refused to authorize counterfire that might have provoked escalation.

There was a bizarre episode when a member of my staff brought a drunken Somali police general to see me. When I rebuffed his persistent pleas to take him and his family with us, he announced that he would kill his wife, his children, and himself outside the gate. He calmed down when I asked Colonel Oates, a six-foot-two Marine in battle dress, to join us, and he left peacefully under the colonel's escort.

As evening came, we learned that we would be going to Oman instead of Mombassa. I do not remember any complaints among those who heard this news before arriving on the *Guam*. We completed the destruction of all the classified equipment except machines we were still using to communicate with the ships and Washington, and then put them out of service as the *Guam*'s helicopters approached. Mike Rugh and his helpers had done a characteristically thorough job preparing the evacuees for departure. Nationals of thirty countries had been organized by helicopter load. Despite our best efforts a number of evacuees had brought pets with them, and one of the more unpleasant tasks was putting them down.

As the pilots would be using night-vision equipment to bring five helicopters at a time into the small landing zone we had created, lights became a problem. The compound's bright lights needed to be on for the pilots to find us, but had to be extinguished as the pilots began their descent to avoid whiting out the night-vision goggles. I vetoed the suggestion that the lights be shot out for the same reason I had refused to authorize gunfire earlier, insisting that switches be found and used.

Last-Minute Escape

Back in front of the chancery, Major Sayed was threatening to signal his Somali troops to fire on any choppers that tried to take off. As I listened through an interpreter to an excited but disarmed Sayed, Bob Noble and several SEALs beyond the circle of light kept Sayed and his radio in their sights. The major had given up his grenade in return for Noble's taking the clip out of his machine gun, not noticing that Noble had chambered a round.

After fifteen minutes of discussion, Sayed agreed that the first wave of helicopters could take off without interference. For the next three-quarters of an hour, I kept him engaged in sometimes insane conversation while walking him toward the landing zone, as other choppers landed, loaded, and took off. Finally, after gaining possession of the major's radio, Noble and I joined the Marines and SEALs in their helicopters and sailed over the compound walls, and our adrenaline rush began to ebb.

It was only after our arrival on the *Guam* that we were told that the radars of the SA-2 battery at the airport had illuminated, and that the helicopter crews through their night-vision glasses had seen intruders coming over the compound walls as we were lifting off. The next day we discovered that rockets had been used to blast open embassy doors within two hours of our exodus; we learned later that several of our Somali colleagues had been killed in associated violence.

Going Home Slowly

As we set off on a five-day voyage to Muscat, we were extremely grateful to the Marines and sailors who had put their lives at risk to save ours. The crews of both vessels were justifiably proud of their achievement, certainly the most exciting event of their five months at sea. The success of this dangerous evacuation mission, called Operation Eastern Exit by the military, restored confidence shaken by the failed attempt a decade earlier to rescue the Tehran hostages.

Officers vacated their quarters to make room for the embassy's senior staff and the chiefs of other diplomatic missions. Other embassy members, including several who had been lodged in officers' quarters when last serving on a U.S. ship, found themselves stacked four high in the enlisted men's compartments.

Two hundred Marines and sailors volunteered within an hour when the chaplain of the *Guam* asked those interested to sign up as evacuee guides and escorts.

For many of them, evacuee children were surrogates for little ones back home. Several extra-large Marines helped bottle-feed Mary Lynda Rugh, the Somali infant Mike and Karen were bringing home to adopt much sooner than planned. After several days at sea, the *Guam*'s Captain Saffell announced the birth of the 282nd evacuee, the Sudanese diplomatic couple's new son, with all the satisfaction of a senior family member. A few ambassadors soon were proudly sporting *Guam* sweatshirts, or were attired in naval uniforms purchased at the ship's store.

During our days at sea we reconciled our evacuee manifest with that made by sailors unfamiliar with foreign names. Sleep and regular meals helped repair the wounds of stress. A snowstorm in the United States delayed the arrival of the plane sent to transport us to Frankfurt—a charter because the approach of war in the Persian Gulf had frightened off the civil airlines. Hospitable colleagues and the first beer in some time made our long wait at the Muscat airport tolerable. U.S. Consul General Pierre Shostal was at the Frankfurt airport to greet us, together with senior German officials and a bin of very welcome army surplus winter clothing.

Twenty-four hours later, most of us were back in Washington, welcomed at a late hour by Davidow and other task force members. And—a month after sending them home—reunited at last with our families.

LEARNING FROM EXPERIENCE

Our successful evacuation owed much to luck and more to the courage and skill of the Marines and SEALs who put their lives at risk to save ours. The calm competent performance of my colleagues in the dangerous days preceding our departure reflected their strength of character, our good fortune in not taking casualties, and the seasoning of the previous months. Though the violence around us was sometimes quite frightening, the slow buildup permitted psychological adjustment. Conducting realistic exercises accustomed everyone to the proximity of arms, the value of cover, and the use of the machinery necessary to destroy classified material.

A perverse consequence of the gradual buildup in the violence was that it deepened the sense of denial some experienced. Even a few of the parents who had seemed most concerned about the danger to their children in the days before we recommended evacuation hesitated to go when the opportunity was provided.

Among the lessons learned by mistakes, the most uncomfortable one was the need to keep a communicator within the chancery at all times to avoid loss of communications with the outside world. Failure to realize how difficult our compound would be to identify from a helicopter flying below the strobe light we had mounted on top of the water tower caused pilots unnecessary anxiety. Profiting from our mistake, the State Department subsequently issued embassies with proper materials to identify landing zones to incoming aircraft.

Although there were twenty-two naval physicians and a larger number of nurses aboard the *Guam*, none accompanied the helicopters. The medical personnel within the compound could have used assistance dealing with the wounded who had made their way to the embassy; they probably would have been out of their depth if the rounds coming into the compound had struck evacuees or U.S. military personnel.

One irony of the evacuation was that in its final hours the Marines received orders, sent via military channels allegedly at the request of the secretary of state, that they not leave until every Soviet national had been accounted for. Fortunately, the Soviets were all within the compound and there was no similar message regarding American or allied citizens—it had been impossible to account for one American and one German, both of whom ultimately left Somalia by other means. Micromanagement at great distance can have perverse consequences.

Sea voyages are rare in today's Foreign Service. But five days aboard ship allowed Mogadishu evacuees to catch up on sleep and otherwise restore psychic batteries close to exhaustion when the Marines and SEALs flew into the compound. After the only debriefing given the evacuees following their return to the State Department, the medical staff remarked on their surprisingly robust mental health.

One issue that remains unresolved is the responsibility of the State Department to its local employees when an embassy is abandoned. My request that our Somali employees and the family members with them in the compound be airlifted to the safety of the countryside outside Mogadishu was rebuffed by Washington. A number of them were killed as the compound was looted immediately following our evacuation. More reportedly starved to death while the department was refusing to allow FSO volunteers to return to Mogadishu with their Somali colleagues' overdue pay.

Notes

1. Embassies at Risk: Learning from Experience

1. U.S. Department of State, *Report of the Secretary of State's Advisory Panel on Overseas Security* (the Inman report), June 20, 1985, p. 9.
2. William Sommers, "Joel Barlow: Hero-Diplomat," *State*, May 1982, pp. 22–26.
3. Historical Studies Division, Historical Office, Bureau of Public Affairs, Department of State, *Offenses Against American Foreign Service Personnel Abroad, 1776–1965*, 1965 monograph.
4. Ibid.
5. Ibid.
6. Inman report, p. 9.
7. David T. Jones, "How This Tribute to Our Fallen Colleagues Got Started," *State*, November 1988, pp. 12–14.
8. Landrum R. Bolling, "Insult to Injury: The Dan Mitrione Tragedy," in Martin F. Herz, ed., *Diplomats and Terrorists: What Works, What Doesn't* (Washington, D.C.: Institute for the Study of Diplomacy, Georgetown University, 1982), p. 66.
9. David A. Korn, *Assassination in Khartoum*, An Institute for the Study of Diplomacy Book (Bloomington, Ind.: Indiana University Press, 1993), pp. 110, 113–15.
10. Grant V. McClanahan, *Diplomatic Immunity: Principles, Practices, Problems*, An Institute for the Study of Diplomacy Book (London: C. Hurst & Co.; New York: St. Martin's Press, 1989), p. 145.
11. Inman Report, pp. 14–15.
12. Ibid., p. 75.
13. "International Terrorism," *GIST*, Department of State, May 15, 1992.
14. Testimony by Ambassador Thomas E. McNamara, Subcommittee on International Security, International Organizations and Human Rights, Committee on Foreign Affairs of the House of Representatives, March 12, 1993.
15. "International Terrorism," *GIST*, May 15, 1992, p. 1.
16. Ibid., p. 1.
17. Ibid., p. 2.
18. Testimony by Ambassador Thomas E. McNamara, March 12, 1993.
19. In this context, "services to U.S. citizens" also means "services to noncitizens with U.S. permanent resident status" wherever possible.
20. Charles Stuart Kennedy, *The American Consul: A History of the United States Consular Service, 1776–1914* (Westport, Conn.: Greenwood, 1990), p. viii.
21. Inman report, p. 82.

22. Harold G. Bean, *Diplomats and Terrorists II—Overseas Security: Our People Are the Key* (Washington, D.C.: Institute for the Study of Diplomacy, Georgetown University, 1987), discusses the Inman report's recommendations and related issues.
23. The Department of State budget for security, which increased dramatically in the years immediately following the Inman report, had declined steadily and substantially by the early 1990s.
24. Indeed, U.S. Ambassador Francis E. Meloy had a bodyguard when he was killed in Beirut in 1976.

2. Crisis Avoidance: Shutting Down Embassy Kampala, 1973

1. Unfortunately, Embassy Nairobi was extremely slow in briefing Embassy Kampala spouses in the safe-haven post about the latest news from Kampala. There is no question that improved procedures are needed in this area, particularly in detailing the responsibilities of the embassy in the safe-haven post for assisting evacuees thrust suddenly and involuntarily into their midst. Nairobi was not unique, for my colleagues and I had similarly distressing experiences with Embassy Bangkok when we were evacuated from Cambodia in April 1975.
2. A protecting power is "a state that agrees to act on behalf of another at the latter's request within the territorial jurisdiction of a third state" in the absence of a diplomatic mission of the requesting state, often but not only when countries break relations. James J. Blake, "Pragmatic Diplomacy: The Origins and Use of the Protecting Power," in David D. Newsom, ed., *Diplomacy Under a Foreign Flag: When Nations Break Relations* (Washington, D.C.: Institute for the Study of Diplomacy, Georgetown University, 1990), p. 6.

3. Crisis After Crisis: Embassy Tehran, 1979

1. Yazdi was a legal permanent resident of the United States.
2. Air Force Major General Philip Gast, who was replaced and departed Iran a few weeks before the November 4 attack.
3. PRG Prime Minister Mehdi Bazargan told Charles Naas that he had never expected such a quick collapse of the shah's regime.
4. By one estimate, the small arms looted from military arsenals in February 1979 were sufficient to equip ten infantry divisions.
5. *Homafars* were a class of noncommissioned officers created by the shah during the period of massive military equipment purchases in the 1970s. They received technical training, often in the United States, to maintain the sophisticated new weapons systems being acquired. Most came from families where traditional Islamic values held sway, often based in the provinces rather than in Tehran. It was a dispute between *homafars* and army officers over the showing of a videotape of Khomeini's return to Iran that set off the fighting that brought down the Bakhtiar government in early February.
6. The radical group were deeply involved in fraud and extortion directed at American firms. Their removal by the PRG at Ambassador Sullivan's request came when the government still had sufficient authority to act decisively.
7. Both Ambassador Sullivan and his deputy, Charles Naas, believe this was the case.
8. Rumors had long circulated that the shah suffered from some illness. In fact, he had been diagnosed several years earlier with lymphatic cancer, but this development had been a closely guarded secret while his doctors achieved some success in containing the disease's progress.
9. Somewhat surprisingly, the initial reaction was more restrained than anticipated, most likely because of uncertainty about the development's significance and factional disagreements on the appropriate response.
10. I was involved nine years later, as country director for Thailand and Burma, in a situation in which Embassy Rangoon personnel experienced similar searing events but personnel were

not changed, to the detriment, in my view, of that embassy's subsequent reporting and analysis. That crisis occurred in August and September 1988, when the people of Rangoon took to the streets to demand democracy and were later brutally crushed by the military. This experience reinforced my belief in the utility of changing personnel following traumatic events that may affect perspective.

11. In addition to these shredded documents that the students pasted together, a large volume of unshredded material fell into their hands. Many of these were papers accumulated by embassy offices subsequent to the February 14 attack that had not been shredded for lack of time. A substantial number, however, *predated* the earlier attack, despite the effort to destroy or ship out virtually all files from the period prior to that attack. Thus, the origin of the pre–February 14 documents is a mystery. It is possible they were in a safe that for some reason had not been opened and emptied after February 14.

12. I had stepped in only at the last minute when the officer who was to accompany Laingen was unavailable. She had been away from Tehran over the weekend, and car trouble on the return trip had delayed her arrival at the embassy that morning.

4. The Murder of Ambassador Dubs, Kabul, 1979

1. "The Kidnapping and Death of Ambassador Dubs, February 14, 1979, Kabul, Afghanistan: Summary of Report of Investigation," prepared by the Special Assignments Staff, Office of Security, Department of State, n.d., pp. 2–3.

2. Former State Department deputy assistant secretary Steve R. Pieczenik alleged in an article in the *Washington Post* "Outlook" section on February 14, 1981, that U.S. officials in the State Department had authorized by phone the assault on the room where Dubs was being held. Three days later the State Department issued a statement saying: "The allegation is not correct. The Department has reviewed the logs of the incident and the recollections of officers directly concerned in Kabul and in the Department. All concur that throughout the incident written and oral communications with the Embassy in Kabul stressed the need for restraint and moderation and the need to avoid any precipitate assault."

3. Department of State, "Kidnapping and Death," p. 5.

4. Ibid., pp. 16–17.

5. Embassy security officer Charles Boles, who was part of the team at the hotel and of the subsequent investigation, strongly believed that Dubs "was kidnapped by the Afghan government and murdered by that government with the active assistance and approval of the Soviet embassy." October 6, 1994, letter from Boles to an author whom Boles had hoped to stimulate to write about the Dubs assassination. The letter was shared with the Institute for the Study of Diplomacy and is quoted here with Boles's permission.

5. Attack on the U.S. Embassy in Pakistan, 1979

1. Actually, two officers were senior to both of us, economic counselor Larry Kennon and public affairs officer Jim Thurber, but they waived their seniority in view of our more direct political and administrative/security responsibilities for dealing with the crisis.

2. Embassy MSG detachments typically number six or more noncommissioned officers (NCOs), including the NCO-in-charge, who is normally at least a staff sergeant in rank. The NCOIC of such detachments, regardless of actual rank, has long been referred to as the "gunny," short for "gunnery sergeant."

8. Saddam's Siege of Embassy Kuwait: A Personal Journal, 1990

1. Following the car bombings of Embassy Beirut in April 1983 and of Embassy Kuwait that December, retired Admiral Bobby Inman chaired a commission on embassy security measures, as noted in chapter 1. As a result of that commission, U.S. embassies worldwide adopted physical antiterrorism measures, including strict rules on perimeter walls.

2. "Human shields" were American, British, Japanese, French, and German civilians, including women and small children, rounded up in Kuwait and placed throughout Kuwait and Iraq at strategic military and civilian installations to preclude coalition military action against these potential targets. In mid-September, Saddam released all women and children, but continued to round up and hold adult men from these countries.

3. The compound included the ambassador's official residence and housing for the U.S. Marine Corps security detachment, in addition to the usual offices and support buildings.

4. The Kuwait airport control tower, unaware that Kuwait had been invaded, cleared a British Air flight to land at 4:00 A.M. on August 2. Most of the passengers and crew were taken hostage by Iraqi forces and transferred to Baghdad to await the tortuous negotiations for their release.

5. "Sitreps" is shorthand for "situation reports"—periodic updates to the Department of State and others on fast-breaking news, the status of employees, families, and private citizens, and similar matters.

6. A "country team" comprises the senior officers and agency heads at an embassy. Core members are the ambassador, the deputy chief of mission, heads of the political, economic, administrative, and consular sections, the security and press officers, and heads of other agency components, such as the Departments of Defense, Commerce, and Treasury, and in Kuwait the Federal Highway Administration and the General Services Administration.

7. It should be noted for the record that French Chargé Jean Pierre Gaultier showed remarkable courage and compassion toward others when he was ordered by his government to close his embassy and depart with the rest of the French community toward the end of October. While the details must remain classified, a number of Americans owe the French a large measure of gratitude.

8. Because of the Rev. Jesse Jackson's visit to Kuwait in early September and the change in Saddam's human shield program, all the women and children and a number of adult men with severe health problems (including the oil executive) were home by the middle of September. Nineteen adult male Amcits stayed on the compound for the duration.

9. In the embassy's switch room two private citizens, Benny Mitchell and Mike Penniman, found a number of direct local lines that were not in use. These numbers were no longer listed for the embassy and did not go through the embassy switchboard. Reconnected, these lines allowed the embassy to reestablish contact with the American community and others outside. International calls were never possible.

10. The well remained in operation on the embassy compound until June 1993, when the embassy had it filled in as a "safety hazard."

11. There were two basic groups of evacuees: U.S.-citizen women married to Kuwaitis and their dual-national children, and native-born U.S.-citizen children (most of them Palestinian) whose parents and siblings, even if not U.S. citizens, were eligible for evacuation with the Amcit child.

12. The men would dictate messages to family or friends by phone to the embassy. These would then be made part of a cable collection of such messages sent every day to Washington, where they were read over the phone to the family or friends. Messages were passed back to the men by the same system.

13. Almost all were able to get out by the end of December, but it was close; a few chose to stay underground in Kuwait.

14. On November 29, 1990, the U.N. Security Council had passed Resolution 678, which gave Saddam an ultimatum: "Get out of Kuwait in forty-five days, or we will push you out." Desert Shield became Desert Storm on January 16, 1991, as promised. By February 27, 1991, Kuwait had been liberated by the combined forces of nearly thirty countries.

15. The three staff members who left on December 9, 1990, were Consul Gale Rogers, general services officer Mark Herzberg, and secretary Mildred Logsden. To leave on December 13, 1990, were Ambassador W. Nathaniel Howell, deputy chief of Mission Barbara K. Bodine,

administrative officer Wayne Logsden, and communicators Jeffrey Jugar and Connie Parrish.

16. Wiesbaden Air Force Base Hospital, near Frankfurt, Germany, served as the receiving and transition point for any number of U.S. hostages upon their release. Among the earliest were the Tehran embassy hostages in 1980; one of the last was Terry Anderson from Lebanon in December 1992.

Index

About the Authors

James K. Bishop, a U.S. Foreign Service officer from 1960 to 1993, with extensive African experience, was vice president of the Parliamentary Human Rights Foundation from 1994 to 1995. He was U.S. ambassador to Somalia from September 1990 until the January 1991 evacuation of Embassy Mogadishu and previously served as deputy assistant secretary of state for African affairs (1981–87) and as ambassador to Niger (1979–81) and Liberia (1987–90).

Barbara K. Bodine, a Senior Foreign Service officer, is dean of the School of Professional Studies at the State Department's Foreign Service Institute. Her career has focused primarily on Southwest Asia and the Arabian Peninsula and on political-military affairs. She was associate coordinator for counterterrorism operations and acting coordinator for counterterrorism from 1991 to 1994, following her service as deputy chief of mission at the U.S. embassy in Kuwait from July 1989 until December 1990.

Richard M. Gannon served five years as a U.S. Navy pilot, with service in Vietnam, before joining the Department of State in 1975. He was regional director for security programs in East Asia, 1991–93, and deputy chief for counterintelligence, 1993–95. In addition to serving in Washington and Brussels, he was security officer at the U.S. embassy in Beirut from September 1982 to July 1983.

Herbert G. Hagerty is an author and retired Foreign Service South Asia expert. He was political counselor at the U.S. embassy in Islamabad from 1977 to 1981, then deputy chief of mission in Sri Lanka. He has been director of the State Department's Office of Pakistan, Afghanistan, and Bangladesh Affairs and acting deputy assistant secretary for South Asia. Before joining the Foreign Service in 1964 he was a U.S. Navy officer and a Central Intelligence Agency analyst.

Dennis C. Jett is the U.S. ambassador to Mozambique. A Foreign Service officer since 1972 and a former U.S. Naval Reserve officer, he has served in Buenos Aires, in Tel Aviv, and, as deputy chief of mission, in Lilongwe, Malawi. He was DCM in Monrovia during the early 1990s phase of the Liberian civil war, then acting special assistant to the president and senior director for African affairs at the National Security Council.

Robert V. Keeley held the rank of career minister in the U.S. Foreign Service when he retired in 1989, after thirty-four years, and was president of the Middle East Institute from 1990 to 1995. He was deputy chief of mission in Uganda (1971–73) and in Cambodia (1974–75); ambassador to Mauritius (1976–78), Zimbabwe (1980–84), and Greece (1985–89); and deputy assistant secretary of state for African affairs (1978–80). He served in the U.S. Coast Guard during the Korean war.

Anthony C. E. Quainton, assistant secretary of state for diplomatic security since 1992, was director of the Office for Combatting Terrorism from 1978 to 1981. A Foreign Service officer since 1959, he has served as U.S. ambassador to the Central African Empire (1976–78), Nicaragua (1982–84), Kuwait (1984–87), and Peru (1989–92). From 1963 to 1976 he served principally in South Asia and was senior political officer for India.

Joseph G. Sullivan, a minister counselor in the Senior Foreign Service, is chief of mission at the U.S. Interests Section in Havana. He has been deputy assistant secretary of state for Inter-American affairs (1989–92) and director for Central American affairs (1988–89) and has also served in political assignments in Mexico, Portugal, and Israel. He joined the Foreign Service in 1970 after serving in the U.S. Public Health Service.

James E. Taylor is a career diplomat who entered the Foreign Service in 1965—after four years as an Air Force intelligence officer—and retired in 1990. He was political officer in Kabul, Afghanistan, from 1977 to 1980, and later served in the State Department's Bureau of Intelligence and Research tracking the prospects for Soviet withdrawal from that country. He has also served in Tehran, Munich, and Moscow and as political-military officer in Tel Aviv.

Victor L. Tomseth, a career diplomat and Asia expert, is U.S. ambassador to Laos. He headed the U.S. consulate in Shiraz, Iran, from July 1976 to February 1979, when he became the U.S. embassy's counselor for political affairs in Tehran, a position he held until January 1981. He has also served as deputy chief of mission in Sri Lanka and Thailand. He joined the Foreign Serice in 1966 after Peace Corps service in Nepal.

William G. Walker, a career minister in the U.S. Foreign Service, is vice president of the National Defense University at Fort McNair in Washington, D.C. From August 1988 to March 1992 he was U.S. ambassador to El Salvador, following service as deputy assistant secretary of state for Inter-American affairs responsible for Central America and Panama. Other posts have included Peru, Okinawa, Brazil, and, as DCM, Honduras and Bolivia. He served two years in the U.S. Army (1957–58).